THINKING FEELINGLY:

SOMATIC APPROACHES TO POETRY

KATY HAWKINS

THINKING FEELINGLY: SOMATIC APPROACHES TO POETRY

ISBN: 978-1-7336232-7-8

Copyright © 2022 by Katy Hawkins

Moving Poetics Publishing

Cover Illustration: Katherine Soutar

Cover Design: Doug Smock

Formatting and Layout: Bryan Simon

Back cover author photo: Justine Stehle

For Daddy
Who nose to nose saw me
Far as the eye can see

CONTENTS

proem

You know what I mean. I wrote this book with the basic assumption that you already know what I mean. It's an attempt to look out from the page and share shivers, like when you grab someone's hand at that moment in the movie where your stomach tightens. Even though this is our experience whenever we encounter something in the world that we somehow already know (which might define what constitutes "art" for each of us), very rarely does any kind of introductiontoabook talk to us this way. But if these pages are in your hot little hands, chances are that you already know why I wrote them. You were the kid with wild dreams and unruly school habits. You spent long hours in your own inner universe, and no one knew quite what you were up to, but it almost always involved spinning imaginative threads with language. Memorizing data was not your forte. You craved other worlds than this one and understood them better.

When you encountered the first poem that knew you, it worked on you like a spell—its sorcery echoing around the white spaces on the page, the truncated sense that entrusted you with its completion, the glancing lateral references that connected this thing with that, the between-the-lines wink that flirted with you, the gut feeling that no explanation could explain. Not all poems knew you, but some did. As Dylan Thomas says, "Poetry is what in a poem makes you laugh, cry, prickle, be silent, makes your toenails twinkle, makes you want to do this or that or nothing...." I hope a few of these entries make your toenails twinkle.

INTRODUCTION

"Dismiss whatever insults your own soul; and your very flesh shall be a great poem, and have the richest fluency, not only in its words, but in the silent lines of its lips and face, and between the lashes of your eyes, and in every motion and joint of your body." — Walt Whitman

"If I feel physically as if the top of my head were taken off, I know that is poetry." — Emily Dickinson

Thinking Feelingly came from a desire to fill a gap in writing and thinking about poetry, which nowhere approaches poems with the same capacities and senses we use when we experience them. This book is a thought experiment, playing with how poems might be engaged with the part of the bodymind that is actually moved by them. Each poem included here was important to me on a given week, selected according to the randomness and kismet by which I encountered it. The poem is followed by a reflection (POETIC THEMES) on its form and meaning and then a suggestion (PRACTICE) for how their language might be experienced at the level of blood, bone, and skin.

We need to bring our writing about poetry up to speed with how we use it. For the last two decades, I've been teaching poetry outside the classroom, mostly barefoot. More recently I have brought this way of teaching, which I call "Moving Poetics," back into the university setting. I've been surprised to find how much my students cherish and need poetry. Maybe it's Amanda Gorman who sparked the observation that poems have a particular draw at this time, but this shift started well before the 2021 inauguration. What is up with the religion of Mary Oliver, or Rumi, in America today? What exigencies have made it possible for Slam Poetry, spoken word, or rap to pull verse out of the ivory tower? People turn to poems in a different way than they might have a generation ago, with more urgency, even desperation, to find wisdom voiced in its own language of mystery—wisdom that just might save our souls.

The entries in this book experiment with ways of writing and thinking about poetry that are more native to its mode of transmission. A sense-based experience of a poem is rooted not just in the forebrain's tendency to pin an idea down like a bug, but also in the intuition's way of turning it in the fingers of the mind like a prism, perceiving how the light catches it differently from each angle. Learning how to abide with a poem's beauty or truth or sublime terror until it rubs off on us and we're changed, however subtly, is a different skill set. What are some alternatives to proclaiming definitive victory over the meaning of a poem? I embarked on a year of trying to capture on the page the kind of organic, serendipitous way poems find us these days, through social media pages of the poets we love, or shared on a friend's post, or by way of curated collections like "The Slowdown" email newsletter, or Pàdraig Ó Tuama's "Poetry Unbound" NPR podcast, or the daily poems from the Poetry Foundation. We chomp into these poems with the little time we might have; maybe we pause and close our eyes over our coffee mug and then email them to ourselves to read later, or maybe we text them to a friend and then go on with our day. What if we were to give ourselves just five or ten more minutes to play with new ways of tasting them? What would we do with them, how would we relate to them, and what would a record of that interaction even look like?

This is a workbook, really, exploring potential ways that the rhythm and resonance of poetic language can seep into the gut-felt instinctual mind. These intuitive ways of feeling into knowledge are based on hunches. Poignant images and sing-song phrases are much more likely to enliven and provide meaning to everyday life when they make their way past the "thinky" brain and seep into the deeper, more primal layers of reflection and feeling. Cozying up to language like this opens the door to understanding, puzzling through, and abiding with poetic nuance. So the weekly entries to follow are inexact on purpose. They are non-authoritative and unfussy, in order to open up to outside engagement rather than close down possibility. They aspire to be something more like splotches of finger paint, or leaf rubbings that capture some skeletal imprint of truth, or the echo of your body's turnings in the rumples of your sheets—the real stuff of a day lived in a human body. They express the surges and "stucknesses" of the bodymind—some entries are longer and more exuberant and others are short and simple, trying to stay

faithful to the full range of embodied experience. I think of Whitman's procla-
mation in "Body Electric" that we must not desert any part of us, which is
followed by a truly prodigious list of physical phenomena from knee-pan to
lung sponges, whatever those are. These "chapters" are not meant to be
admired but used, the way one might use an avocado for guacamole, or a deck
of cards to play solitaire, or a hammer to hang a painting. Like a poem, they
are meant to be completed by your imaginative engagement. In fact, maybe
you could use this workbook a little differently than you would a start-to-
finish chapter book. These ideas might be best served up in the form of a
spiral-bound notebook, some kind of Rolodex, that could begin at the week
you happen to open it. The winter reflections tend to be more intricately
conceptual compared to moody March or the voluptuous summer flights of
fancy. Such is the way, when we move with the season and the planets and the
moon, rather than forcing equal productivity at all times. I'm choosing to begin
on the first week of March as a lesser-known first month of the year, largely to
accentuate the arbitrary nature of when we begin new stuff, based on the
complexities of our lives.

    Breaking from stylistic rigidity as it pertains to punctuation, capitalization,
or strict grammar is a purposeful attempt to align this body of thought with
innovative writing that challenges normative methods of inquiry. For similar
stylistic reasons, I try to steer clear of academic footnotes. To kick sentences
alive, I'll experiment with textual practices that upset the little rickety boat of
logic and codified "rigor" in favor of splashing around in the actual waves of
Mind, with its vagaries and imperfections and crosscurrents. And speaking of
oceans: many of these poems are chosen for a given week based on a seasonal
change that is happening in the Northern Hemisphere. Others are chosen for
American holidays. Wherever you happen to be, I trust in your creative
powers to take liberties as you flip the Rolodex. Other, more sinister biases and
limitations to my imaginative reach will be found everywhere, which I speak
to directly in the next section.

WHAT'S IN THE SOUP

"Axiom 1: People are different from each other"
— Eve Kosofsky Sedgwick

I'll begin the work of positioning myself by giving a little context for my interest in how poetry elicits gut feeling. The title of the book plays with a phrase from *King Lear*, "seeing feelingly," explaining to a king the perspective of a blind man. This was an important phrase to my dad, Sherman Hawkins, a Shakespeare scholar who taught me poetry. Just two months before he died, we were making tweaks to *Promised End*, his book on *Lear*, and he lingered with this phrase, eyes welling up. He was a brilliant scholar and a complex thinker, but what people really celebrated and remembered about him was his unique teaching style, which quite simply helped students feel things. I can't separate my understanding of poetry from my dad's influence on learning through feeling. He taught me poems at the dining room table from such a young age that, ultimately, I had to tease apart my own thinking from his Prospero-like influence.

Fast forward to grad school, where I was struggling to stick with my topic of study for the last decade or more, in thorny connections and dissonances between Queer and black experiences of alterity. It was a time when the Left was eating its own even more than today and call-out culture loomed larger. When I got wind that Eve Kosofsky Sedgwick, one of the primary architects of Queer Theory, had moved to New York, I signed up for her year-long seminar on Proust. My brain exploded. Eve's late work was all about the domain of feeling and how it encompasses both emotional/psychic processes and bodily sense experience. Her scholarship offered imaginative alternatives to the knowingness of critical work at the time. Her study of creative process and the wilderness of touch restored for me an attention to the body's wisdom that had gotten lost somewhere. She also showed us the subtlety possible in the affinities one person can feel for what would seem foreign to their experience, while still resisting the elision or subsumption of otherness into the self. She bravely articulated her identification with gay maleness through a first-person nakedness that helped her readers understand where she was coming from. In doing so, she carved a path for others to make coherent many as-yet-unimagined Queer identities. This appealed to me, as someone for whom polymorphous perversion has always been central. Eve became my intellectual hero, my guide, and my friend.

In trying to describe how this book sources its interpretive MO from Eve, I'm super aware of the risk of launching into a certain mode of academic writing that can create distance. So as simply as I possibly can, I'm going to try to describe how Eve's ideas about an interpretive mode that attends to texture lines up with these questions about identity politics. In her book *Touching Feeling*, Eve invited us to take a break from our tendency to think always in terms of a meaning hidden beneath or beyond or behind something and replace it with an approach that acknowledges that multiple truths can exist alongside each other. The idea that two things can co-exist happily beside one another isn't some facile way of getting around conflict. It actually invites us to think more subtly about the nature of difference. When several things are co-presenting, we are called to look into the nature of their relation, where there's always so much going on: including mimicry, rivalry, aggression, warping, differentiation, paralleling, desiring, and twisting. Paying attention to the way multiple elements are tangled up is usually harder than disproving falsehood in order to uncover some single "real" meaning of something. This "alongside" way of looking at things can be imagined as a textural approach. Experiencing the texture of something engages, rather than denies, our relationship to it. To explore the texture of the relation of elements in, say, a poem—as we might attend to, like, the bones of an insect's legs or a scarf someone knitted for us—is to examine patterns and their discontinuities in a way that includes our response. ("These knee-joints are so incredibly carefully designed… ewwww, little yucky sticky feet!" "Aw, she used green yarn when she ran out of blue, even though it's fuzzier, because she knows I like green.") So instead of trying to hide inconsistencies and subjective response, exploring texture helps us see more valences, more ways something can be interesting or unique. In Sedgwick's words, "We needed for there to be sites where the meanings didn't line up tidily with one another, and we learned to invest those sites with fascination and love."

So what you can expect to find here are untidy but hopefully generative readings that invest poems with fascination and love. I learned from Eve that the more precise and forthright we can be in presenting our "come from," the clearer and more available will be the blind spots, presumptions, and fertile relational dynamics in our thinking. So I want to underscore that my early intellectual heritage is super white. We learned the Greek alphabet at the dinner table fer Chrissakes. In addition to my Shakespearean dad, I was raised by my Medievalist mother, who happened to be my father's student in college. So there is no doubt that these entries will recapitulate habits we are outgrowing. I do my best to resist the classic strategies Prentis Hemphill has identified in attempts to establish innocence: stretching truths, obscuring intentions, omitting information, and claiming allies as a defense. Still, many of my methods might only serve as compost, in adrienne maree brown's language, for the new ones we're building. In the process of writing, I have come to know a writerly style very different from my academic voice, and I have chosen to keep the traces of that growth process as a palimpsest, rather than smoothing out the rough edges. I try to remain as transparent as possible about my motivations, which I hope will serve the worthy goal I first learned from Eve: diversifying possible modes of human connection.

Many of these concepts and exercises stem from the impactful work of those at the intersection of somatics and cultural change, which I have referenced to the best of my abilities, although much of this work has seeped into my consciousness in ways that makes it hard to source. Many of these practices uproot non-Western traditions from their cultural context. I try to approach these practices, from yogic breathing techniques to ancient Egyptian science to Chinese medicine to Sufi circling to Ayurvedic purifications, as whole universes of which I have glimpsed a star-speck, rather than making assertions of authority or mastery. Still, the presumptions at work in uprooting a poem or practice from a cultural context of which I know little may be problematic and triggering. I want to encourage a practice of deep listening to the messages from your own body, which we're now able to see as manifestations of cultural and ancestral inheritance. Any embodied spelunking needs to be approached with these intimacies in mind. Part of holding your truth, and your pace in touching it, is to stay open to the cues and firings of your own personal associative bodymind network. By engaging these practices, you might touch down on something that makes you wince or worse, and so I want to be very, very clear: these are merely offerings! Take what serves, discard what doesn't, cut and paste at will, modify, or recreate these practices freely. These entries invite you to breathe and move and hearseetastetouchfeel your way into a poem. I'm honored to be in the playground with you as we co-create new generative modes of worlding. KT language

MARCH WEEK 1

BEFORE THE GRASS IS RIZ

William Carlos Williams
"Spring and All [by the road to the contagious hospital]"

I
By the road to the contagious hospital
under the surge of the blue
mottled clouds driven from the
northeast-a cold wind. Beyond, the
waste of broad, muddy fields
brown with dried weeds, standing and fallen

patches of standing water
the scattering of tall trees

All along the road the reddish
purplish, forked, upstanding, twiggy
stuff of bushes and small trees
with dead, brown leaves under them
leafless vines—

Lifeless in appearance, sluggish
dazed spring approaches—

They enter the new world naked,
cold, uncertain of all
save that they enter. All about them
the cold, familiar wind—

Now the grass, tomorrow
the stiff curl of wildcarrot leaf

One by one objects are defined—
It quickens: clarity, outline of leaf

But now the stark dignity of
entrance—Still, the profound change
has come upon them: rooted, they
grip down and begin to awaken

———

Jane Hirshfield
"Counting, This New Year's Morning, What Powers Yet Remain To Me"

The world asks, as it asks daily:
And what can you make, can you do, to change my deep-broken, fractured?

I count, this first day of another year, what remains.
I have a mountain, a kitchen, two hands.

Can admire with two eyes the mountain,
actual, recalcitrant, shuffling its pebbles, sheltering foxes and beetles.

Can make black-eyed peas and collards.
Can make, from last year's late-ripening persimmons, a pudding.

Can climb a stepladder, change the bulb in a track light.

For four years, I woke each day first to the mountain,

then to the question.

The feet of the new sufferings followed the feet of the old,
and still they surprised.

I brought salt, brought oil, to the question. Brought sweet tea,
brought postcards and stamps. For four years, each day, something.

Stone did not become apple. War did not become peace.
Yet joy still stays joy. Sequins stay sequins. Words still bespangle,
bewilder.

Today, I woke without answer.

The day answers, unpockets a thought from a friend

don't despair of this falling world, not yet

didn't it give you the asking

———

Jane Hirshfield
"Today, When I Could Do Nothing"

Today, when I could do nothing,
I saved an ant.

It must have come in with the morning paper,
still being delivered
to those who shelter in place.

A morning paper is still an essential service.

I am not an essential service.

I have coffee and books,

time,
a garden,
silence enough to fill cisterns.

It must have first walked
the morning paper, as if loosened ink
taking the shape of an ant.

Then across the laptop computer—warm—
then onto the back of a cushion.

Small black ant, alone,
crossing a navy cushion,
moving steadily because that is what it could do.

Set outside in the sun,
it could not have found again its nest.
What then did I save?

It did not move as if it was frightened,
even while walking my hand,
which moved it through swiftness and air.

Ant, alone, without companions,
whose ant-heart I could not fathom—
how is your life, I wanted to ask.

I lifted it, took it outside.

This first day when I could do nothing,
contribute nothing
beyond staying distant from my own kind,
I did this.

Cheater, cheater, pumpkin eater! Did you open this book to the first entry instead of skipping to the week you're in? Obstinate! Headstrong! Rock on with your bad self. I want to celebrate your choice to be at choice by letting you in on a little secret. I have no idea where I actually started writing this book, but it wasn't on March first (as convenient as it would be to start writing on what was New Year's Day according to the old Roman calendar).

When I started writing, it was with the intention of relearning how to analyze poetry, and new skills only emerged with practice. My first go-round on this first week of March was about William Carlos Williams' "Spring and All," and its downward camera sweep from the inchoate sky, down through the muddy fields, and then further down to the underground roots and the life that is quickening there. I find in this poem the elemental movement Chinese medicine perceives in the spring: from water (chill, mud, wind, sky) to wood (as "one by one objects are defined" from vague "stuff" to the precise, stiff carrot leaf). I do feel this transition physically, emerging "sluggish and dazed" from winter but intuiting a kind of potential quickening somewhere deep inside. It's kind of the perfect description of the beginning of a book, no?

I'd love to use Williams' neat camera sweep to describe the writing of this book: the dark, formless, introspective months of gestation yielding to action and disciplined doing! But y'all... creative work is never like that. Growing something new is a mess. It's a muddy, bleary-eyed swing back and forth. Like the weather—one day we are all action, the next we are hunkered down with tea and hot pad. One day we get a glimpse of OurNextBoldMove and the next it's mush again. The learning curve in writing these entries was steep, as I resisted the inclination to wrestle dissonance into neatness and tried instead to stay true to the limits of my own perceptive reach and my sensual reckoning with a poem's overflow. The truth is always richer than the tidy anyway, and the actual progress of spring isn't a clean transition from chaos to form. It's kind of a mess.

So I'd like to engage a different poem to start, one that speaks to the aims and intentions of starting something new, rather than clean and masterful execution. Jane Hirshfield's poem for the New Year poses a question rather than answering it—the question this world is asking each one of us: "what can you make, can you do, to change my deep-broken, fractured?" Instead of answering this question, the speaker builds an altar to it, bringing salt and postcards and stamps. Waking without answers to the daily question, admitting the limitations of the power to turn stone to apple and war to peace, the poet instead counts "what remains." In doing so, the poem *becomes, itself,* the altar it describes. We could say of the poem what its final line says of the world: "didn't it give you the asking."

I'd like to borrow Hirshfield's question as the "thought from a friend" that this New Year's Day "unpockets": what can we make or do to create change in the world? We don't yet need a perfect answer, and this book sure isn't one. I have tried to remain stubbornly open to the shifting modes of inquiry in writing and in rewriting entries as I find new poems or can't afford to anthologize old ones. As a result, many entries contain within them the movement from familiar modes of close reading to stranger, more unwieldy ones. Maybe we could just *be in* this queer flux between mud and emergence, without concretizing what precisely we are growing just yet.

But enough with the self-reflexive stuff! This is starting to read like another intro. Maybe it is, in fact, your first week of March, dear reader, and you're looking to define your own springtime action! Hirshfield has an equally forgiving poem about opening our spidey senses to the hunches from the world on what needs doing. She released "Today, When I Could Do Nothing" in the middle of the disorientation of Covid lockdown. Many of us had coffee, books, time, a garden, and "silence enough to fill cisterns." And yet we, unlike Hirshfield's unfrightened ant, weren't doing so hot. If we weren't one of the brave fighters on the front line, if we could "contribute nothing beyond staying distant from [our] own kind," we had time aplenty to scan around for the small action. Saving an ant, who may not have been saved otherwise! These lines mark the sacredness of the small action—the local, the humble, the compassion-driven effort. That truth sticks around longer than any pandemic could. What do you do when you feel powerless? Check in on your mom. Get groceries for your sick friend. Write that letter to your city official. Pet your dog. Challenge a hometown acquaintance to talk through some racist shit. Oh, and pet your dog some more.

But/And! Some hours need to be devoted to letting the creative field lie fallow so it can birth new life. We can only generate solutions to the mess of our world by returning to the ant's pace for a time. If we are gentle with ourselves and our pacing, merciful in defining the blossoming thing within us that could maybe help this planet of ours, we just might find an answer one of these spring mornings. The human hand that moved the ant "through swiftness and air" is contrasted to the insect's own slow progress, from newspaper to laptop (warm!) to cushion—"moving steadily because that is what it could do." The poem was and is an invitation to move steadily, deliberately, with attention to warmth and ink and softness. Our contribution may just be a small thing, but together small things can carry the heaviest loads.

Maybe you could Just.Plain.Slow.Down. Simply fetching coffee at an ant's pace is incredibly instructive. Or if you're drawn to the messy springtime transition from underground stirrings toward form and structure, you might embody it! Seated or in slow movement, try exploring a dividing line at the waist, where upper-body movements are isolated from the stillness of the lower body, as though it were buried underground. Attend to the specific angles in your orientation to space—to the edges and corners of the room around you, ceiling, floor, and furniture. The amygdala likes to know where it stands, so to speak, and will be helped by clear, symmetrical, determined planting of the feet, legs, and hips.

Perhaps, in your breathing, you might embody the elemental up/down play of spring more subtly. Picture your underground lower body gripping down on the exhale and then inhaling the stem of the spine, chest, and skull upward, as though everything above the waist were reaching up for the sun. Perhaps close by visualizing one small action from your week, tantamount to ant-saving. It's only a beginning. You could just remain open to hunches from the world around you about what your winter hibernation might yield this spring, what might be coming into definition for you. How could you take action to give it what it needs to emerge?

MARCH WEEK 2
UN-HIBERNATE THE ANIMAL BODY

Margaret Hasse, "Day After Daylight Savings"

Blue numbers on my bedside clock
tell I forgot to change the hour.
This sets routines on haywire.

Like a domestic goat staked
to its circle of earth,
I don't do well untethered.

I have no hunger for early dinner,
become confused by the sound
of children who seem out

too late for a school night.
They've found an extra helping
of daylight to romp on new grass

and can't contain themselves,
strip off jackets, scatter
like a rag of ponies.

Whatever time says,
their joy insists
on springing forward.

————

Adrie Kusserow, "Mary Oliver for Corona Times"

You do not have to become totally Zen,
You do not have to use this isolation to make your marriage better,
your body slimmer, your children more creative.
You do not have to "maximize its benefits"
By using this time to work even more,
write the bestselling Corona Diaries,
Or preach the gospel of ZOOM.
You only have to let the soft animal of your body unlearn
everything capitalism has taught you,
(That you are nothing if not productive,
That consumption equals happiness,
That the most important unit is the single self.
That you are at your best when you resemble an efficient machine).

Tell me about your fictions, the ones you've been sold,
the ones you sheepishly sell others,
and I will tell you mine.
Meanwhile the world as we know it is crumbling.
Meanwhile the virus is moving over the hills,
suburbs, cities, farms and trailer parks.
Meanwhile The News barks at you, harsh and addicting,
Until the push of the remote leaves a dead quiet behind,
a loneliness that hums as the heart anchors.
Meanwhile a new paradigm is composing itself in our minds,
Could birth at any moment if we clear some space
From the same tired hegemonies.
Remember, you are allowed to be still as the white birch,
Stunned by what you see,
Uselessly shedding your coils of paper skins

Because it gives you something to do.
Meanwhile, on top of everything else you are facing,
Do not let capitalism coopt this moment,
laying its whistles and train tracks across your weary heart.
Even if your life looks nothing like the Sabbath,
Your stress boa-constricting your chest.
Know that your antsy kids, your terror, your shifting moods,
Your need for a drink have every right to be here,
And are no less sacred than a yoga class.
Whoever you are, no matter how broken,
the world still has a place for you, calls to you over and over
announcing your place as legit, as forgiven,
even if you fail and fail and fail again.
remind yourself over and over,
all the swells and storms that run through your long tired body
all have their place here, now in this world.
It is your birthright to be held
deeply, warmly in the family of things,
not one cell left in the cold.

POETIC THEMES

Feeling pessimistic? "The more things change the more they stay the same" kinda thing? Consider: when I first encountered these two poems in March of 2020, we were all trying to "spring forward," wandering unstaked in the midst of a Covid lockdown, without any secure tether to our routines. It was like daylight savings confusion cubed. And now—now! By the time you are reading this, the practice is probably a thing of the past! The same kids who were freed from their school cages in 2020 will barely remember losing an hour of sleep every March.

The mechanistic, post-industrial view of time as money created this practice, with the crazy notion of shifting the number of daylight hours—something determined by the planet's orbit and axis, not our wee alarm clocks. And everyone moaning and groaning about waking up in darkness will have to soon consider... hmmm... why do we begin school and work so damn early? And then maybe we'll consider... hmmm... how could we shift those structures to honor the movement of nature around and in us? And so it goes, like dominoes!

The "new paradigm" that is preparing to be birthed isn't just composing itself within our individual minds, but also in communities building practices where we model human behavior on the patterning of nature. Part of our work in resisting alienation from our bodily wisdom is to restore our experience of time as instinctual, sacred, harmonized with natural cycles. "Day After Daylight Savings" illustrates the contrast between what we all knew as kids and our confused, brainwashed state after being trained to a capitalist approach to time. To return to an intuitive experience of early spring might be to acknowledge that it's hard to feel mudluscious in the brrr. It's a long ride from March to April, when we begin to feel puddle-wonderful springtime in earnest. But maybe we could invite an inner thawing by imagining something is stirring deep within us, some hibernating animal.

Kusserow's playful rewriting of Mary Oliver's poem "Wild Geese" gives us a little prod to reawaken to feeling-first enjoyment, even in these chilly, not-so-sensuous mornings. We might, in re-membering Oliver, call up the bear emerging from hibernation in one of at least two Oliver poems entitled "Spring." Tooth and claw, this poem invites us to experience our corporeal awakening as nature, not apart from it. Breath and taste and sharp nails and touch are a way of coming down, descending into a wordless primal state, a place in the animal world. When we enter our body's experience, our *thingliness*—beyond despair or language at all—is the very definition of perfect love. This is the answer to the question posed, in true Oliver style, splat in the middle of "Spring," about how to care for the globe. We are not visitors, observers through binoculared distance, but part and parcel of the natural cycles around us. Our animal nature, our gut instinct, will guide us in repairing a broken planet, if we can reawaken to it.

Maybe part of returning to the soft animal body is recovering a reverence for stillness. The push of the remote leaves "a loneliness that hums as the heart anchors." The strange capacity for loneliness to anchor the heart has a dissonance echoed in the poignant line: "remember, you are allowed to be still as the white birch, stunned by what you see, / uselessly shedding your coils of paper skin / Because it gives you something to do." During this time where the sacred and the beautiful coexist so seamlessly with the pointless and the nonsensical. The phrase "Our place" reframes the body as a cozy home base, in contradistinction to the claustrophobic or heavy feeling of hibernation, a weight "boa-constricting" "across our weary heart" or "through our long tired body." In these cold March mornings, we are being "held warmly" in Oliver's thingly ecology, "not one cell / left out in the cold." And let's all agree how lovely it feels to be told we are forgiven for our failures, our limitations—"even if [we] fail and fail and fail again."

PRACTICE

I'd like offer what I think of as a kind of animal power walking for embodying our primal thingliness. Spring invites movement that is faster-paced, heating, and more muscular, like a vigorous walk that awakens the big muscles of quads, biceps, and core. In addition, power walking cleanses the lungs, heating and drying the body. The uptick of heart rate, breath pace, and blood flow can feel like a real-time awakening from hibernation, especially in the morning. If we imagine awakening a particularly fierce and wild spirit animal within, the movement changes. This might be the walk of your animal soul.

Quaker theologian Parker Palmer envisions the soul as a beast in the wilderness, one we only catch sight of once in a while. Hunting down the soul is no easy business, but catching sight of it is like rounding a tree to come face to face with steady, all-knowing eyes that seem to recognize you. Can you think of a moment of "soul-whispering," when you caught sight of yourself inside an animal's mojo? Are there qualities of this animal that can manifest in your way of walking, helping you imprint this superpower into the softest beast that is your body?

MARCH WEEK 3
SPRING EQUINOX NEW YEAR

Robert Frost
"Putting in the Seed"

You come to fetch me from my work to-night
When supper's on the table, and we'll see
If I can leave off burying the white
Soft petals fallen from the apple tree.
(Soft petals, yes, but not so barren quite,
Mingled with these, smooth bean and wrinkled pea;)
And go along with you ere you lose sight
Of what you came for and become like me,
Slave to a springtime passion for the earth.
How Love burns through the Putting in the Seed
On through the watching for that early birth
When, just as the soil tarnishes with weed,
The sturdy seedling with arched body comes
Shouldering its way and shedding the earth crumbs.

This poem is in the public domain.

Octavio Paz
"Proem"

At times poetry is the vertigo of bodies and the vertigo of speech and the
    vertigo of death;
the walk with eyes closed along the edge of the cliff, and the verbena in
    submarine gardens;
the laughter that sets on fire the rules and the holy commandments;
the descent of parachuting words onto the sands of the page;
the despair that boards a paper boat and crosses,
    for forty nights and forty days, the night-sorrow sea and the day-sorrow
    desert;
the idolatry of the self and the desecration of the self and the dissipation of
    the self;
the beheading of epithets, the burial of mirrors; the recollection of
  pronouns freshly cut in the
  garden of Epicurus, and the garden of Netzahualcoyotl;
the flute solo on the terrace of memory and the dance of flames in the cave
    of thought;
the migrations of millions of verbs, wings and claws, seeds and hands;
the nouns, bony and full of roots, planted on the waves of language;
the love unseen and the love unheard and the love unsaid: the love in
    love.

Syllables seeds.

Muriel Rukeyser
"Elegy in Joy" [excerpt]

We tell beginnings: for the flesh and the answer,
or the look, the lake in the eye that knows,
for the despair that flows down in widest rivers,
cloud of home; and also the green tree of grace,
all in the leaf, in the love that gives us ourselves.

The word of nourishment passes through the women,
soldiers and orchards rooted in constellations,
white towers, eyes of children:
saying in time of war What shall we feed?
I cannot say the end.

Nourish beginnings, let us nourish beginnings.
Not all things are blest, but the
seeds of all things are blest.
The blessing is in the seed.

This moment, this seed, this wave of the sea, this look, this instant of love.
Years over wars and an imagining of peace. Or the expiation journey
toward peace which is many wishes flaming together,
fierce pure life, the many-living home.
Love that gives us ourselves, in the world known to all
new techniques for the healing of the wound,
and the unknown world. One life, or the faring stars.

POETIC THEMES

The ancient Babylonians and Persians marked the turning of the year sometime around the vernal equinox. In my neck of the woods, at least in the moment of global warming in which this book was written, around now is generally considered a safe time to plant seeds, especially if you are looking to harvest edible things in the summer. But there are many ways to plant a seed, as these poems illustrate.

Frost's "Putting in the Seed" represents gardening as solitary labor through which "Love burns" (his wife making him dinner is not configured this way). The petals he's fingering are pretty suggestive: "not so barren quite, / Mingled with these, smooth bean and wrinkled pea." Hm. "Putting" (an odd, neutral choice of verbs for this otherwise sexy poem) seeds into the ground is seen to be the demonstration of his "springtime passion for the earth." He is such a "slave" to passion that he may or may not decide to come eat the dinner prepared for him. His wife is, however, invited to the early birth, when the "sturdy seedling" will shoulder its way into the world.

Contrast this to Octavio Paz's expansive vision of planting seeds. A poem about the action of writing poetry as an analogy for seed-planting would seem to point to a certain self-reflexivity. The horizon expands and expands further in the far-reaching scope of what poetry can be: vertigo cliff-walk of bodies, speech, and death. Words parachuting onto the page are depicted in Biblical proportions of sorrow and despair, which would seem to aggrandize the poet. But then, admitting this "idolatry of the self" is itself a kind of desecration. And in this play of expansion and contraction, the small self of the poet is dissipated into something much larger. Poetic creation is figured here in terms of destruction, before anything new can be possible: epithets are beheaded, rules and commandments are set on fire. Even the poem's nostalgic homage to the ancient world of Plato and Epicurus forces open the Western ancient world to include the gardens of Netzahualcoyotl, a poet and philosopher from pre-Columbian Mexico.

Language isn't configured as the poet's spawn, a product of his labor pains, but instead as something wild, set free, far beyond and outside of him. Verbs migrate with "wings and claws," nouns are "bony and full of roots," language is a sea of waves. The mystery of creation isn't an act to be claimed or owned here. For Frost, the middle of the sonnet holds the love act that breeds its creation: "Love burns through the [capitalized act of] Putting in the Seed." But love only emerges at the end of Paz's poem, so mysterious as to be invisible, unheard, and unspoken. The involuted line "love in love" comes back to the final, solitary, italicized line: *Syllables seeds.* The poem created, for Paz, is what comes before, like a proem. The love for creation seeds, in turn, more love.

Is it far-fetched to perceive in "Elegy in Joy" echoes of the watery despair, engendering love, roots and flame of "Proem"? Rukeyser's articulations of a liberal politics might owe just as much to Octavio Paz as her poetry does. I've only dipped a toe in it, so I'm not the one to say. But in the foreword to her translations of his early poetry, she describes finding in his work a fusion of politics and art: "In coming to the poems of the young Octavio Paz, I found that voice of the meeting-place for which many of us were looking in those years. Meeting-place of fever and the cold eye, in a passion which could hold together with his own arms the flying apart of his own time." She describes, in the foreword, how translating him transformed her. Her grace and humility in admitting her limitations, not being of Mexican descent, exemplify a keen awareness of the messiness of intersubjectivity ahead of its time. She recounts her awkward "stumbling" through the task of bringing the full range of meanings, carrying Nahuatl as well as Mexican nuances. She confesses to having made many "mistakes in my frenzy and ignorance," and speaks directly to appropriative violence: "…the traces of my attempt to move from this poetry toward an English poem have left wounds, scars where we need healing." She closes the foreword by restating her conviction that "The translator must be exposed to this extent; fully, that is"; ending not with her own conclusions, but with Carlos Fuentes' description of Paz's "lucid expression of Mexican tragedy."

But back to "Elegy in Joy"! Rukeyser's elegies were her response to the confusion of World-War-II-era America. They are part of an oeuvre that, like Paz's, wrestles with the nitty-grittiesies of a commitment to pacifism in the context of savage political realities. And this poem is the last of the elegies. It is the work of a mature poet and anti-fascist activist, no longer naive to the ways of the world. As such, this poem swims in grief, aware of its own limitation in offering nourishment or answers to wide-eyed children in wartime. Still, it isn't an elegy *for joy*, but an elegy *in joy*. Like a small raft on the flowing river of despair, joy persists in new beginnings. The "green tree of grace" gives a blessing in the form of a seed. The seed here is configured as a metaphor standing for new beginnings, of whatever kind, which we are called to nourish and which in turn promise nourishment. Anything sullied, tainted, made toxic by ordinary human cruelty, can be recreated: "Not all things are blest, but the / seeds of all things are blest."

After spending "Years over wars and an imagining of peace," the nowness of the present moment is the seed for peace, an instantiation of "fierce pure life." All of us collectively caring about the broken world, "which is many wishes flaming together," holds the possibility for our "expiation journey / toward peace." The first word of the poem is, after all, WE. Frost's labor of love in sowing a seed creates new life, configured as progeny. Paz's poem is the creative seed that generates a love so expansive that the smallness of humanity disappears in it. For Rukeyser, Love itself appears to be the nourishing seed that "gives us ourselves": we are recreated in and through the very notion of beginning anew. The blessing of "this instant of love" makes possible "new techniques for the healing of the wound, / and the unknown world." And then the magnificent final line about the reach and import of each mortal incarnation, as far-flung as any surrealistic sweep of Paz's imagination: "One life, or the faring stars."

PRACTICE

The most literal way of exploring your relation to seed-planting would be... um... to plant an actual seed. Frost's poem is the most grounded in embodied movement and earthy detail. You could come back to earth by feeling the dirt under your fingernails. Or you might instead plant an emblematic talisman, a meaningful object of some kind, referencing the magic of something you're ready to birth this spring. You could mark it with a stone, dig it up at the end of the summer, wash it off, and see what has come into the world through you. Or you could render the action of planting a seed metaphorically, as Paz does with the analogy of writing, through some creative act. It seems very fitting to mark the new year by generating something new, and perhaps it could renew your love for painting, or journaling, or dancing. Or you could "nourish beginnings" in Rukeyser's way, through letting grace drop its seed in a single act of loving. Who needs you in this moment? How could you contribute to healing the world's wound by reaching out to them in love?

MARCH WEEK 4
SPRINGTIME ANNUNCIATION IN-SPIR-ATION

Denise Levertov, "Annunciation"

We know the scene: the room, variously furnished,
almost always a lectern, a book; always
the tall lily.
       Arrived on solemn grandeur of great wings,
the angelic ambassador, standing or hovering,
whom she acknowledges, a guest.

But we are told of meek obedience. No one mentions
courage.
       The engendering Spirit
did not enter her without consent.
       God waited.

She was free
to accept or to refuse, choice
integral to humanness.

. . .

Aren't there annunciations
of one sort or another
in most lives?
          Some unwillingly
undertake great destinies,
enact them in sullen pride,
uncomprehending.
More often
those moments
          when roads of light and storm
          open from darkness in a man or woman,
are turned away from

in dread, in a wave of weakness, in despair
and with relief.
Ordinary lives continue.
                God does not smite them.
But the gates close, the pathway vanishes.

————————————

She had been a child who played, ate, slept
like any other child–but unlike others,
wept only for pity, laughed
in joy not triumph.
Compassion and intelligence
fused in her, indivisible.

Called to a destiny more momentous
than any in all of Time,
she did not quail,
  only asked
a simple, 'How can this be?'
and gravely, courteously,
took to heart the angel's reply,
the astounding ministry she was offered:

to bear in her womb
Infinite weight and lightness; to carry
in hidden, finite inwardness,
nine months of Eternity; to contain
in slender vase of being,
the sum of power–
in narrow flesh,
the sum of light.
                    Then bring to birth,
push out into air, a Man-child
needing, like any other,
milk and love–

but who was God.

This was the moment no one speaks of,
when she could still refuse.

A breath unbreathed,
                    Spirit,
                              suspended,
                                        waiting.

_____

She did not cry, 'I cannot. I am not worthy,'
Nor, 'I have not the strength.'
She did not submit with gritted teeth,
                              raging, coerced.
Bravest of all humans,
                         consent illumined her.
The room filled with its light,
the lily glowed in it,
                         and the iridescent wings.
Consent,
        courage unparalleled,
opened her utterly.

"There is a vitality, a life force, a quickening that is translated through you into action. As there is only one of you in all time, this expression is unique, and if you block it, it will never exist through any other medium; it will be lost. The world will not have it. It is not your business to determine how good it is, nor how it compares with other expressions. It is your business to keep it yours, clearly and directly, to keep the channel open. You do not even have to believe in yourself or your work. You have to keep open and aware directly to the urges that motivate you. Keep the channel open."

— Martha Graham, in a quote remembered by Agnes de Mille

POETIC THEMES

Of all the major Christian holidays, the day marking the visitation of the angel upon Mary is the only one centering around a woman. Levertov's insidious first line: "We know the scene." Oh, and how.

Let me just say now: to wrestle with this poem is hard. Really hard. It's a Christian poem celebrating the ostensible power of consent in the idea of a virgin mother. The costs of this myth, with its violent regime of white female purity, have been catastrophic—part of the weaponry of colonialism that has left so.many.people.destroyed. Lingering with this poem uses more parts of me than I'm comfortable using.

I want to join Levertov in disrupting the narrative of Mary's "meek obedience," in favor of the notion that God "did not enter her without consent." I really want to. I want to believe that "She was free / to accept or to refuse," and I wholly agree that this freedom is a "choice / integral to humanness." But y'all… it feels like such a stretch, in spite of the beauty of her languaging.

An ethic of toughness shames us for turning away "in a wave of weakness" from what we might not want to take on. Levertov associates "no" with despair and the relief of the ordinary. To blunder through the hard questions about power and yielding, we could revisit our own stories of pressured consent. After all, most of us would respond in the affirmative to Levertov's central question: "Aren't there annunciations / of one sort or another / in most lives?" How could we design some fresh strategies for imagining openness, receptivity, and the power to take in otherness?

Levertov reconfigures Mary's consent to bring something sacred into the world as the power of creativity. The visitation of the divine is muse-like, an instantiation of literal inspiration: taking in spirit, breathing it in, to gestate it and birth something new. There is something so soothing about this reconfiguration of openness. It's a recognizable, gender-neutral experience of being "opened...utterly" by a form of power that is distinctly outside of us—"other."

Speaking of "courage unparalleled," I'd like to bring Martha Graham to the stage. Isn't it ironic that the movement legacy of this non-procreative woman is *the contraction*? Creativity requires radical openness, for Graham as for Levertov. Maybe we could divorce the idea of creation from actual pregnancy and childbirth, to reconfigure springtime themes that inhere in the Annunciation. Mary is known, in Christian thought, as the Queen Bee, the ubiquitous symbol of fertility, rebirth, and a transition from rest to work. Listening for the buzzing of the divine voice in our ears might sound like Graham's "vitality" or "life force" or "quickening that is translated through you into action." It's a call to listen, a call to "keep the channel open," "clearly and directly," to stay "open and aware directly to the urges that motivate you." This is, for Graham, the divine visitation. Graham and Levertov lead us to consider what we are being asked to open ourselves to. What is the work we are being called to undertake? Sometimes the call to create appears as Levertovian "moments when roads of light and storm / open from darkness," and other times it appears as an itch that needs scratching, Graham's "queer, divine dissatisfaction, a blessed unrest." This is more like the feeling of something waiting to get free of us. Either way, if we don't respond to the call of our work in the world, we are given the stakes. Levertov's assertion that "the gates close, the pathway vanishes" is echoed by Graham: "it will not exist through any other medium; and be lost. The world will not have it." This is an angle that configures creativity from a process of output to an art of input. Perceiving the generativeness of the spring in this way draws the focus away from producing or amassing resources, and toward openness and receptivity.

I want to witness Queen Bee Mary as a figure who reinvigorates time-worn clichés about fertility with a courageous openness to our work in the world. I really do. But it's not easy to neutralize the painful associations that attend a figure who has caused a world of harm, even for someone like me whose religious upbringing didn't feature Mary. But if we can listen for the divine buzz, maybe with practice we might come to witness openness and receptivity with new eyes. Perhaps it could even help revise the idea of a "work ethic" as a collaborative, celebratory promiscuity: pollinating and cross-pollinating sweet, sticky stuff to spread more life around!

I began offering humming as a closing practice in my somatics classes before I learned that it soothed the vagus nerve. I just knew it was helpful to bridge the gap between the quiet mindfulness practices and the way we show up in the world. Opening eyes, greeting one another, and making sounds in the space seemed to help us all import the qualities we were cultivating into the rest of our lives and interactions. So I settled on humming together—no wrong notes, no scripted rhythm, just humming for the length of our exhale and then starting again.

Yoga calls this practice "bee breath" (*brahmani pranayama*). Much of the power of Sanskrit, particularly the "Om," is attributed to vibration, and when we hum, we actually feel it vibrating the skull, the sinus cavity, and the brain—our second womb. To summon our bee powers speaks to all the themes I've been playing with here. It's pretty empowering to watch, over time, as a practice builds our capacity to calm our inner state, sedimenting a fresh foundation from which to put something new out there. Over time, the clean categories of input and output get kerfuffled even further: the quiet buzz of a hum is a form of output that, when removed, makes us aware of all that inhabits the silence that we didn't take in before. When the avant-garde composer John Cage first entered an anechoic chamber (a room designed to deaden sound), he identified two distinct concurrent sounds, and the engineer told him that one corresponded to the nervous system, the other to blood flow. This can be a whole practice unto itself.

Would you be willing to test out humming, perhaps at different registers and tones, as a way of clearing fresh inroads to the brain? Then you might pause in the stillness and listen to the white noise until you hear not just the static buzz, but a lower register, like a bottom-end bass tone. It can be deeply centering to toggle the attention between the bass and the "treble," if that's what you want to call the static sound. It can also allow for an experiential reconfiguring of what's inside and what's outside the soma. Deep listening is a practice of opening up to the messages that might be reaching out for us. Might you then differently hear the messages reaching out for you? What else in your life helps clear the pathway for visitation, inspiration, communion? Are there other ways you might cultivate the openness and receptivity that invite spirit in?

APRIL WEEK 1

THE GREENING OF THE TREES

Ada Limón
"Adaptation"

It was, for a time, a loud twittering flight
of psychedelic-colored canaries: a cloud
of startle and get-out in the ornamental
irons of the rib cage. Nights when the moon
was wide like the great eye of a universal
beast coming close for a kill, it was a cave
of bitten bones and snake skins, eggshell dust,
and charred scraps of a frozen-over flame.
All the things it has been: kitchen knife
and the ancient carp's frown, cavern of rust
and worms in the airless tire swing,
cactus barb, cut-down tree, dead cat
in the plastic crate. Still, how the great middle
ticker marched on, and from all its four chambers
to all its forgiveness, unlocked the sternum's
door, reversed and reshaped until it was a new
bright carnal species, more accustomed to grief,
and ecstatic at the sight of you.

———

Ada Limón
"Instructions on Not Giving Up"

More than the fuchsia funnels breaking out
of the crabapple tree, more than the neighbor's
almost obscene display of cherry limbs shoving
their cotton candy-colored blossoms to the slate
sky of Spring rains, it's the greening of the trees
that really gets to me. When all the shock of white
and taffy, the world's baubles and trinkets, leave
the pavement strewn with the confetti of aftermath,
the leaves come. Patient, plodding, a green skin
growing over whatever winter did to us, a return
to the strange idea of continuous living despite
the mess of us, the hurt, the empty. Fine then,
I'll take it, the tree seems to say, a new slick leaf
unfurling like a fist to an open palm, I'll take it all.

POETIC THEMES

Our 2022 Poet Laureate! Praise be! What joy to hang out with Ada Limón's lifesaving words for a bit. Both these poems are about maturity, about how our banged-up winter bodies and love-battered hearts could dream to still hope, hope to still dream. I suppose I should say at the outset that my experience of seasonal depression, and clinical depression in general, will always color my need for and way of reading both poetry and the shifting seasons. It's as much a part of my subject position as anything else. But I promise next week I'll cheer up—or try to. For now though, I'd like to confess that both these poems speak to the part of me that wants to die every day between four and five in the afternoon. Both poems also speak to what gets me through it: every day the feeling passes. The Buddhist teaching of impermanence has special use value for depressives, which could be chalked up to… like… survival.

The human heart in every life has on taken so, so many different shapes. "Adaptation" gives a litany of heart incarnations, weird and wonderful and dark. Shape-shifting from startled canary to carnivorous moon-eye to kitchen knife to the "ancient carp's frown." Each is more evocative than the next. For me, the most compelling metaphors find a way to describe the heart darkly, in some kind of cage, like the dead cat in the crate, or the worms and rust inside the tire swing. Oh, the ways and ways our heart can incarnate darkness.

And then, right in the middle of a line, comes the cutting word "still"! What comes next is the sweetest of promises, the certainty that the "great middle ticker" will reemerge yet again, in new form, "from all its four chambers / to all its forgiveness." We know the relief in experiencing inner movement after emotional stuckness, like rain after a long drought. We are reassured of our heart's capacity for tenaciously marching forward. We are lifted, palpably, out of our pain when the door of the breastbone is unlocked and the heart escapes to *feel* again, stronger in its grief-resilience.

Finally, magically, the very last word reveals this to be a love poem. Entering the scene, refreshing everything: you! We have no idea to whom—or to what—this poem is written. But the heart appears, "reversed and reshaped until it was a new / bright carnal species" (perhaps the source of the title of the collection, *Bright Dead Things*). What or whom is being witnessed to inspire this change? Perhaps "you" is a private matter, or maybe it's us, the reader! Or maybe "you" is the world perceived again as new, the way it is when rebirthed in spring. In any case, when renewed, the heart can once again escape the cage of the self and behold the other. This is ecstasy in its true sense (from the Greek *ekstasis,* standing outside oneself).

"Instructions on Not Giving Up" strikes me as the twin poem to "Adaptation," both about the capacity for renewal that allows us to remain open. Limón redefines strength: true grit is a kind of flexibility of feeling, a tenacious emotional openness to otherness within and without. Forget the showy fabulousness of cotton candy confetti cherry blossoms—that's not really what spring rebirth is about. It's about something deeper, more authentic, slower, less obvious: the ability for something huge and strong and old to sprout something new and humble and alive—something green. This perspective shift celebrates, again, the body that has been through it, the hurt and empty mess returning "to the strange idea of continuous living." Acknowledging "the mess of us, the hurt, the empty" is step one to actually not giving up; step two is reminding us of our capacity for growing new skin. Skin, the biggest and the least acknowledged organ in the body. The boundary between what is and is not us. Skin, at once our defensive barrier and our porous, sensate mode of making contact with the outside world. In touching our potential for renewal, for continuance, we might open back up to the world, like a fist to an open palm, and move forward toward life.

PRACTICE

If you're called to move, it might be lovely to develop a movement sequence from big, showy shapes toward a deeper, slower, more subtle, contemplative mode. You could experience the contrast of splayed-open movements and poses by taking up as much space as possible, with extravagant flourishes that mimic Limón's fist unfurling to open palm through flamenco-style wrist circles that reach out and up. Movement choices that make use of action words like "shoving," "breaking out," "shock," and "strewn" might dial down to something slower and subtler, like stroking the fingertips of one hand along the heart meridian, from the end of one limb to the end of the other. For example, right fingertips explore the skin by gliding from left fingertips, up the arm, across the heart center, to unfurl to the right, then the left fingers take a turn.

It might make sense to finish just by attending to the heart's beat. As you lay your fingertips on the wrist, carotid artery, or the great middle ticker itself, you might call to mind a few heart metaphors from your own past, to acknowledge the banged-up mess but also to re-source your allies. The metaphors don't have to be anything fancy, just meaningful objects or people: ballerina-doll heart, dodgeball heart, jungle-gym-trickster heart. What might be the next carnal species calling to your ticker this spring? We need to open ourselves to all the heart-shapes that might rebirth our ability to love.

APRIL WEEK 2
THE HAPTICS OF DELIGHT

Ross Gay
"Sorrow is not my Name"
—*after Gwendolyn Brooks*

No matter the pull toward brink. No
matter the florid, deep sleep awaits.
There is a time for everything. Look, just this morning a vulture
nodded his red, grizzled head at me,
and I looked at him, admiring
the sickle of his beak.
Then the wind kicked up, and,
after arranging that good suit of feathers
he up and took off.
Just like that. And to boot,
there are, on this planet alone, something like two
million naturally occurring sweet things,
some with names so generous as to kick
the steel from my knees: agave, persimmon,
stick ball, the purple okra I bought for two bucks
at the market. Think of that. The long night,
the skeleton in the mirror, the man behind me
on the bus taking notes, yeah, yeah.
But look; my niece is running through a field

calling my name. My neighbor sings like an angel
and at the end of my block is a basketball court.
I remember. My color's green. I'm spring.

—*for Walter Aikens*

———

Ross Gay
"Ode to Buttoning and Unbuttoning My Shirt"

No one knew or at least
I didn't know
they knew
what the thin disks
threaded here
on my shirt
might give me
in terms of joy
this is not something to be taken lightly
the gift
of buttoning one's shirt
slowly
top to bottom
or bottom
to top or sometimes
the buttons
will be on the other
side and
I am a woman
that morning
slipping the glass
through its slot
I tread
differently that day
or some of it anyway
my conversations

are different
and the car bomb slicing the air
and the people in it
for a quarter mile
and the honeybee's
legs furred with pollen
mean another
thing to me
than on the other days
which too have
been drizzled in this
simplest of joys
in this world
of spaceships and subatomic
this and that
two maybe three
times a day
some days
I have the distinct pleasure
of slowly untethering
the one side
from the other
which is like unbuckling
a stack of vertebrae
with delicacy
for I must only use
the tips
of my fingers
with which I will
one day close
my mother's eyes
this is as delicate
as we can be
in this life
practicing
like this
giving the raft of our hands
to the clumsy spider and blowing soft until she
lifts her damp heft and
crawls off
we practice like this

pushing the seed into the earth
like this first
in the morning
then at night
we practice
sliding the bones home.

POETIC THEMES

Ross Gay teaches the mechanics of how to train our curiosity in order to cultivate delight as a discipline. "Fleeting intense attentions," he explains to Krista Tippett in the *On Being* podcast, are the "butterflies of delight" which land on the thing that is joy. Notice what's *not* a part of this process: he does *not* demand that we say thank you! Neo-spiritual gratitude practices can be so damn guilty-making, y'all. When we dutifully make our gratitude lists in our journals each morning, we are called back to the feeling of the child unwrapping the gift and plastering on the smiley face for Aunty Linda. I remember when my kids' cousin opened his Christmas present and obediently repeated, in a robotic tone, the forced acknowledgement he had been taught: "thankyousomuchitissperfectitisjustwhatiwanted." The gift was, like, a book or something. The notion of delight frees us from the "should" of gratitude as groveling at the gift of the world by dissolving our attention into it. We actually, temporarily, become one with it, in a non-dual merging of self and our surround.

Gay's trademark modality of practicing delight as a discipline offers a welcome respite from the unachievable happiness model. And no, this isn't a mode of bypassing, but rather a way of allowing our joy to co-exist alongside all that is crappy in our world. Like parallel play. The subtitle of "Sorrow is not My Name" refers to an assertion by Gwendolyn Brooks: "I have no right to sorrow" (from "Another Girl, 1936"). The pull of darkness is no match for tree-green. Gay acknowledges with a "yeah, yeah" the world's suckiness; he remains fully aware of the creepy guy behind him on the bus taking notes, as a black man in this twisted culture must. Then he turns our attention—"But look"—to two million naturally occurring sweet things.

Because we need to believe that, ultimately, the wind will carry away the vulture, poems like this should be taken like vitamins. Gay (note the titular play on his name) reminds us of okra, agave, and persimmon. He's irresistible, and we want to be with him in joy, and decide too that our color is green, and that we too are spring.

All the phenomena in "Sorrow Is Not My Name" are visual or aural. But "Ode to Buttoning and Unbuttoning My Shirt" introduces the sense of touch. This ode to touch achieves a rounding out of focus, a spatial generosity on the page, even through the vertical stack of these short button-like lines. The poem shifts from front body, to hemispheric split, to back body, to the line between living and dead, human and animal, above and underground. It even invites gender shifts, just in the act of slipping in the glass buttons from the opposite side, as women's shirts do. The car bomb slicing through people places harsh reality firmly at the center of the poem, co-existing with the sweetness of the legs of the honeybee "furred with pollen." The poem itself functions as fingertips, delicately spiderwalk-touching this thing and then that thing.

Playing with the thin disks on our shirts is a touching example (wink, wink) of the joy to be found in the little things. "Untethering" the two sides of fabric is described in terms of pleasure, in the sexiness of "unbuckling / a stack of vertebrae" (aka, let your backbone slip). The pleasure here, for Gay, seems to lie in the delicacy of what fingertips can feel and do. Our fingers learn by practicing, and the practice of subtle touch has real-world applications: we will use that delicacy to free a spider or to close the eyelids of those we lose. Anyone who has done this gentle maneuver must feel shivers upon reading this line. My dad's eyelids were stubborn, unyielding, and I held my hand over them for a long time before the imprint was made. This association can only persist in echoing and re-echoing in the subsequent action of "pushing the seed into the earth." The poem's final action—"we practice / sliding the bones home"— brings us home to our participation in the practice: we become aware that even in reading the poem we are rehearsing a way of being. Gay's poem brings together shirt-buttoning and closing our beloveds' eyelids in death. Buttoning together multiform meanings, tangles of associative networks, changes and enriches our experience, making us more sensitive. Each micro-action of our fingertips, even turning this page, is an opportunity to hone our awareness to nuance and to practice delicacy in all things.

PRACTICE

I love the idea of buttoning two things together as an alternative to dualistic thinking. These new combinations can be galvanizing, like trying on a new and fabulous outfit. For example: I'm not a good mom or a bad mom, instead I'm a part of a generation of good-enough moms whose kids suffer from experiencing the full range of emotion (because they have been given permission), and so those kids also have extraordinary compassion for the suffering of others. In the context of Ross Gay's magical notion of delight, co-existing realities, and the sensitivities of touch, we might choose a practice that plays with the expansive modes enabled by pleasure.

Pleasure activist Kai Cheng Thom teaches a somatic exercise that seems to fit here. The practitioner touches one hand with the other, focusing first on giving the touching hand pleasure, then giving the receiving hand pleasure. Simple but deep, this activity can be used to explore many different embodied skill sets like consent, or giving, or serving. It fits well inside a Queer framework that explores the potential of non-normative desire to create ingenious new modes of meaning-making. (I could queer this section further by contextualizing this exercise where I first encountered it, in a session with an Estonian sex therapist where this was one of the most erotic, and least overtly sexual, of all the things she did with me.) Kai Cheng Thom framed the practice as a "bottom-up" exercise, in the language of somatics, as privileging the experience of the body before assigning any interpretation. Fusing the somatic with the linguistic, as this book seeks to do, you might dissolve this line by inviting a few of Gay's wonderful action verbs into the experience of touch. In fact, you could smudge that body/mind boundary further by trying out Lucina Artigas' Butterfly Hug, a bilateral stimulation exercise that neatly embodies Gay's butterflies of delight. Cross your thumbs, laying the hands over your chest with the fingertips just under the collarbones, and alternate hands as the four fingers together softly tap the chest. Remember, your color is green.

APRIL WEEK 3
OUT IS THROUGH

Kazim Ali
"Ramadan"

You wanted to be so hungry, you would break into branches,
and have to choose between the starving month's

nineteenth, twenty-first, and twenty-third evenings.
The liturgy begins to echo itself and why does it matter?

If the ground-water is too scarce one can stretch nets
into the air and harvest the fog.

Hunger opens you to illiteracy,
thirst makes clear the starving pattern,

the thick night is so quiet, the spinning spider pauses,
the angel stops whispering for a moment—

The secret night could already be over,
you will have to listen very carefully—

You are never going to know which night's mouth is sacredly reciting
and which night's recitation is secretly mere wind—

POETIC THEMES

"Ramadan" is a poem about religious ecstasy (from the Greek *ekstasis*, the state of standing outside of oneself, to echo last week's entry). The yogic and Muslim spiritual practices that pepper Kazim Ali's poetry facilitate an experience of the body deep enough to transport the practitioner beyond the worldly plane. The "hidden sweetness in the stomach's emptiness," to quote Rumi's "Fasting," is an evacuation of the self that makes way for a more expansive state. In Ali's poetry, identity presents as diffuse and prismatic; now a river, now an angel, selfhood can manifest as stairs, hunger, a bowl for rain, or the rain itself. The shapeshifting seems rooted, paradoxically, in an excruciatingly precise awareness of one particular body. In the first line of "Ramadan," for example, one could travel into hunger so deeply as to "break into branches." One truth at the heart of embodied spiritual practice is that the only way out is through. In the words of Nomi Stone, "Make no mistake, you leave the body only / through the body" (from "Many Scientists Convert to Islam," a Jewish take on Ramadan).

Not surprisingly, what draws Ali to Ramadan is its mystery and complexity, not just in its angel visitations or its spiders weaving protective webs, but even and especially the liturgical ambiguity about which day is sacred. If identity is a shifting field, there's also a temporal unmooring. This might have something to do with surrendering to an inherited faith, where childhood memories flicker inside spiritual practices. The ghostly presence of precognitive awareness or even epigenetic memory engender a multiplicity of view. Ancestors and family members float through Ali's poems, variously angelic or bedeviling. But this shifting field of reference orbits around a strong spiritual center.

In his gut-wrenching poem "Home," Ali wrestles to expand what might fit within the boundaries of the religious practices he grew up with. He opens up the confines of which languages might be sacred to include Hebrew, Latin, Sanskrit, and Arabic. He finally dismisses the notion that divine messaging could ever even "fit into the requirements of the human mouth." Ultimately, the poem asserts, the divine transcends the limits of language: "I learned God's true language is only silence and breath." Fasting is one way of gaining entry into this extra-ordinary world, where one learns secret skills, like how to harvest fog. Among these superpowers is a linguistic or sonic hyper-refinement, where fasting allows us to access patterns at the limits of language and recitations in the deep quiet. "You will have to listen very carefully," Ali tells us. Listening for God is seen as something that one refines over time. It seems right, in treating a religious poet who stays true to his heritage, to offer a practice of sense deprivation from my own. Quakers, too, regard the realm of silence as communion with the divine.

PRACTICE

Like fasting, the cultivation of deep quiet stores up the energy we typically disperse with sense experience. And for some, the practice of observing silence has the capacity to reveal God's true language. At Pendle Hill, the Quaker hub of the East Coast, the practice is common; there are even lanyards available to hang a sign around one's neck: "Observing Silence." I often wish I had that sign to wear at my local food co-op. When I offer a day of silence on retreats, nearly everyone who is new to the practice dreads it, and yet never has anyone regretted having tried it. The practice of silence offers one somatic entryway into communion with the divine, but, like fasting, it requires time. What would be another way of diving deep into the body to be transported beyond it, into the Queer Sublime?

If you are looking for a practice that takes minutes, not hours, here's a centering technique I learned from Staci Haines and Patrisse Cullors, with a Quaker twist. Haines talked us through the practice of orienting the body on the vertical, horizontal, and sagittal planes to align heart and mind toward our purpose in the world. Practitioners orient themselves downward into gravity, upward in dignity, outward toward connection, and sagittally in time (the personal and ancestral histories behind us, the present-moment happenings inside the body, and the future we're leaning into). There's a fourth plane related to an all-over experience of longing, related to touching in with our purpose.

Cullors named centering as her number one strategy for unlearning her strategic defense of numbing out to challenging feelings. As a trauma survivor, this resonated with me; it was the Zendo, not my home Quaker Meeting, that helped me build tolerance for difficult feelings. Perhaps that was because in First Day School (our equivalent of Sunday School), no one gave me step-by-step instructions on "centering down," which I've subsequently learned is typically just a simple body scan. The very idea of bringing any technique into worship is hotly contested, not being a part of the ministry of early Friends. The first use of the term "centering" came late, maybe from the controversial minister Elias Hicks, who was the endless source of fascination, verging on worship, for Walt Whitman.

I can't imagine how I might be different if First Day School had taught me an actual centering technique at an early age, to balance myself down and up, out and in, and between past present and future. I imported the practice into Meeting for Worship, and over the course of a few months, spontaneously my breath began to synch up with my centering. Exhaling outward into connection, inward into the somatic present, backward into the past, and forward into the future, yielded a different orientation. It wasn't my purpose, exactly. It was a transcendent experience where "centering down" became a natural extension of the vertical plane upward into the divine. Perhaps experimenting with centering breath might also help you to drop in to sense experience, to be transported beyond.

APRIL WEEK 4

APRIL SHOWERS–SLOW DOWN GENTLE

Elizabeth Bishop
"Song for the Rainy Season"

Hidden, oh hidden
in the high fog
the house we live in,
beneath the magnetic rock,
rain-, rainbow-ridden,
where blood-black
bromelias, lichens,
owls, and the lint
of the waterfalls cling,
familiar, unbidden.

In a dim age
of water
the brook sings loud
from a rib cage
of giant fern; vapor
climbs up the thick growth
effortlessly, turns back,
holding them both,
house and rock,

in a private cloud.

At night, on the roof,
blind drops crawl
and the ordinary brown
owl gives us proof
he can count:
five times–always five–
he stamps and takes off
after the fat frogs that,
shrilling for love,
clamber and mount.

House, open house
to the white dew
and the milk-white sunrise
kind to the eyes,
to membership
of silver fish, mouse,
bookworms,
big moths; with a wall
for the mildew's
ignorant map;

darkened and tarnished
by the warm touch
of the warm breath,
maculate, cherished;
rejoice! For a later
era will differ.
(O difference that kills
or intimidates, much
of all our small shadowy
life!) Without water

the great rock will stare
unmagnetized, bare,
no longer wearing
rainbows or rain,
the forgiving air
and the high fog gone;

the owls will move on
and the several
waterfalls shrivel
in the steady sun.

———

Conrad Aiken
"Beloved, Let Us Once More Praise the Rain"

I

Beloved, let us once more praise the rain.
Let us discover some new alphabet,
For this, the often praised; and be ourselves,
The rain, the chickweed, and the burdock leaf,
The green-white privet flower, the spotted stone,
And all that welcomes the rain; the sparrow too,—
Who watches with a hard eye from seclusion,
Beneath the elm-tree bough, till rain is done.

II

There is an oriole who, upside down,
Hangs at his nest, and flicks an orange wing,—
Under a tree as dead and still as lead;
There is a single leaf, in all this heaven
Of leaves, which rain has loosened from its twig:
The stem breaks, and it falls, but it is caught
Upon a sister leaf, and thus she hangs;
There is an acorn cup, beside a mushroom
Which catches three drops from the stooping cloud.

III

The timid bee goes back to the hive; the fly
Under the broad leaf of the hollyhock
Perpends stupid with cold; the raindark snail
Surveys the wet world from a watery stone...
And still the syllables of water whisper:
The wheel of cloud whirs slowly: while we wait
In the dark room; and in your heart I find
One silver raindrop,—on a hawthorn leaf,—
Orion in a cobweb, and the World.

Aiken, Conrad "Beloved, Let Us Once More Praise the Rain" from *Selected Poems*. NY: Oxford University Press, 1961. Reprinted with permission of Oxford University Press through PLSclear.

POETIC THEMES

Three true words: introverts dig rain. These three poems offer rainy-days experiments that can bring about three magical effects: protected solitude, detached witness, and slow time. The promise of rain is the potential for renewal. With the "forgiving air / and the high fog gone," in the words of Elizabeth Bishop, we can "rejoice! / For a later / era will differ." We are, after rain, wondrously returned to our big-s-Selves.

The first line of Bishop's poem captures so well the peace of isolation that it makes an introvert like me drool: "Hidden, oh hidden." Amen. The "dim age of water" is always magical and "rainbow-ridden." Rainy days entrance us with the mysterious seclusion of house and rock and the private cloud that holds them both. Undercover stuff of lichens and dark owls, "familiar, unbidden," are secret worlds that awaken when we get a reprieve from the garish sun. We ease up on trying to get anywhere; instead of feeling driven to get from point A from point B, we meander like the rainy-day vapor, which "climbs up this growth effortlessly, [and] turns back."

Then there's the delicious aural sense experience of rainy days! The streams sing like Bishop's brook, "loud from a rib cage of giant fern"—or the urban corollary, gutter gurgles. Aiken's "syllables of water whisper" describe rain-speech. The language of rain provides a "new alphabet / For this, the often praised." The title of Aiken's poem, "Beloved, Let Us Once More Praise The Rain" points to its double duty, functioning both as a praise song for rain but also a love song. Intimacy lies inside and underneath all the secluded witnessing—the sparrow, the oriole, the timid bee, the fly, all surveying the scene from a place of remove. Aiken gives us, in the place of majesty, The Rain-dark Snail. Who Is Now My Spirit Animal. The camaraderie of sister leaves, hanging together "in all this heaven / Of leaves," marks a celebration of intimate companionship, which does not negate solitude as a mode of self-companioning. And the whirring wheel of the poem takes us around and down, and brings us to the private love scene of the final lines, in the darkened room: "and in your heart I find / One silver raindrop,—on a hawthorn leaf,— / Orion in a cobweb, and the world." If Mx. Raindark Snail didn't get you, this final sing-songy phrase will. So akin to a children's rhyme, this line rests in a place governed by magic, as opposed to logic and rational meaning. The beloved's heart, as leaf, or as cobweb, or both, holds a mysterious silver rain-drop, which is also Orion the Hunter, or the Star. In fact, the dark room of rainy waiting is all of it—cobweb and star and hive and spotted stone and more—because the beloved's heart is and holds the World, capitalized. The endless regress of holding, like the rings in a tree trunk, one thing in another in another is a scene of nurturing embrace.

I'm reminded of Mary Oliver's "Last Night the Rain Spoke to Me," where a long moment of holding hands extends to holding a tree, which is in turn holding raindrops, on up to the astral plane. These concentric circles of care rhyme with Aiken's, where the leaf, and the leaf it holds, are interwoven with heart and cobweb, Orion and stars. At the same time that rainy days connote holding environments, safe and cozy, they also open our vista to the wider world around us, unto the stars! So let us actually once more praise rain; its waiting stillness reveals the everything that the beloved's heart can hold. And what if, my introvert friends, what if that heart so worthy of love were, in fact, your own?

PRACTICE

How can we let our attention meander (free of any direction toward anything, à la Bishop), and also rock softly between outer and inner, the space holding us and the inner concentric layers of self? You might just play with this notion of holding hands with our (future, post-rain, renewed) self, until it has the sense of being accomplished and real. What is the feeling state—both emotionally and in sensation—of simply lifting one limp hand with the other, to place them somewhere the body needs touch? Or, shifting the field of reference from detail to broad picture, try toggling your attention between an area of tension (in the shoulders, for example) and someplace else that feels relaxed (like the ear cartilage), and try to hold them both in your consciousness at once. Then expand your attention beyond the physical body, and to the space around you. You might even find online rain sounds to pull your focus out if there are no real April showers to be had. Many different meditative traditions teach strategies for moving from focused concentration on what we're doing to un-self-aware suspension inside the doing of it. Compare the "feel" of the deliberate, one-pointed focus on these areas of tension and ease to the dissolution of self-awareness into your surround, always around and holding you. Is it possible to abide with both simultaneously?

MAY WEEK 1

MAY DAY

Patrick Rosal
"Brokeheart: just like that"

When the bass drops on Bill Withers'
Better Off Dead, it's like 7 a.m.
and I confess I'm looking
over my shoulder once or twice
just to make sure no one in Brooklyn
is peeking into my third-floor window
to see me in pajamas I haven't washed
for three weeks before I slide
from sink to stove in one long groove
left foot first then back to the window side
with my chin up and both fists clenched
like two small sacks of stolen nickels
and I can almost hear the silver
hit the floor by the dozens
when I let loose and sway a little back
and just like that I'm a lizard grown
two new good legs on a breeze
-bent limb. I'm a grown-ass man
with a three-day wish and two days to live.
And just like that everyone knows

my heart's broke and no one is home.
Just like that, I'm water.
Just like that, I'm the boat.
Just like that, I'm both things in the whole world
rocking. Sometimes sadness is just
what comes between the dancing. And bam!,
my mother's dead and, bam!, my brother's
children are laughing. Just like—ok, it's true
I can't pop up from my knees so quick these days
and no one ever said I could sing but
tell me my body ain't good enough
for this. I'll count the aches another time,
one in each ankle, the sharp spike in my back,
this mud-muscle throbbing in my going bones,
I'm missing the six biggest screws
to hold this blessed mess together. I'm wind-
rattled. The wood's splitting. The hinges are
falling off. When the first bridge ends,
just like that, I'm a flung open door.

———

Craig Santos Perez
"Ars Pasifika"

   when the tide

   of silence

   rises

   say "ocean"

   then with the paddle

of your tongue

rearrange

the letters to form

"canoe"

———

Lucille Clifton,
"blessing the boats"
          (at St. Mary's)

    may the tide
    that is entering even now
    the lip of our understanding
    carry you out
    beyond the face of fear
    may you kiss
    the wind then turn from it
    certain that it will
    love your back   may you
    open your eyes to water
    water waving forever
    and may you in your innocence
    sail through this to that

May Day, the celebration of all things sensual, is essentially the victory of life against death. The central way to celebrate the holiday is by dancing. The language of "Brokeheart" is a mature maypole dance, all rhythm section, beating out the dance of sliding "from sink to stove in one long groove / left foot first then back to the window side / with my chin up and both fists clenched...." It's not until late in the poem that the dancer confesses he's older than he'd like to be. In the first half, we're just let loose and lost in the movement with sassy lines of slippery enjambments interspersed with staccato end-stops like "I'm a lizard grown / two new good legs on a breeze- / bent limb." "Just like that" keeps operating like the high hat, breaking up the tongue-twister consonance. But then—"bam!"—it all comes flooding in. The sadness, the age, the vulnerable, injured, falling-apart self who can't sing and has no mother. This "grown-ass man / with a three-day wish and two days to live" reveals his aching, throbbing hurts and limitations, because, as the poem so succinctly points out, "Sometimes sadness is just / what comes between the dancing."

But what's perfect is the way we have been suspended in the music of the poem enough to forget our own aches and pains, and when we are reminded of them, maybe we can still feel these lines from the inside: "but / tell me my body ain't good enough / for this." And speaking of good-enough bodies, what a wonderful message of solace in the "Just like thats" of becoming water and boat and both, just rocking. Be your own boat!

To bring home Rosal's comforting boat-ification, I'd like to synch it up with these two short boat poems, by Lucille Clifton and by Craig Santos Perez. Santos Perez instructs, lovingly: when you feel thrown around by the rising tide, rearrange "with the paddle of your tongue" the letters of the word "ocean" to form "canoe." Clifton gives us a blessing. Less than 60 words, in small letters with no punctuation, just the lulling repetition of "may the..." "may you..." "may you..."—like waves on the ocean. And in a time when the future is uncertain, this symbol of eternity is welcome, this "water waving forever." She gives us four simple blessings: that we be carried beyond fear, kiss the wind and trust it, open our eyes, and sail. This is past the lip of our understanding, she says. We are innocent, she tells us. There is another shore, she tells us. We will make it, she tells us. The feeling of the wind in our sails. Open heart, brave face to the wind, all.

PRACTICE

To embody a flung-open door, we could try to open every little molecule of the torso to breath. Cracking the heart open, could we create enough space to feel that strange ache behind the sternum? You might lay yourself out supine on pillows, so your chest is buoyed and your head is slightly higher, feet together with knees open, and imagine your body as a boat, rocking on water. Three-part breathing gives the impression of a watery wave. As though filling up the container of your torso, breathe one third into the pelvis and low belly, two thirds into the upper abdomen, and fill up to the notch of the throat, and empty out each chamber sequentially from the top to the bottom. Moving from the bowl of the hips, the seat of water, on up to the base of the breastbone, it's lovely to visualize the bob of the sternum on your breath, like a canoe on the waves.

MAY WEEK 2

MOTHER'S DAY

Ada Limòn
"The Raincoat"

When the doctor suggested surgery
and a brace for all my youngest years,
my parents scrambled to take me
to massage therapy, deep tissue work,
osteopathy, and soon my crooked spine
unspooled a bit, I could breathe again,
and move more in a body unclouded
by pain. My mom would tell me to sing
songs to her the whole forty-five minute
drive to Middle Two Rock Road and forty-
five minutes back from physical therapy.
She'd say, even my voice sounded unfettered
by my spine afterward. So I sang and sang,
because I thought she liked it. I never
asked her what she gave up to drive me,
or how her day was before this chore. Today,
at her age, I was driving myself home from yet
another spine appointment, singing along
to some maudlin but solid song on the radio,
and I saw a mom take her raincoat off

and give it to her young daughter when
a storm took over the afternoon. My god,
I thought, my whole life I've been under her
raincoat thinking it was somehow a marvel
that I never got wet.

———

Jason Schneiderman
"In the End You Get Everything Back (Liza Minnelli)"

The afterlife is an infinity of custom shelving, where everything
you have ever loved has a perfect place, including things
that don't fit on shelves, like the weeping willow from
your parents' backyard, or an old boyfriend, exactly as he was
in your second year of college, or an aria you love, but without
the rest of the opera you don't particularly care for.
My favorite joke: Q: You know who dies? A: Everyone!
Because it's true. But ask any doctor and they'll say that
prolonging a life is saving a life. Ask anyone who survives
their surgeries, and they'll say yes, to keep living is to be saved.
I do think there's a statute of limitations on grief, like, certainly,
how someone died can be sad forever, but who can be sad
simply about the fact that Shakespeare, say, is dead, or Sappho,
or Judy Garland, or Rumi. There's a Twitter account called
LizaMinnelliOutlives, which put into the world a set of thoughts
I was having privately, but the Twitter account is kinder than
I had been, tweeting things like "Liza Minnelli has outlived
the National Rifle Association which has filed for bankruptcy"
and "Liza Minnelli has outlived Armie Hammer's career" to take
the sting out of the really painful ones, like "Liza Minnelli
has outlived Jessica Walter," or "Liza Minnelli has outlived
George Michael" or "Liza Minnelli has outlived Prince."
In my own afterlife, the custom shelves are full of Liza Minnellis—
Liza in *Cabaret*, Liza in *Arrested Development*, Liza singing

"Steam Heat" on *The Judy Garland Christmas Special*, Liza
on the *Muppet Show*, Liza in *Liza's at the Palace*, and because this is heaven,
Liza won't even know she's in my hall of loved objects,
just as I won't know that my fandom has been placed on her shelf
for when Liza Minnelli has outlived Jason Schneiderman,
waiting for Liza Minnelli when Liza Minnelli has outlived
Liza Minnelli, which is what fame is, and what fame is not,
and if Jason Schneiderman outlives Jason Schneiderman,
and your love of this poem waits for me on one of my shelves,
and will keep me company for eternity, thank you for that.
I promise to cherish your love in that well-lit infinity of forever.
In one theory of the mind, the psyche is just a grab bag of lost objects,
our wholeness lost when we leave the womb, when we discover
our own body, and so on and so on, our wholeness lost and lost and lost,
as we find ourselves smaller and smaller, which is why heaven
is an endless, cozy warehouse, where nothing you loved is gone,
where you are whole because you get everything back, and by everything,
I mean you.

"In the End You Get Everything Back (Liza Minnelli)" © Jason Schneiderman, first printed in *American Poetry Review*, Nov/Dec 2021. Used by permission of the poet.

POETIC THEMES

Mother's Day. This week our culture celebrates the maternal powers of birthing, nurture, and attention. It attempts to mark the near-impossible demands of contemporary mothering (I think of Billy Collins' poem "The Lanyard"—as if one holiday, like his useless bit of plastic, could make up for the societal lack of structural support for mothers). Mothering feels to me, at least, depleting, disorienting, and impossible to do with elegance or finesse. The canned sentimentality of this holiday fetishizes biological mothering over all other maternal expressions. And oh my God the guilt! If there's any way to make guilt beautiful and moving, Ada Limòn's "The Umbrella" accomplishes it. The speaker's childhood voice, unspooling like her spine, sings to us of the protective shelter that we all want to have and to be. In fact, we crave this maternal cover so hard that we make ourselves crazy. Sometimes I wonder if this holiday might cause more hurt than it's worth. But rather than claiming to speak for a collective, I'll "mind my own business" as Rev. angel Kyodo williams teaches, and split into a picture of my own annual experience:

Every Sunday I wait for my children to be
returned to me.
And so I wait now, pausing for a drag
before vacuuming up last week's lice,
and the grass that came in
clinging to their perfect, rounded toes.
grass at the prow of my new orange electric mower
before forecasted rain
grow my basil some roots
(maybe me too)
find capillaries into earth's lung to breathe me new
Let it wash all this: the cigarette stink
the crayola contract never to smoke again
so mommy won't die
the now-useless blood
one moon closer to dry
the promise of the crone in me
a second coming.

Mothering is by far the hardest work, and I can only hope my kids become my best friends, as my own mother has become mine. But if they do, it's by pure luck, not by virtue of my maternal capacities, which I prefer to imagine as a creative power available to anyone—a kind of witchy, mysterious, two-way sorcery, as in Sharon Olds' "The Enchantment."

For *sure* it's transformative to become a mother—that crazy deep, crazy-making form of human love. But also many of us find the thorniest deep-dives into the shadowy parts of our psyche through our relationship to other mother figures. Writ large, the nurturing, life-giving figures in our lives are our heroes, whose consciousness is blended in with our own. In an attempt to explode the boundaries of how we configure the maternal figure, I'd like to offer Jason Schneiderman's poem for this week's meditation. This homage breaks the conception of influence and nurture as a one-way street, even as it expands the strictures of mortality, selfhood, linear time, and the fourth wall between poet and reader. Our wholeness is lost at birth, along with our dear, wrinkled, weird placenta, "lost and lost and lost." Our selfhood shrinks into the size of a figurine that might fit on an afterlife shelf, and that's a comfort. The second-person address of the final line gathers us under the umbrella of this poem because of our love for it! What could be more nurturing than the notion of maternal care as an endless regress, or a forward proliferation, of the capacity to just love stuff? If we hone this capacity, and promise to cherish one another's love as Jason does, we will keep one another company for eternity.

PRACTICE

There's a Buddhist meditation Eve (Sedgwick) taught me and wrote about someplace, where you imagine everyone everywhere, at one point or another, in one lifetime or another, as having been your mother—or your child! This meditation seeks to cast a spell of tenderness between us and anyone, cultivating an instinct of care toward all people, alive and "in that well-lit infinity of forever." Maybe *that* is the loveliest power to celebrate on Mother's Day.

Or, if this feels disembodied and abstract, to explore the seat of creativity in the physical body—any physical body, any way it's gendered—we might focus on the pelvic bowl and low belly. Any form of caretaking has its demands and its costs. You might toy with contracting the abdomen, Martha-Graham-style, while stirring the cauldron of the belly. Sweeping one hand like a scoop to the belly embodies not just cauldron-stirring but also the way we actually carve out of our bodies what's needed to generate beauty, contribute to new worldings, or nurture life—not just with biological wombs and breasts, but also with the daily rhythm of doling out our life force.

You might close by testing out the magic of *yoni mudra* (thumb and pointer fingers join, extend in opposite direction, with the other fingers interlaced and tucked into the palms), placed in front of low belly, pointer fingers facing down. Consider jotting down what's behind the feeling in your wombed-up fingers—what and whom are you gestating, at present? What and whom are you cherishing with your nurture, what's the endless regress of figures contributing to your magic, and how can you cultivate the trust that you will get all of you back, whole?

MAY WEEK 3

SHADOWY GARDENING

Paisley Rekdal
"Happiness"

I have been taught never to brag but now
I cannot help it: I keep
a beautiful garden, all abundance,
indiscriminate, pulling itself
from the stubborn earth: does it offend you
to watch me working in it,
touching my hands to the greening tips or
tearing the yellow stalks back, so wild
the living and the dead both
snap off in my hands?
The neighbor with his stuttering
fingers, the neighbor with his broken
love: each comes up my drive
to receive his pitying,
accustomed consolations, watches me
work in silence awhile, rises in anger,
walks back. Does it offend them to watch me
not mourning with them but working
fitfully, fruitlessly, working
the way the bees work, which is to say

by instinct alone, which looks like pleasure?
I can stand for hours among the sweet
narcissus, silent as a point of bone.
I can wait longer than sadness. I can wait longer
than your grief. It is such a small thing
to be proud of, a garden. Today
there were scrub jays, quail,
a woodpecker knocking at the white-
and-black shapes of trees, and someone's lost rabbit
scratching under the barberry: is it
indiscriminate? Should it shrink back, wither,
and expurgate? Should I, too, not be loved?
It is only a little time, a little space.
Why not watch the grasses take up their colors in a rush
like a stream of kerosene being lit?
If I could not have made this garden beautiful
I wouldn't understand your suffering,
nor care for each the same, inflamed way.
I would have to stay only like the bees,
beyond consciousness, beyond
self-reproach, fingers dug down hard
into stone, and growing nothing.
There is no end to ego,
with its museum of disappointments.
I want to take my neighbors into the garden
and show them: Here is consolation.
Here is your pity. Look how much seed it drops
around the sparrows as they fight.
It lives alongside their misery.
It glows each evening with a violent light.

Paisley Rekdal, "Happiness" from *Animal Eye*, by Paisley Rekdal, ©2012.
Reprinted by permission of The University of Pittsburgh Press.

A.R. Ammons
"The City Limits"

When you consider the radiance, that it does not withhold
itself but pours its abundance without selection into every
nook and cranny not overhung or hidden; when you consider

that birds' bones make no awful noise against the light but
lie low in the light as in a high testimony; when you consider
the radiance, that it will look into the guiltiest

swervings of the weaving heart and bear itself upon them,
not flinching into disguise or darkening; when you consider
the abundance of such resource as illuminates the glow-blue

bodies and gold-skeined wings of flies swarming the dumped
guts of a natural slaughter or the coil of shit and in no
way winces from its storms of generosity; when you consider

that air or vacuum, snow or shale, squid or wolf, rose or lichen,
each is accepted into as much light as it will take, then
the heart moves roomier, the man stands and looks about, the

leaf does not increase itself above the grass, and the dark
work of the deepest cells is of a tune with May bushes
and fear lit by the breadth of such calmly turns to praise.

POETIC THEMES

I'd like to use this week's entry to mark the seasonal shift from springtime flowering into something mulchier. What new habits, projects, connections, and modes of being have we been growing, and what is ready to return to the earth?

"City Limits" shines an unflinching light on the darker side of nature, shifting the way we see the exploding blossoms on May bushes. A sharp, intense, transcendentalist-style "radiance" is the subject of every other stanza. The light is doing the action here. Radiance "does not withhold itself," but rather "pours its abundance without selection into every / nook and cranny." This flashlight of attention shines on bird bones, guts of a slaughter, and coils of shit. Ammons is challenging us to see our mortal coils, employing a laser beam that "will look into the guiltiest / swervings of the weaving heart and bear itself against them, / not flinching into disguise or darkening."

In our attempts to grow something new, maybe there are also old habits, outdated modes of being or behaving, that are dying. Ammons offers that we open to shining a light on these inner demons. Our capacity is limited; we can accept into ourselves only "as much light as [we] will take." But if we can build the resilience to shine a light on our darker side, the poem assures us that the "heart moves roomier." The promise goes something like this: when we let the light in to reveal and maybe aerate our guilty heart-swervings, they are returned to their rightful place in the category of the transcendent. The final stanza—wherein the "leaf does not increase itself above the grass"—alludes to the pun of Whitman's "Leaves of Grass" (leaves as pages of writing, and also the blades of grass they describe). The man perceives self-referentially the limits of the written word to capture the beauty it describes. We feel "in the deepest cells" of our body, rather than the leaves of our poems, the processes of deterioration happening secretly within the May bushes. Our body is one with it all, everything in Ammons' Whitmanian list: "air or vacuum, snow or shale, squid or wolf, rose or lichen."

I'd like to add daffodils to this list, as an early spring blossom that's already prepping to mulch in May. Paisley Rekdal's mention of the narcissus seems to give a visual for the dying yellow stalks and the newly living green tips snapping off in her hands. It's no accident that this lover of Ovid uses the term "narcissus," a myth illustrating that "There is no end to ego, / with its museum of disappointments." What is the lesson of the daffodil according to the teachings of biomimicry? I'm no gardener. Both my thumbs are black. From my friends' reports, although cutting back the stems and leaves of daffodils after the flowers are spent makes the garden tidier, they shouldn't be cut back until late in the spring when they have turned yellow. This is because the leaves continue to photosynthesize, producing energy that will be stored in the bulb for the following year. The life cycle of daffodils creates some unsightly dead stuff around this time, which gardeners strategize to hide. This mash-up of light and dark, life and death, echoes Ammons' unflinching acceptance of the whole of nature. And the title "Happiness" must be partly ironic, for a poem that progresses from the image of a gardener wildly ripping out the living and the dead, to the offended, angry neighbors stalking away, to the seeds dropped around battling sparrows. This gardener shows open disdain for the dudes coming around to seek her pity, one "with his stuttering fingers" and another "with his broken love."

This naked (and not-so-tacitly gendered) view gives way to more savage accuracy in the lines to follow. Gardening might look like pleasure, but in this poem it's fitful work, executed "by instinct alone." The speaker chooses to work instead of giving her neighbors their "accustomed consolations." She makes a case for the right to "only a little time, a little space." Against the expectation that vitality should "shrink back, wither, / and expurgate," she sets a modest plea: "It is such a small thing / to be proud of, a garden." Even if there is pride, there doesn't seem to be much peace for this gardener. Hers is a burning, dark intensity of view, where the grasses turn color like "a stream of kerosene being lit." Still, she distinguishes between the unconscious working of bees and the compassion for others made possible by gardening. It's not, the poem seems to say, that we can't empathize, it's that we can't do it incessantly! We need time and space to regenerate, like the daffodils. The consolation to be found in the garden is the simple fact of life's dogged continuance alongside human misery. The poem's ending somehow rhymes with Ammons' image of bird bones lying "low in the light as in a high testimony": in the final line, the garden becomes something eerie and a little sinister: "It glows each evening with a violent light." If this is happiness, it's got teeth.

Maybe the point here is that we not be too aggressive in our pruning. It's akin to all the familiar analogies we've heard before: a snake doesn't just rip off its skin on a whim, and butterflies need to strengthen their wings before they can come free of their cocoon. Our foibles and learned habits and little stuck-nesses can be fodder for new growth. The daffodil lesson: don't sweep away your ugly dead leaves; they need to be broken down, taken apart, their life energy extracted, to pass on to the next generation.

PRACTICE

Here's one way to embody mulchification: reclining supine, rapidly flex and point the feet so that the back body scrubs up and down. Let your parts jiggle—that's part of it. You'll tap in to the root system of the feet, ankles, calves, and the musculature surrounding the shins. Imagine the sticky, garbagy habits and mishaps and blunders sifting down and mixing up with your magic and beauty. Generative moments of cluelessness are fodder for new stuff. Let them lie fallow for a bit before rising to greet whatever is rising to greet you today. Or, if it's bedtime, try meeting each thought of regret or shame with an act of turning your body in the bed, as though mixing the mulch pile of your psyche.

MAY WEEK 4

MEMORIAL DAY NOSTALGIA

Gregory Pardlo
"For Which it Stands"

For a flag! I answered facetiously. A flag of tomorrow,
fluent in fire, not just the whispers, lisps, not just the still there
of powdered wigs, dry winds. Who wants a speckled
drape that folds as easy over smirch as fallen soldier?
This is rhetorical. Like, "What to the Negro
is the fourth of July?" A flag should be stitched with a fuse.

Jefferson said for each generation a flag. Maybe
he said Constitution. I once raised a high-top flag
of my hair, a fist, a leather medallion of the motherland.
I studied heraldry and maniples (which are not
what you might guess), little sails and banners
down to the vane of a feather. Because his kids were
rebel cities my father loved like Sherman. Because
I wanted history I could touch like the flank of a beast.

My wife's people are from San Salvador. They sent us
with a guard, his AK shouldered like a mandolin, among
anil-tinted shawls and jerseys, across tiled and pocked

concrete, and the gated stalls of El Centra. I felt sacred
as a goat there, too, as I did below the Mason-Dixon
where our only protection was the Fourteenth Amendment.

Afraid our Yankee plates would be read aggressive as a Jolly
Roger we rented a compact in Atlanta. Charleston, Savannah,
Montgomery, and after Birmingham we were broke.
Skipped Selma. Slept at B&Bs where my dreams power-
washed layers of footnotes and Februaries, revealing
the surreal sheen of Apollo Creed's trunks, the apocalyptic
Americana of Jacko moonwalking around a tinfoil Buzz
Aldrin planting the corporate ensign. Years passed. I grew

youthless in my dad-pants, but still puffed at pinwheels
and windsocks, launched glyphs of grillsmoke and one day
it came to me, as if commissioned, Theaster Gates's *Flag*
from old fire hoses, a couple dozen, like vertical blinds, no,
like cabin floorboards of canvas colored rusty, brick dust, some
cheerless drab-and-custard, beside a medley of vespertine
blues, hoses evoking landscapes of sackcloth and gunny,
texture of violence and tongues inflamed by shine, holy ghost.

Ross, Duchamp, Johns, et al., are integrated here with officers
of the peace, their dogs, and, in evidence, their pretend
tumescence Gates has hung to cure like pelts
or strips of jerky.

How did it feel to shield spirit with flesh? I mean,
what did it do to the body, water furry as the arm
of an arctic bear? What thirst did it ignite?

Gates's salute is a torch song, a rhythm
of hues marching over a pentimento of rhyme.
I approve its message, its pledge to birth a nation
of belonging and to teach that nation of the fire
shut up in our bones.

Maggie Smith
"Accidental Pastoral"

I must have just missed a parade—
horse droppings and hard candy
in the road, miniature American
flags staked into the grass, plastic
chairs lining the curb down this

two-lane highway, 36 in the open
country, briefly Main Street in town.
When I was small, I sat on a curb
only a dozen miles from here, my feet
in the ashtray-dirty gutter, and watched

stars-and-stripes girls wheeling
their batons, slicing the sun-dumb
air into streamers. I can still hear
the click of cellophaned candies
on pavement. I didn't want to

leave town, not then, and I never left.
I am not a parade, my one car passing
through Centerburg, Ohio, too late.
The chairs are empty. The children
are unwrapping golden butterscotches

in the cool, shuttered houses.
But look up—the clouds are stories
tall, painted above Webb's Marathon,
and flat-bottomed as if resting on something
they push against though it holds them.

Memorial Day—the unofficial start of summer. The flavor of summertime is the taste of nostalgia, the season of childhood. No one (no, not even teachers) experiences summer freedom the way kids do. Kind of like a Memorial Day parade, which is as much about childhood memory as it is about who died for us... and also why. This is a holiday named for remembering, re-membering the lost—but without any formal recognition in the rites and rituals of our country's military history. Nostalgia is a funny thing, etymologically rooted in the ache of homesickness (from the Greek *nostos*, to return home, and *algos*, pain). The tension between joy and violence, aggression and play, vitality and death, is a kind of ambivalence that colors memory itself. We remember the sounds and smells and thwonking hard candy of the parades from our childhood, alongside freedom from school, beach and pool openings, and the promise of summer hijinks. (Charles Wright somewhere describes helicopters "thwonking" back to marine bases, and that verb somehow for me captures the buzz and chaos of the parade and re-invents it darker.) That's what happens, over time: as we learn more, our experience of childhood, like the Memorial Day parade... changes.

Gregory Pardlo's poem is really written for July Fourth, and its governing theme of fire depends on it. He asks, "Who wants a speckled / drape that folds as easy over smirch as fallen soldier?" He refers to another seething critique of "Independence Day" given by Frederick Douglass (which flatly declares, "your celebration is a sham"). But many folk feel that whether it's in the heat of July or on Memorial Day, "A flag should be stitched with a fuse." Like a tick-ticking time bomb, the poem marks the passage of time, held in the holiday, grilling along and puffing at pinwheels... until suddenly it catches the spark of a new, more appropriate national flag. Pardlo hits on Theaster Gates' seminal artwork from 2011—eerie, dark flags made of decommissioned fire hoses, linked to the violent treatment of civil rights protestors. He refers to Gates' work as a "torch song," apt for a poem like this one, so "fluent in fire." Memorial Day 2020, Minneapolis was in flames in response to the murder of George Floyd. In 2021, American support of Israeli military efforts contributed to the exploding violence in Gaza. But somehow Memorial Day isn't a holiday of fireworks quite like July 4th, and what most of us remember about it is—the parade.

We might have caught on to the ruse of the 'Murica myth later in life. Some of us have privilege, unlike Pardlo, where we don't have to pray to the Fourteenth Amendment below the Mason-Dixon Line. "Accidental Pastoral" (which is actually also written about July 4th) is a nostalgic trip back to the childhood scene of a midwestern small town the poem's speaker hasn't felt the need to get far from—a dozen miles, to be precise. It's unclear whether it's ghost-town-creepy or sweet. The poem's solitary car passes by horse droppings, empty plastic chairs, and "ashtray-dirty gutters," while the kids suck on butterscotches and the houses are cool. Inside the hints of emptiness, there are multisensory echoes of the child's jubilant view of summer: hard candy hitting the pavement and, perhaps the most beautiful line, the batons "slicing the sundumb / air into streamers." The clouds at the end of the poem, "stories tall," offer a pretty apt analogy for memory itself: we push against our stories, and yet they hold us (down? back? accountable? in tender embrace?). What is the fall from idealism when we try to recreate a moment from our childhood and find it changed, textured differently? Reading Smith's poem after Pardlo's, one might wonder—can flags staked into the grass and stars-and-stripes girls ever be innocent? If we are disenchanted with America's story, do we, inevitably, also come to disbelieve the innocence or sweetness of our own?

PRACTICE

Is our childhood self attached to us, like some creepy Peter Pan shadow? Or is it an endless regress within us like so many Russian dolls? Or are we held in its atmosphere, like Maggie Smith's flat-bottomed cloud? Where does memory live in the body? Does nostalgia share the same home, or is it different? Or is the pleasure and/or violence of remembering not something that can be housed, but instead an action; and if so, how does it move? Does remembering something broken in our "inner child" ever fix her? What is the gestural language of that tender tending?

Some different possibilities to explore in simple hand gestures:

—squeezing out the dregs of memory, like squeezing out a toothpaste tube

—holding, molding, parsing (test the QiGong practice of separating the hands to feel for the energy between them, as if stretching bubble gum between the palms)

—pushing away what doesn't serve and gathering in what does (or supine crunches: extend head and limbs upward, then ball yourself up and clutch them tightly)

—touching our history like the flank of a beast (experiment with a pillow—how do you touch your history? Do you honor its danger? Soothe its wild side? Or do you climb on to ride to battle?)

—honoring with awareness the subtlety of body temperature: start simply by touching hands and feet and perceive whether there is hemispheric balance in your body temperature.

Progress through simple self-touch to explore where you feel cool, shuttered safety and where you feel heat. Is this simply circulation, or does it correspond to areas of injury, associations with experiences of comfort or safety, or movement patterns that have built particular strength?

JUNE WEEK 1

DA BEACH!

Dan Albergotti
"Things to Do in the Belly of the Whale"

Measure the walls. Count the ribs. Notch the long days.
Look up for blue sky through the spout. Make small fires
with the broken hulls of fishing boats. Practice smoke signals.
Call old friends, and listen for echoes of distant voices.
Organize your calendar. Dream of the beach. Look each way
for the dim glow of light. Work on your reports. Review
each of your life's ten million choices. Endure moments
of self-loathing. Find the evidence of those before you.
Destroy it. Try to be very quiet, and listen for the sound
of gears and moving water. Listen for the sound of your heart.
Be thankful that you are here, swallowed with all hope,
where you can rest and wait. Be nostalgic. Think of all
the things you did and could have done. Remember
treading water in the center of the still night sea, your toes
pointing again and again down, down into the black depths.

Dan Albergotti, "Things to Do in the Belly of the Whale" from *The Boatloads*. Copyright © 2008 by Dan Albergotti. Reprinted with the permission of The Permissions Company, LLC on behalf of BOA Editions, Ltd. boaeditions.org.

Devin Kelly
"Conditionally"

Sometimes I remember summer in California,
just 12, army father, & the way he left me
alone at the hotel, & how, taken to nothing
but wanting love, I wandered the beach,
not knowing what to do with an ocean.
I wore socks with my sneakers & sat,
thinking myself older, clutching a book
I didn't read, wanting to read, but not,
& then looking up, & wanting to read again.
A lot has changed since then, & nothing.
I don't wear socks. I know what it's like
to be high. Sometimes I have wanted
to know if there is an underside to life,
& if it is inverted, so that there, we live
inside of light rather than below it.
I have found it better to believe in everything
than nothing—like the old man each day
on the beach, scavenging with the metal
extension of his arm for gold or bits of
valuable scrap. Each day I thought him
doing something else: sometimes searching
or forgiving or even blessing, sometimes
longing for something more than this, & yet
something still, head turned toward this soft
ground that offered nothing but *would* or *maybe*.

"Conditionally," by Devin Kelly, first printed in "The Slowdown" (July 22, 2022).
Used by permission of the poet.

Donika Kelly
"The moon rose over the bay. I had a lot of feelings."

I am taken with the hot animal
of my skin, grateful to swing my limbs
and have them move as I intend, though
my knee, though my shoulder, though something
is torn or tearing. Today, a dozen squid, dead
on the harbor beach: one mostly buried,
one with skin empty as a shell and hollow
feeling, and, though the tentacles look soft,
I do not touch them. I imagine they
were startled to find themselves in the sun.
I imagine the tide simply went out
without them. I imagine they cannot
feel the black flies charting the raised hills
of their eyes. I write my name in the sand:
Donika Kelly. I watch eighteen seagulls
skim the sandbar and lift low in the sky.
I pick up a pebble that looks like a green egg.
To the ditch lily I say *I am in love*.
To the Jeep parked haphazardly on the narrow
street *I am in love*. To the roses, white
petals rimmed brown, to the yellow lined
pavement, to the house trimmed in gold *I am
in love*. I shout with the rough calculus
of walking. Just let me find my way back,
let me move like a tide come in.

As the springtime buzz gives way to summer chill, it's time to come unsprung and slow down the doing. Come walk along the shore and bury your feet in the sand. What if we take a moment to imagine that what we've done is enough? Or maybe the truth is that the world is enough not because of what we have or have not done. It grows in its enough-ness in proportion to our growing attention. These three poems mark a progression in the work of slowing down, beginning with a kind of listless discomfort, giving way to hopeful reverie, which then starts to glimmer enough that we can really attune to it, until it finally peels open to pure presence.

The first poem is the darkest. In the belly of the whale, we can just catch a glimpse of sky through the spout. By this dim glow, the other senses come alive: when we can "be very quiet, and listen for the sound of gears / and moving water. Listen for the sound of [our] heart." The beach is something we only dream of, remember vaguely, nostalgically. Albergotti's list of ThingsTo-DoWhileNotDoing is randomly assembled, because that's how it goes in free-float. And that's how it is, in this cultural moment of reckoning, where we are in between what's dying and what is yet to emerge. In the blind bungling in between, our attention meanders from reviewing our life's "ten million choices" to categorically destroying the "evidence of those before" to listening for our heartbeat and back again. It would be lovely to write these wisdom nuggets on sticky notes to hang around the house: "Be nostalgic." "Try to be very quiet." "Call old friends." But also: "endure self-loathing"! It's not easy, thinking of all we did and could have done. All of us are Jonah in our own deep sea.

Albergotti's image of being swallowed captures the sometimes-claustro-phobic experience of tapping into the intense emotional world of the body. The image of being "here, swallowed with all [our] hope" is like being dropped into our own belly, one holding environment where we harbor all the ancient, early lessons of not-enoughness (perhaps even generational lessons that predate our birth). Think of what we learned in Covid lockdown: the shifts between claustrophobia, on the one hand, and the feeling being held in a safe, warm, structured place. Over the course of each long day, sometimes we were grateful for permission to "rest and wait," and other times the emptiness was excruciating. I'd put one last sticky note right on the bathroom mirror with the marvelous final lines, reminding us of our ability to tread water. It's a pretty scary place to be, in the middle of the ocean at night, dark and still. But we continue the pedaling action of our legs, "toes / pointing again and again down, down into / the black depths." We are reaching down into the darkness with our feet, some of the most sensitive receptors we've got, keeping us afloat.

Enter Devin Kelly, whose writing has broken me and my understanding of masculinity in sixteen different ways. His poetry describes something "inside of every man," like Albergotti's Jonah, lying "still at night waiting for change" —and yet the image of pedaling feet make me think instead of Kelly's devastatingly vulnerable essays about endurance running. Running, he confesses in "Running Dysmorphic," saved his life in fifth grade when his mother left his father to raise two boys alone. That's the 12-year-old kid depicted in "Conditionally," left at the hotel by his father and faced with the enormity of the ocean, lost.

The poem focuses on his feet. Jokingly, he claims the only thing that changes with his adulthood is that he no longer wears socks with his sneakers. But between the ground floor of his running shoes and the adult knowledge of "what it's like / to be high" he plays with flipping the world on its vertical axis: "Sometimes I have wanted / to know if there is an underside to life, / & if it is inverted." He turns this into useful spatial paradigm to explore the existential-ish notion of living "inside of light rather than below it," where it's "better to believe in everything than nothing."

Flipping the light around, as a mysterious underground glimmer we need to root around to find, gives way to the mythical figure of the old man on the beach, "scavenging with the metal / extension of his arm for gold or bits of / valuable scrap." The preadolescent boy projects into the old man's divining rod the tasks of "searching / or forgiving or even blessing." These three primary functions of the heart lead to a fourth occupation: "longing for something more than this, & yet / something still, head turned toward this soft / ground that offered nothing but *would* or *maybe*." This is the final labor of the heart: turning downward to hunt for the possibility of gold that might be right under our feet. The conditional promise of this poem points the heart downward toward the earth and beneath it.

Enter Nietzsche, one of Eve Sedgwick's favorite Queer thinkers, who imagines the "genius of the heart" (with all the attendant freight of the otherworldy, spritely genii bouncing around the 19ᵗʰ-century imagination)—as a divining rod!

...the genius of the heart, which imposes silence and attention on everything loud and self-conceited, which smoothes rough souls and makes them taste a new longing—to lie placid as a mirror, that the deep heavens may be reflected in them;—the genius of the heart, which teaches the clumsy and too hasty hand to hesitate, and to grasp more delicately; which scents the hidden and forgotten treasure, the drop of goodness and sweet spirituality under thick dark ice, and is a divining-rod for every grain of gold, long buried and imprisoned in mud and sand; the genius of the heart, from contact with which every one goes away richer; not favoured or surprised, not as though gratified and oppressed by the good things of others; but richer in himself, newer than before, broken up, blown upon, and sounded by a thawing wind; more uncertain, perhaps, more delicate, more fragile, more bruised, but full of hopes which as yet lack names…

  — (*Beyond Good and Evil*, article 295 trans. Helen Zimmern, Project Gutenberg).

Yay to the heart's genii, smoothing our souls with the longing to lie placid. Yay for the divining rod that perceives the mortal body as a mirror for the divine, then drops right on through it to go down, down, to long-imprisoned underground riches. Yay for the generous, unspecial, connected, blown-open soul. Yay for new, broken, delicate, bruised, fragile, hopeful regeneration into forms for which we don't yet have names.

Enter Donika Kelly, who brings us back into the living, thriving, loving present moment. Albergotti perceives a tiny porthole of light above a sea of darkness, our toes pointing downward to keep us afloat. Devin Kelly imagines this worldly plane as light, rather than the sky above, a premise as tenuous as the possibility of finding gold under the sand, but one that enables heart behaviors like forgiveness, blessing, and longing. Nietzsche turns this around: the behavior of the heart *is* the divining rod, and through its capacity for finding gold in the muck, we become placid, hopeful, still, new, delicate—a mirror for the heavens. But to this vertical cosmology Donika Kelly adds time and horizontal space. No longer are we dreaming of some past or future beach, or recollecting childhood heartbreak to redefine our present.

The first words of this poem are "I am." The poet's name, the thrice-repeated fact of her present-moment-being-in-loveness, stand out in italics as though written in the sand of the poem. There's no love object in the poem, besides the hot animal of her skin. The magical ability to move her limbs rises above her injuries. She doesn't linger long enough with death to touch it, instead turning her attention to seagulls above and pavement below and green egg pebbles in her hand and roses and gold all around. Walking like water, she asks only to find her way home. The movement of a tide come in takes everything in its wake, black flies and ditch lilies and all, sweeping everything back to the sea of now.

In spite of it all, inside it all, there's the ability to "have a lot of feelings," in the language of the facetious title that refuses to take life and love too seriously. We might translate the message written in the sand of the poem to read: we can, like Donika Kelly on the particular day of this poem, insist on existing inside the state of loving. We too can mark the present moment with our existence, walking forward like a high tide that can hold it all. We can be/persist in/within... love. Happy Pride y'all.

PRACTICE

There are so many somatic practices embedded in these images. Exploring them with other beings and other bodies, my students found different physiological entry points for light. We played with treading-water-walking, pointing our toes as thought bicycling into each step. Moving into the floor in slow motion from the pointed toes through the balls of the feet to the heels definitely slows down the autopilot and gives the fresh experience of "dipping a toe in" to each step. Someone suggested that we visualize a footprint of phosphorescent light left behind.

We experimented with myriad divining rods: sitting with one hand on the chest and the other on the earth, as though a current were running between them. One begins to sense that the heart could see, feelingly, through the extended arm and into the ground. Experiencing the actual sternum as a divining rod required a bit more gymnastics, and we experimented with how to both be close to the ground and also stand the breastbone upright. Some movements were yoga backbends: bridge, bow, upward-facing bow, and fish, which definitely gives the heart a rush of something like optimism or light. My personal favorite for experienced yogis is dolphin pose, supported by a yoga block wedged between the upper back and a wall. From a kneeling position, place your elbows shoulder-width on the ground, right up against the baseboard, with the forearms reaching up the wall. Hold a block between your palms, vertically up the wall. Then tuck your toes and straighten your legs to lift your hips, pressing the thoracic spine up against the block. Be sure the head is suspended or at least bearing no weight at all.

If you want something more impressionistic, try going for a Donika Kelly walk: what does it mean, in your particular body, to "move like a tide come in"? Perhaps it's not a physical action but a more subtle shift of focus, sweeping everything you pass into the wake of your attention. Whatever you do, consider making yourself some Albergotti-style sticky notes afterward. What might be *your* ThingsToDoWhileNotDoing?

JUNE WEEK 2
FATHER'S DAY

Ashley M. Jones
"Photosynthesis"

When I was young, my father taught us
how dirt made way for food,
how to turn over soil so it would hold a seed,
an infant bud, how the dark could nurse it
until it broke its green arms out to touch the sun.
In every backyard we've ever had, he made a little garden plot
with room for heirloom tomatoes, corn, carrots,
peppers: jalapeno, bell, and poblano—
okra, eggplant, lemons, collards, broccoli, pole beans,
watermelon, squash, trees filled with fruit and nuts,
brussels sprouts, herbs: basil, mint, parsley, rosemary—
onions, sweet potatoes, cucumber, cantaloupe, cabbage,
oranges, swiss chard and peaches,
sunflowers tall and straightbacked as soldiers,
lantana, amaryllis, echinacea,
pansies and roses and bushes bubbling with hydrangeas.
Every plant with its purpose.
Flowers to bring worms and wasps. How their work matters here.
This is the work we have always known,
pulling food and flowers from a pile of earth.

The difference, now: my father is not a slave,
not a sharecropper. This land is his and so is this garden,
so is this work. The difference is that he owns this labor.
The work of his own hands for his own belly,
for his own children's bellies. We eat because he works.
This is the legacy of his grandmother, my great-granny.
Ollie Mae Harris and her untouchable flower garden.
Just like her hats, her flowerbeds sprouted something special,
plants and colors the neighbors could only dream of.
He was young when he learned that this beauty is built on work,
the cows and the factories in their stomachs,
the fertilizer they spewed out—
the stink that brought such fragrance. What you call waste,
I call power. What you call work I make beautiful again.
In his garden, even problems become energy, beauty—
my father has ended many work days in the backyard,
worries of the firehouse dropping like grain, my father wrist-deep
in soil. I am convinced the earth speaks back to him
as he feeds it—it is a conversational labor, gardening.
The seeds tell him what they will be, the soil tells seeds how to grow,
my father speaks sun and water into the earth,
we hear him, each harvest, his heartbeat sweet, like fruit.

———

Gustavo Hernandez
"Marte"

Around the time
        the first holiday billboards
                go up

    I raise a finger to a point in the night.

To my eldest sister say,
        look   that red light is Mars.

We have been more than one year
            without him, and just now
                        we are starting to see things again.

        So much of our knowledge
about the skies is gone.
                Chart-blind,
                        codices black—all questions
            we have forgotten to ask:
                the color of the orbs
                the slabs of moonlight.

I tell her the planet has been
            floating there for weeks,
and I really mean to say,
            we must try to hold on
                        to everything we can still recognize,
                                even the need to look
            for our fathers
    in the
                                    sky.

———

Bayo Akomolafe,
"Epilogue: Re / Turn"
(A prose piece appearing here as a poem, with his generous approval)

Home is such a slippery concept.
Maybe there are no words to finally rope her in.
In the stead of words, a gasp:
home is then the moment when
in a fit of sovereignty
you would have given names
to the glory-weary sun

and to the council of mountains that hum
gently in his praise
and to the sea
and the bulbous shapes that hang from trees
names for all
only to hear behind your ears
the whisper of the world
"You! We shall give you a name too!"
It is not enough to find one's way home.
The things that stand in our way
are aspects of our ongoing reconfiguration
enemies, bottlenecks, seething memories, gnarling fetishes, haunting
        creeds, howling specters, grumbling boogeymen, careening splinters,
        frowning clouds, green giants, gaping holes, chuckling forests.
A good journey is about dismemberment, not arrival.
Look for the path with the dead end
the unmapped one
haunted by Sphynxian riddles
And yellow slit-eyed peering shadows.
Encircled by crumbling fences and by an encroaching wildness
without maps and without answers
surrender to the journey
let the loamy fingers of this dark soil
envelope you unmake you fiddle with you disturb you unsettle you
        conspire with you
and birth you.
The world needs you to fly
to wait for guidance from a tree
to do something preposterous
to tell us why one and one could equal sixteen.
The future is not fixed, and the past is yet to come.
This home that is a dance with exile
drives us to find new kin
the cow down the street
the wet anointing she spills on everything
the moon that nods as we stroll by.

For me, this feeling of home
it looks like my father—your grandfather…
Dear Dad,
Mummy told us the week before we set sail

that you might not come back with us to Nigeria
the government needed you there
in the raging wars of Kinshasa.
But we knew.
This heavy gravity that pulled down everything within
as if I had swallowed a wrecking ball.
We drove in the embassy's Pajero SUV to the busy docks.
We got on the ferry across the Congo River
And when the boat started to drift away from the quay
You stood there on the platform, your legs
an actionable distance apart — a long cool figure
cut out from the pestilence of the background,
Silhouetted against he din of the ordinary.
I feel your prickly mustache as you press your face into mine
the anchoring hopes come undone
and the ferry drifts out,
dancing on the currents
in the wake of other departing vessels.
You did come home
many times after that
until the day you came home in a box.
I have a daughter now.
I'm sure you know that because you haunt me.
I write you to let you know
I see you standing on the quay even now
when leaves rustle with passing wind
when your granddaughter asks about you
I see you when I remember the promise
to think with her
to listen to the ghosts that wander the streets
as they whisper about world forgone,
And to live in small places
where I never forget
that to be Alethea's father is the deepest honor
the universe bestows on me.
I love you. Don't leave me alone.

This, all of this,
is how home feels.
Home is your mother
in whose entrails and dust I will be entangled

long after memories are congealed into new stars.
So take these letters
pack them in a neat heap
and burn them in a fire
put the ashes in with us,
where we now lie,
in the single pot
release us into the ocean wind
let her carry us away
so we will always be close to you.
Run through the fields, my darling.
Run to your new kin.
To your new fathers and mothers.
To the ones who hold you close
as our dust churns a new night.
Gather your children close—if you have any—
and tell them of your mother and me.
Especially your mother.
Tell them of your mother.
And when you dance through the wisps
of Thursday's bright morning
know you will not dance alone.
For we will haunt you.
We are cool like that.

Bayo Akomolafe from *These Wilds Beyond Our Fences: Letters to my Daughter on Humanity's Search for Home*, North Atlantic Books. Copyright © 2017 by Bayo Akomolafe. Rewritten as a poem here with permission of the author.

POETIC THEMES

Maybe we're finally ushering in a time of "Parent's Day." If I try to hunt down what fatherhood is, somatically and essentially, I guess it might be rooted in a seed and then in the practice of cultivating its growth. In a beautiful bridge to Juneteenth next week, Ashley Jones' poem recuperates the image of her father working the earth from its history in slavery and returns it to a "conversational labor" of love. Pouring elements of light and water into the earth is likened to speech, the soil has a voice, and the seeds speak back with what they want to become. In this ecology of heart work, there is a comingling of the elemental and the auditory. Our father's voice grows inside us, so sown into us that we can taste it: "we hear him, each harvest, his heartbeat sweet, like fruit." "Photosynthesis" helps us see how one thing becomes another, across generations. Sharecropping transmutes into a mode of dropping worries like grain. Great-granny's love of color shapeshifts from hats and flowers into food. Work becomes power becomes energy becomes a heartbeat.

If "Photosynthesis" inspires us to listen for our fathers in the earth, "Marte" invites us to look for them in the sky. In fact, this poem is more than an invitation—it's a plea. The poem's jagged lines seem to be shaking us, jostling us back to an awareness of the old ways of our fathers, and ancestors further back. The grief of loss leads us into a kind of blindness, a forgetfulness that threatens to take away our maps, our customs, even our questions. Hernandez encourages us to "hold on" to our need, squinting to find traces of "everything we can still recognize"… even our fathers in the sky.

Which leads me to Bayo Akomolafe's *These Wilds Beyond Our Fences: Letters to my Daughter on Humanity's Search for Home*. In the book's foreword, Charles Eisenstein adopts the metaphor of a crystal for the way home refracts prismatically in Akomolafe's letters: "It isn't like the bull's-eye, the destination, heaven, home, doesn't exist. It is only that it doesn't exist in linear time. It is like a crystal hanging above our entire timeline, refracting partial images of itself onto our world that we recognize as home."

I feel fatherhood, too, in Akomolafe's work, as something exploded, expanded, and dissolved into the sense experience of the whole world, from the humming mountains to the "loamy fingers" of the soil to the nodding moon to the wet-anointing cow to the "bulbous shapes that hang from trees." The *universe* gives us our name. Fatherhood is bestowed like a gift and then re-gifted generously. Nurture must be shared with new kin, those who will hold us close when our "real" parents are turned to dust. This beautiful paradox of holding on to our hauntings (his own father's ghost, waving his tall and noble goodbye from the quay), and the need to let go of the finite (the ashes of our parents and the proverbial letters they have written us) is the mystery of Bayo's worlding project. We must release our tight grip on the past so that we can open ourselves to being haunted in new, just as intimate ways: "let [the ocean wind] carry us away so we will always be close to you." Kinda like his response to me when I sheepishly apologized for presuming to re-sculpt a prose passage so personal to him, so foreign from my own experience. He responded,

No, you are not writing to me about *my own* daughter or *my own* father's death; you are writing to me about yours, about his, hers, theirs. Somehow, in re-presenting those lines to me like a poem, you brought it to me in a new way—in a way that wasn't mine to begin with, but was and has always been a collective, affective, sociomaterial swirl of homemaking/place-sensing becomings. I say yes to this, sister.

#goals: to be, even for a day, cool like *that*.

Bayo is doing what he describes, by unsettling, disturbing, and dismembering fatherhood as a home-base. He destabilizes any single, static, *in situ* ground or moment—even the image of his own father on the quay—and sets it into a movement migration. The ferry, the ashes, invite us to configure our own, tentative, temporary definition of home, in turn to be disturbed, burned up, and recycled.

PRACTICE

How do we invite homemaking/place-sensing becomings into our daily practice? Maybe we could call up a seed memory of a paternal figure and consider an associated sense experience. This might be one of the five senses like listening for a heartbeat in a garden or peering out at the night sky to find Mars, but it also might be a subtler sense impression like the feeling of being ferried away from a static figure. Look for this perceptual experience in your world right now, this day, this week.

If we could shift a parental memory from a moment into a whole field of perception, we might feel more cared for in this world. Right after my dad died I had to walk the dog, and I felt companioned by his spirit in the open horizon of the playing fields by my house. For a while, every morning and night I would visit with my dad at those fields. Now every big open sky carries his imprint, every horizon holds me. We *need* these re-homing patterns—what's yours?

JUNE WEEK 3

SUMMER SOLSTICE, JUNETEENTH

June Jordan
"In Memoriam: Martin Luther King, Jr."

I
honey people murder mercy U.S.A.
the milkland turn to monsters teach
to kill to violate pull down destroy
the weakly freedom growing fruit
from being born

America

tomorrow yesterday rip rape
exacerbate despoil disfigure
crazy running threat the
deadly thrall
appall belief dispel
the wildlife burn the breast
the onward tongue
the outward hand
deform the normal rainy
riot sunshine shelter wreck
of darkness derogate

delimit blank
explode deprive
assassinate and batten up
like bullets fatten up
the raving greed
reactivate a springtime
terrorizing
death by men by more
than you or I can

STOP

II

They sleep who know a regulated place
or pulse or tide or changing sky
according to some universal
stage direction obvious
like shorewashed shells

we share an afternoon of mourning
in between no next predictable
except for wild reversal hearse rehearsal
bleach the blacklong lunging
ritual of fright insanity and more
deplorable abortion
more and
more

Gbenga Adesina
"Surrender"

A mercy puts a thing
on my palm and
it is my childhood
Its tiny endless moth city
Its rind like grace
or tenderness or sorrow
∞
In the red brick room, my father cries.
His cries are small, lonely animals.
I carry them with me
like an inheritance.
∞
Once, I ran out
of a room
because the song
on the radio
was a fist
in the nook of my neck.
I stood
on the street
quietly weeping.
Though when a woman said to me:
"Child, are you well?
I said it was the waters
within me that wanted to
make themselves known.
∞
Some nights are like that. They do not let you go
until they have broken into the secret July in your heart where you hide all
    things.
∞
All I wanted
was to be home,
so I dipped myself
under the earth.
By which I mean
I entered the subway station.

∞

It was there I heard him.
A man that was also a sound.
He was singing. Tree
branches broke
inside his voice.
∞

There was, in his chorus, the quietude of a thing that was coming to an end.
This song he was singing, he said it was not a dirge.
Though he sang it to a thing that was dying.
∞

Which in a way
was the kind of song
my father sang
as he lay dying.
My father said
his song was not a dirge.
Though he sang it
to a thing that was dying
in himself.
He said son.
my song is a joy.
But a joy with sharp knives.
∞

So, my laughter is a thing with a sharp edge.
And my joy a trembling.
∞

This man I saw,
his locks of hair
which ran down
to his neck
were the
visible borders
of a country
that was inside him.
And the sound he made
was the secret language
of a nation unto which
immigrants were called.
∞

It was as though I had sliced through the ocean and arrived here,

only to run into my childhood.
And I did not want to make myself open. But I was made open
for certain songs do not ask your permission.
∞

I raised my hands
and moved toward him,
naked before the song.
I said:
Dear Music, dear childhood.
Take me.
Take me.

POETIC THEMES

Can we talk about anger for a minute? Juneteenth corresponds to the celebration of the sun at the moment of the summer solstice. Solar fire, somatically speaking, is said to be manifest in the circular current of digestion / transmutation. We all are called to metabolize righteous anger into action and tend the flames to keep our passion alive. Deliberate, discerned action is a way of processing, metabolizing, and expelling anger. The Quaker charge to speak truth to power, given to 18th-century Friends, justifies the place of anger in spiritual practice. Although love is opposed to hate, it is not a synonym for retreat. Quakers believe that as we love, so we act. Rage teaches us when and where.

These two poems offer two very different experiences of anger and its relationship to power, which instead of intellectualizing, we can *feel*. That is to say, we can perceive our physiological response to the poem at the level of breath or goosebumps. June Jordan's first stanza depicts the "honey people" in America's "milkland" as monsters, with a battery of violent verbs—murder kill violate destroy—and couches it all in an unsettling analogy of a country pregnant with (faint) possibility: "the weakly freedom growing fruit / from being born." Mercy in this land of milk and honey grows weakly.

Gbenga Adesina's first stanza also contemplates mercy, placing his childhood on his palm like some rare fruit with a "rind like grace / or tenderness or sorrow." Jordan's verbs grow more vivid—rip rape despoil disfigure deform assassinate explode—and the body burns, breast, tongue, and hand. Her whole battering ram of a second stanza only stops with the next stanza's single word in caps. But the context of that word is framed by its impossibility: "death by men by more / than you or I can / STOP." In contrast, Adesina moves to a specific scene of a father weeping in a red brick room. The speaker carries his father's cries (his inheritance) into a scene of his own weeping, when a song on the radio "was a fist / in the nook of my neck." After George Floyd's death, he might have imagined a knee there.

Part II of "In Memoriam" proceeds from the gorgeous, gutted image of sleeping escapists like dead shells scattered, on to its end, which is also the end of Mercy's fetus. The last stanza is a kind of scrambled funhouse of nightmares, the only thing predictable being the proliferation of violence: "more and / more." The end of the poem aborts the weakly growing freedom in America's womb. Adesina's poem ends in death, too, and similarly widens its scope to encompass the tragic state of this country. But its tone is different. The speaker descends into the underworld of the subway where he hears the singing of a man with locks that were the "visible borders / of a country / that was inside him." The sound of the subway singer connects back to the speaker's father, who sang "to a thing that was dying / in himself." The borders of this nation, calling out to immigrants with its "secret language" is sliced open like the ocean the speaker has crossed, like the fruit of some childhood innocence lost, "a joy with sharp knives." Raising his hands, the speaker moves toward the singer, "naked before the song." The last line, blending violence and the erotic, is one of being forcibly opened, hands up naked—"Take me. / Take me." Joy with knives for sure.

These poems are a visceral kick to the gut. Juneteenth, which celebrates an incomplete freedom, maybe should feel just like that. Maybe the holiday invites us, at the beginning of the season of fire, to get this gutsy in exploring our own anger, so that we can speak our own truth to power.

PRACTICE

These poems thrust out the daunting challenge to examine how and where anger lives in our bodies:

Jordan: womb, breast, tongue, hand, abortion, rape

Adesina: palm, fist in notch of the throat, tears, heart broken into, voice like branches breaking, locks of hair, nakedness, raised hands

Can we feel the difference between the tummy-burbling of a threatened ego (Ross Gay calls this part of the psyche his "sad little annoyance monster") and the knot in our belly when our gut tells us something is really wrong? Can we develop metaphors for the relationship of anger and grief and how we experience each somatically? What would your "STOP" gesture be, à la June Jordan?

Try standing, establishing absolute stillness in the steadiest, most grounded stance from which to punch or kick at the air. Supine, seated, or prone on the belly, beating softs fists or open palms on the ground can tap you into anger.

Resmaa Menakem's techniques for "Warning and Warding," like baring your teeth, growling, and widening your eyes can be found in his most recent book, *The Quaking of America: An Embodied Guide to Navigating Our Nation's Upheaval and Racial Reckoning*. Chapter Six of this indispensable book suggests that practitioners "soul scribe" from the experience of the body's intelligences, using the acronym VIMBA: vibrations (any felt charge or energy), images (memories, fantasies, or visions), meanings (like explanations, connections, stories), behaviors (what the body does or wants to do but doesn't), affect (emotions), and sensations (pressure, tightness, temperature, numbness, for example). This week might be an excellent time to soul scribe, without judgment, about your experience of anger.

JUNE WEEK 4
MIDSUMMER

Derek Walcott
"Love After Love"

The time will come
when, with elation
you will greet yourself arriving
at your own door, in your own mirror
and each will smile at the other's welcome,

and say, sit here. Eat.
You will love again the stranger who was your self.
Give wine. Give bread. Give back your heart
to itself, to the stranger who has loved you

all your life, whom you ignored
for another, who knows you by heart.
Take down the love letters from the bookshelf,

the photographs, the desperate notes,
peel your own image from the mirror.
Sit. Feast on your life.

George Herbert
"Love (III)"

Highlight Actions Disable annotations
Love bade me welcome. Yet my soul drew back
      Guilty of dust and sin.
But quick-eyed Love, observing me grow slack
      From my first entrance in,
Drew nearer to me, sweetly questioning,
      If I lacked any thing.

A guest, I answered, worthy to be here:
      Love said, You shall be he.
I the unkind, ungrateful? Ah my dear,
      I cannot look on thee.
Love took my hand, and smiling did reply,
      Who made the eyes but I?

Truth Lord, but I have marred them: let my shame
      Go where it doth deserve.
And know you not, says Love, who bore the blame?
      My dear, then I will serve.
You must sit down, says Love, and taste my meat:
      So I did sit and eat.

The poem to celebrate the official beginning of summer on the 21st would be Mary Oliver's "The Summer Day," a poem that begins with a question about God and ends with a recipe for prayer. We don't need to know our creator; we just have to commit to feeling its creation, moment by moment. This is the religious imperative of Oliver's oeuvre as a whole—an agnostic worship of the world. And I do mean worship in its etymological sense: what is worthy of our attention. We pay attention, like cash money; we devote our attention, the most precious of gifts. The poem is not about a summer's day; it's entitled *"The Summer Day."* This one you're in. It's not just any grasshopper, it is a *particular* one.

This difference could be illustrated via a longstanding debate about how to translate a famous (perhaps the most famous) haiku. The story is that Basho, the renown Japanese poet of the Edo period, was challenged by his Zen master with a Koan (or riddle), and he responded with a haiku about mindfulness. Here's the literal translation: *Fu-ru* (old) *i-ke* (pond) *ya, ka-wa-zu* (frog) *to-bi-ko-mu* (jumping into) *mi-zu* (water) *no o-to* (sound). Do we liken the pond to the mind and the splash to a thought? If so, should it be *a* pond or *the* pond? *A* frog, or *the* frog? Is the focus on the water, the jump, or the sound? You can google the Basho translation debate and find a whole world there. But suffice it to say, the message of "The Summer Day," like the frog haiku, is about presence. Our singular existence is not all human life, it's this one we're living. Every one of us is just as strange and complex, ethereal and earthy. And Oliver's famous second person address to discern what you'll do with *your* time on earth is exportable to every calling that brings us into the immediacy of what we are meant to be and do. We are challenged to drop to our knees and surrender to that calling, offering our lives like a prayer.

But since Mary Oliver's angle on devotion is pretty well known, I want to offer a slightly different angle in a poem by Derek Walcott. Why Walcott's poem for midsummer? Well, first because hunting around for poems about this pagan-turned-Christian holiday (which takes place between June 21st and June 26th in various places over the globe), I found Walcott's book entitled *Midsummer*. But then I swam around in the book's Biblical allusions for a while —most beautifully in a scene of Caribbean yellow butterflies "stuttering 'yes' to the resurrection" in "Midsummer LIV." The bitter, brilliant manipulation of Christian doctrine in *Midsummer* rang a bell. I was called back to "Love after Love" as the perfect poem for this tension between earthly and Christian love at work in this weird June holiday.

Walcott is famous for his reappropriations of canonical Western texts. I'm not sure if anyone has ever noted that "Love after Love" speaks to George

Herbert's "Love III." This is the final poem in this 17th-century poet and priest's collection about spiritual conflict, *The Temple*. God-as-Love issues an invitation to the poem's sinful Everyman: "You must sit down, says Love, and taste my meat: / So I did sit and eat." Herbert's poem consigns human love to a Christian realm, from which Walcott rescues it.

The holiday of Midsummer is rife with these tensions. The pagan focus on sexual bonds and romantic love (mating in midsummer means a convenient birth in spring!) become entangled with the birthday of St. John the Baptist and his divine bond with Jesus. This mishmash yields some mighty strange rituals. Somewhere, this week, lovers are jumping over a ceremonial St. John bonfire with their wrists tied together, to cement a bond said to be stronger than blood. Somewhere a man is eating snails to avoid being cuckolded (long story). Somewhere a woman is putting a beauty elixir called "St. John's Water" on her face or placing a bouquet of carefully-selected magical flowers under her pillow. Some kinky stuff is happening in an all-night vigil somewhere —even in the U.S., according to Louise Glück's "Midsummer"!

Walcott adopts the dialogue form of "Love III" to concoct his own magical brew from these tensions between religious and earthly love. We reclaim communion to learn to love our own soul. The bread and wine serve to "Give back your heart / to itself." What more could one ask of Midsummer's purported capacity for lifelong bonds than a comingling union with our soul and heart? Body and blood returned to same. In "[The midsummer sea...]" Walcott asks, "Where's my child's hymnbook, the poems edged in gold leaf, / the heaven I worship with no faith in heaven, / as the Word turned poetry in its grief?" He provides his own answer: "Ah, bread of life, that only love can leaven!" Only love, Walcott teaches, can leaven the bread of our life. Maybe that's the message of Midsummer.

PRACTICE

We might explore the embodied act of reuniting a self divided in two—body hemispheres, past and present selves, mind and heart, body and soul, thoughts and witness mind. We could use a mirror like the poem's doorway, where one part of the self greets the other. In tandem with movements that strip down, like actions of "peeling off" layers or "taking down" imaginary facades, we are looking for somatic experiences of melting resistance in forms of surrender, like smiling, sitting, and receiving (gifts, food). We could unburden our shoulders or our neck or wherever we are weighed down by massaging them and flicking the excess tension off the fingers. We could peel off clothing or splay the limbs open to unpeel the core. What would gestures of receiving/feasting look like?

Finally, to explore the act of mirror-gazing, consider this. I used to sit and touch noses with my dad. A quick google search reveals that the touching of noses and foreheads is an ancient greeting involving the transmission of spirit, practiced across many spiritual traditions: the Maori call it *Hongi*, the Hawaiians name it *Honi;* and it is practiced in certain parts of Scandinavia, among Tibetans, the desert Bedouins in Southern Jordan, the Inuit, and who knows where else. If it resonates with you that the eye could indeed be the window to the soul, stand with your nose and forehead in contact with a mirror, and as you stare into your own eyes, envision an exchange of power with the image you face. End in some form of relaxed rest, the stillness like a banquet prepared by the soma, to just be savored, "feasting" on your life.

JULY WEEK 1
INDEPENDENCE DAY

Tony Hoagland
"America"

Then one of the students with blue hair and a tongue stud
Says that America is for him a maximum-security prison

Whose walls are made of RadioShacks and Burger Kings, and MTV
    episodes
Where you can't tell the show from the commercials,

And as I consider how to express how full of shit I think he is,
He says that even when he's driving to the mall in his Isuzu

Trooper with a gang of his friends, letting rap music pour over them
Like a boiling Jacuzzi full of ballpeen hammers, even then he feels

Buried alive, captured and suffocated in the folds
Of the thick satin quilt of America

And I wonder if this is a legitimate category of pain,
or whether he is just spin doctoring a better grade,

And then I remember that when I stabbed my father in the dream last
    night,
It was not blood but money

That gushed out of him, bright green hundred-dollar bills
Spilling from his wounds, and—this is the weird part—,

He gasped "Thank god—those Ben Franklins were
Clogging up my heart—

And so I perish happily,
Freed from that which kept me from my liberty"—

Which was when I knew it was a dream, since my dad
Would never speak in rhymed couplets,

And I look at the student with his acne and cell phone and phony ghetto
    clothes
And I think, "I am asleep in America too,

And I don't know how to wake myself either,"
And I remember what Marx said near the end of his life:

"I was listening to the cries of the past,
When I should have been listening to the cries of the future."

But how could he have imagined 100 channels of 24-hour cable
Or what kind of nightmare it might be

When each day you watch rivers of bright merchandise run past you
And you are floating in your pleasure boat upon this river

Even while others are drowning underneath you
And you see their faces twisting in the surface of the waters

And yet it seems to be your own hand
Which turns the volume higher?

Aria Aber
"America"

America the footsteps of your ghosts are white stones weighting my center

America the old girls' campus in the heart of Oakland where I teach
Grows quiet as glass marbles rolling between my feet

I pick one up, I say It's pretty
And my students laugh, cheering Welcome to America

I have no one to look to this summer, I light a candle, burn the
      proposedly holy wood

And God does not come when summoned

Just the scent of bonfire in my hair
Gold light flooding the bay window sure as a divination

America I divine nothing
In the other country, my parents wear their silence like silk robes each
      morning, devoted to the terrible sun

Day after day, I weep on the phone, saying Even the classroom is a prison
And still my father insists But it is good to become an American

And so I cement my semantics
I practice my pronunciations, I learn to say This country
After saying I love

I rinse my aquiline face, wring my language for fear

I feared what had happened in your forest, the words that pursued the
      soft silk of spiders

The verbs were naturalize, charge, reside
The nouns were clematis, alien, hibiscus

America I arrived to inhabit the realm of your language
I came to worry your words

What you offered is a vintage apartment, an audience for poems
Pills the color of dusk
To swallow so as not to collapse when I read the poem about my uncle

The reading of which I owe him, to everyone who antecedes me

No, I mean who haunts me

The haunting of which is a voice

The West is too young to be haunted, an ex-lover assures

Still, every night I listen to your voice scraping against my walls

And in the mornings, trivial offerings on my pillows
I pick the spiders from my bed, flush their curled transparence down the
    drain

America I don't know what to make of my ordinary cruelty
Or my newly bourgeois pain

Venom lacing each crack of the historic apartment
Venom lacing the porcelain plates we hand out at parties

In the hallway I let someone touch me under my mask
Three fingers in my mouth
My back pushed against the door, the cold sink

The mind plays where it leads, a dark hour, the weight of a body on indigo
    tiles

America the scale says not thin enough

America my lawyer suggests to keep quiet about certain things
About you and me

So I write in my notebook your name, I write Country of
Cowboys and Fame

America I have no cowboy

And I have no fame

All I gather is the scratching of ink against paper, the laugh of a skeptic

There are nights we hear something likened to fireworks lighting up the
    humid campus
And my students cheer, they laugh Welcome to America

Later in the empty corridor, the disembodied voice of my uncle

Saying   The classroom is not a prison
Saying   Go, go home now and so I go

Past vetiver and cedar, past eucalyptus declaring the shoreline

Until I shiver on the soft-stoned coast on which my father once lay
And I proclaim what he did, I say This land is my fate

America who am I becoming here with you
If I wander the same as without you, barely visible amid your indigenous
    trees

POETIC THEMES

Here are two poems with the same title, both describing American pedagogical scenes of exchange. One is a conversation between white males, a blue-
haired undergrad preaching anti-capitalism to a Marxist professor whose
initial perception of the student's hypocrisy becomes an admission of his own.
The second is a heartbreaking portrait of the micro-aggressions of American
students toward a female professor who is an Afghan refugee. Very different
currents of power obviously are coursing through these two scenes, which
share thematic explorations of power, belonging, and complicity.

The white-on-white anti-capitalist exchange starts as a lofty dismissal that
refuses to acknowledge that we are all poisoned by the same history and
mythos. Hoagland's poem invites us to look into the anatomy of scorn, that
funny mix of ego and intellectualizing pain, a skill set required for and maybe
representative of straight white male normativity. Since suffering lives in the

reptilian brain and body, the forebrain is overstepping its bounds in attempting to wrestle it down. So how to temper the frontal lobe's scorn and get back to the body's authentic relationship to suffering?

Hoagland's poem models a pretty simple tripartite process. The poem is divided into three groups of six stanzas: the first six focus on the other, the second six on the self, and the last on the collective. The depiction of other—a classic pierced and blue-haired radical youth—is rife with (bad) metaphor: rap music is "like a boiling jacuzzi of ballpeen hammers." In fact, the most effective analogy of the bunch is the kid's own description of feeling "suffocated in the folds / Of the thick satin quilt of America," in a transitional stanza that leads the speaker to contemplate something actually touching his own emotional vulnerability, in the dream of stabbing his own father. It's not so much that Hoagland lets go of his typical sardonic style, but rather his humor (about the rhymed couplets) serves as a backlight that accentuates the power of the central, visceral image in the poem (money instead of blood flowing from the father's wounds). And the final third of the poem segues via Marx to describe the collective pleasure boat of the privileged, where the second person address forces us to see the twisted faces of those underwater. In the final couplet, Hoagland brings the reader into the scene by gesturing back at the rap metaphor in a way that makes everyone with any power complicit in floating above it all: "And yet it seems to be your own hand / Which turns the volume higher." The pronouns in the poem move from third person to the first person singular to first person plural and ends with a second person direct address—and a question. Talk about calling the reader to consider his or her place in the mess! The somatic disarmament here slows the rational mind's rat-a-tat-tat judgment and softens ego armor via an opening inward to painful scenes, like one's own father bleeding. Only then can we find an authentic, emotion-based identification with suffering, and that's the only space from which to initiate true connection and change.

And then there's Aber's version of America. It's full of despair and panic at being sucked into the fireworks of American "ordinary cruelty." It's shocked by the ease with which the venom of its "bourgeois pain" can creep into the psyche, like a spider. The images of indigenous trees and burning wood splinter through the poem—like the mocking refrain, "Welcome to America!" —begging the question of what's "natural" and what's "foreign." Language, for one thing, is foreign—and labored, and mandated. Loved ones are absent. So is God. Alongside the discombobulation, invisibility, and sorrow of the outsider, there's an intertextual reference to another poem with another classroom scene, this one about her uncle's death, which haunts her.

Once read, this referenced poem, "Nostos," will never un-haunt, depicting a mass grave outside Kabul that might contain the bones of Aber's uncle and great-grandfather. In a chilling moment, a student who is an ex-marine student spits violence toward Afghan bodies. The poet decides that grief "has a heart and thus will love, / and learn, and thusly / learn to hate." Is there an alternative to this sequence of the heart of grief learning to hate? Having never lost a loved one in such an incredibly gruesome way, it's not my place to say. But if our collective American heart still holds any potential for healing, it is through the blight of grief when we reckon with hard truths like these—a woman weeping on the phone, pushed against a door with three fingers under her mask, awake to the ghosts of her bound blindfolded raped and murdered ancestors. How can we let these images in to cultivate the tenderness required to initiate change?

PRACTICE

What is the anatomy of scorn, of ordinary cruelty? Where does it live in the body? If we can perceive ourselves as a thread in "the thick satin quilt of America," how does our complicity in exploitation haunt us, somatically? How can we relieve the holding patterns that build rigidity in the body, softening its hardened defenses so we can feel and respond to scenes of suffering? How could we de-gunk, or soften, aerate, or cool the places where we hold on to our need for power? We might explore these questions through a simple exercise that engages somatic seats of dominance and tenderness. The next task you undertake today, whether it's brushing your teeth or preparing a meal, perform it with your non-dominant hand, and maybe swaddle your dominant hand in a soft sock.

Or, to engage a different mode of perception, use a scarf to cover your dominant eye. (To find it, extend your thumb hitchhiker style to cover an object across the room. Close each eye in turn. The eye that is open when the object is covered is your dominant eye.) One of the central symbols of America is the Eye of Providence on the Great Seal of the United States, atop an unfinished pyramid. It is the symbol on every dollar bill that, according to Hoagland's "America," courses through our veins. If we strip away the Masonic appropriation of this symbol, we arrive back at the Egyptian origin of the disembodied eye. The importance of the dominant and non-dominant eye is couched in the myth of Horus. Osiris was killed by his brother Set, and his son, Horus, avenged him in battle. In the struggle he lost his left eye, which was then divinely restored. So the Eye of Horus became a symbol of healing, mystery, and the kind of divine gift that only comes with wounding. It is associated with the moon, whose power is periodically destroyed and then magically returned to us, like the eye. We're only beginning to understand the discoveries of Egyptian science; a recent discovery is that when superimposed on a sagittal image of the brain, the six sites the Egyptians associated with the senses actually correspond perfectly to the anatomical sense-centers of the brain. Might experimenting with seeing through your non-dominant side give you an experience of the world not through force, but through the power of vulnerability and intuition?

JULY WEEK 2
FIREFLIES

Natasha Rao
"Old Growth"

Backward crossovers into years before: airy
afternoons licking the wooden spoon, pouring soft blades
of grass from a shoe, all ways of saying I miss
my mother. I wish I could remember the gentle lilt
of my brother's early voice. Instead I hear clearly
the dripping of a basalt foundation. What gets saved—

My father fed my sick goldfish a frozen pea and it lived
for another six years. Outside, pears swathed in socks
ripened, protected from birds. Those bulbous
multicolored days, I felt safe before I knew
the word for it. But how to fossilize a feeling, sustain it
in amber? I keep dreaming in reverse until I reach
a quiet expanse of forest. The dragonflies are large
and prehistoric. Mother watches from a distance
as I move wildly, without fear.

Natasha Rao, "Old Growth" from *Latitude.* Copper Canyon Press / The American Poetry Review. Copyright © 2021 by Natasha Rao. Reprinted by permission of the poet.

Marilyn Kallet
"Fireflies"

In the dry summer field at nightfall,
fireflies rise like sparks.
Imagine the presence of ghosts
flickering, the ghosts of young friends,
your father nearest in the distance.
This time they carry no sorrow,
no remorse, their presence is so light.
Childhood comes to you,
memories of your street in lamplight,
holding those last moments before bed,
capturing lightning-bugs,
with a blossom of the hand
letting them go. Lightness returns,
an airy motion over the ground
you remember from Ring Around the Rosie.
If you stay, the fireflies become fireflies
again, not part of your stories,
as unaware of you as sleep, being
beautiful and quiet all around you.

POETIC THEMES

Here we are in the heart of summer. If you can't feel Rao's torrent of summery muscle memories *this* week, you never will—from "back-crossovers" (as we used to call it) on rollerskates, to dumping grass from our shoes, to time enough for batter-licking. But the summer memories are troubled in "Old Growth," playing in the tension between freedom and safety, fearlessness and protection. The poem recollects a feeling of childhood safety that evades the adult, attainable only in dreams. "But how to fossilize a feeling, sustain it in amber?" This, the poem's central question, expresses a frustration we can all relate to, hoping for more in the category of "what gets saved" in our memory bank. But the frustration of this wish appears when, in the place of a beloved's voice, the speaker gets stuck with the sound of dripping basalt. The slow drip that builds a foundation is a powerful image for accruing memories that stick. We use the foundation of memory to build a safe structure. The unwieldy, dangerous flow of memory, like lava, is cooled into basalt, an igneous rock. These are all ways of keeping things forever frozen, fossilized. And yet... and yet! When one approaches memory in this way, things get lost, like the lilting, motile voice of a loved one. Rao's poem is perfect for describing the ache of wanting it all back. Kallet offers us an alternative.

Adult fireflies live only three to four weeks; by mid-July firefly season is already fading fast. As if bioluminescence itself weren't mysterious enough, the transience of these little phosphorescent dancers makes them all the more magical. Fireflies have been likened to ghosts in many traditions, although perhaps most poetically in Japanese haiku. So no surprise when the poem first compares these ephemeral, vanishing sparks to ghosts. But then! Kallet extends the analogy to encompass the flashes of fleeting memories that fireflies can themselves spark in us. Anyone who experienced fireflies as a kid is visited by the ghosts of memory with the glimpse of the summer's first firefly. The use of the second person—"*your* street in lamplight"—includes the reader in this shared memory of catching lightning bugs, holding them in our hands even as we were "holding the last moments before bed," and "with a blossom of the hand / Letting them go." Like Proust, Kallet offers a model of remembering itself. She suggests that when we catch a memory, we first free it from our clutch and then stay with it, following where it leads. That is to say, when we hold onto our story too tightly, poking it repeatedly in the hope that it will light up for us, it becomes engrained in our psyche in one particular way. It loses beauty, spark, life. But rather than actively doing the thing that is remembering, as agent, we can instead soften our grip and just let ourselves be bewitched by recollection. When we let memory enchant us in this way, we are being remembered, or re-membered. If we allow a memory to fly free and simply linger with its natural drifting patterns, it can move and shapeshift into something new and different. Our stories are freed up to change, changing us on the way, not unlike a dream: "As unaware of you as sleep, being / beautiful and quiet all around you."

The key here, in our approach to memory, is in the pun of lightning/light-ening. The independent life of a memory depends on a light touch. The metonymic chain of light witness sets the light presence of memory free from sorrow, remorse, and our heavy-handed recollection. We look up and around —rather than down at a captured memory—to follow the glancing movement: "Lightness returns / an airy motion over the ground / you remember from Ring around the Rosie." Stephen Cope notes that the enthusiasm of a child, whose spirit leaps up toward the object of interest, is a perfect reflection of the word's etymology (*en theos*, the god within). If we were to take our childhood mode of interest as a sign of divinity within us, how would our memories reach us differently?

PRACTICE

Maybe the dying of the fireflies suggests a reprieve from adulthood, where we instead linger with the simpler, more joyful moments from summers past to remind us of that childhood way of being—remembering who we were in those moments when we were lucky enough to feel safe and surrounded by quiet beauty. To be clear, this practice does not depend on a happy childhood. In fact, memories of lightness might be easier to find when they sparkle out from the rubble of trauma. "Do what you loved at ten" is a practice I learned from my mother. When she retired from academia, and found she was unable to calm her racing forebrain with anything but Tetris, she turned to the one activity that afforded her ten-year-old mind some ease and chill: collecting reptiles and amphibians in her backyard. Observing and tending to these animals calmed her. So she began, at sixty-four, to collect frogs, fish, and turtles. The turtles, especially, became her teachers, with their slow, steady, determined, dinosaur-ancient wisdom. She amassed twenty-three turtles, including Homer, a one-hundred-pound tortoise. Eventually her home became a state-certified turtle refuge. She duct-taped broken shells, tenderly handed frozen shrimp to their chomping beaks, constructed complicated homes for them, and watched. And watched. My mother learned a new way of being from her rediscovered enthusiasm for turtles. In her crone years I actually think she has achieved enlightenment, as en-light-ening. She was always a spiritual seeker; from her first book on spiritual conversion narratives to her last book studying the lives of foster parents caring for (and releasing) children with HIV, she hunted down the spirit within. Until she found it. A couple of years ago when I asked her about her current Quakerism she replied:

> I'm not really interested
> in spirituality anymore...
> I'm more interested in the weather
> The sun at every time of day, and rain
> I love rain.
> I really like weather.

En theos finds us, dances for us, enlightens us, inside the simplicity of interest.

So what did *you* love at ten years old? Picture yourself at ten and imagine a slideshow of photographs, real or imagined. What is an image in the carousel that stands out particularly vividly? Place yourself in the Star Trek beam and allow yourself to be transported. Where are you? What are you doing? Who are you with? What are the conditions: the season, the color or tone of the light, any smells or ambient sounds, the weather? Can you identify any distinct sensations in the child's body?

A cliché in American yoga classes is that we hold our past in our hips. Let's just try on a playful frame of mind, and some suspension of disbelief, for approaching this. Here's a doozie I found online, whose author is unknown, about wanting to be a glow worm: "A glow worm's never glum. / 'Cause how can you be grumpy / when the sun shines out your bum?!"

What if you tried childlike movements like skipping, hopping, or galloping, but backward, leading from your firefly bum? If tush-centric actions aren't calling you, consider the general area of the hips as your light source. As a young child of five or six, I learned dance professor Cheryl Cutler's trademark movement style, which initiates movement from the hips. She taught us to imagine our hip points like headlights. You might quite simply take a walk, imagining the two bony protrusions at your hips steering and guiding your body. How does your state of mind shift with your gait when you initiate movement from the ground floor of the torso? Perhaps sneak in some earnest expressions of catching fireflies and setting them free. Just be sure to keep your exploration light (pun intended). Sometimes when we grant ourselves permission to play, those moments of lightness dip deep and scoop up poignant memories.

JULY WEEK 3

CRICKETS TO CICADAS

Lisel Mueller
"Cicadas"

Always in unison, they are
the rapt voice of silence,
so singleminded I cannot tell
if the sound is rich or thin,
cannot tell even if it is sound, the high, sustained note
which gives to a summer field
involved with the sun at noon
a stillness as palpable
as smoke and mildew,
know only: when they are gone
one scrubbed autumn day
after the clean sweep
of the bright, acrid season,
what remains is a clearing of rest,
of balance and attention
but not the second skin,
hot and close, of silence.

Martin Walls
"Cicadas at the End of Summer"

Whine as though a pine tree is bowing a broken violin,
As though a bandsaw cleaves a thousand thin sheets of
titanium;
They chime like freight wheels on a Norfolk Southern
slowing into town.

But all you ever see is the silence.
Husks, glued to the underside of maple leaves.
With their nineteen fifties Bakelite lines they'd do
just as well hanging from the ceiling of a space
museum—

What cicadas leave behind is a kind of crystallized memory;
The stubborn detail of, the shape around a life turned

The color of forgotten things: a cold broth of tea & milk
in the bottom of a mug.
Or skin on an old tin of varnish you have to lift with
lineman's pliers.
A fly paper that hung thirty years in Bird Cooper's pantry
in Brighton.

———

John Blair
"Cicada"

A youngest brother turns seventeen with a click as good as a roar,
finds the door and is gone.
You listen for that small sound, hear a memory.
The air-raid sirens howled of summer tornadoes, the sound

thrown back against the scattered thumbs
of grain silos and the open Oklahoma plains
like the warning wail of insects.
Repudiation is fast like a whirlwind.

Only children don't know that all you live is leaving.
Yes, the first knowledge that counts is that everything stops.
Even in the bible-belt, second comings are promises
you never really believed;

so you turn and walk into the embrace of the world
as you would to a woman, an arrant
an orphic movement as shocking as the subtle
animal pulse of a flower opening, palm up.

We are all so helpless.
I can look at my wife's full form now
and hope for children,
picture her figured by the weight of babies.

Only, it's still so much like trying to find something
once lost. My brother felt the fullness of his years, the pull
in the gut that's almost sickness. His white
smooth face is gone into living and fierce illusion,

a journey dissolute and as immutable
as the whining heat of summer.
Soon enough, too soon, momentum just isn't enough.
Our tragedy is to live in a world

that doesn't invite us back.
We slow, find ourselves sitting in a room that shifts so slightly
we can only imagine the difference.
I want to tell him to listen.

I want to tell him what it is to crave darkness,
to want to crawl headfirst into a dirt-warm womb
to sleep, to wait seventeen years,
to emerge again.

POETIC THEMES

Anne Lamott said the sound of crickets is like the sound of infinity, lightly sawing away. This week their sound has been drowned out by the hissing waves of cicadas, supremely finite. The death rattle of summer, Blair's "warning wail," dials back eerily to silence. Lisel Meuller calls this sound "the rapt sound of silence," like the wind revealing the presence of air. She compares the sound to smoke or mildew—trace things indicating something that existed before them. And cicadas do evoke the past, returning as they do like a memory. Husk-like, the sound of the cicadas wraps around silence like a "second skin, / Hot and close." When the sound is scrubbed away by "the clean sweep" of autumn, there's a renewed awareness of the silence that remains behind, "a clearing of rest." But now in late July, those gorgeous rainbow bodies are beginning to manifest as creepy exoskeletal husks scattered across the trees and the ground. Martin Walls' description of the husks like "crystallized memory" is melancholic, its detailed shell "the shape around a life turned / the color of forgotten things." The poem's list of things brings us to a strip of fly paper hanging in a specific place, for a specific time period. As we move toward August, we become more keenly aware of time and place, a newborn sense of summer as nearly dead.

In this short cicada time, according to John Blair, drinking in the whining waves of sound is "so much like trying to find something / once lost." Blair's poem, which compares the seventeen-year life cycle to a seventeen-year-old brother leaving home, conveys the reality that "all you live is leaving." Any journey in time—backward or forward—is a repudiation of this precious moment. Everything else is dead and gone and the future just as uncertain: "Second comings are promises / you never really believed." But Blair's poem isn't just a pithy message about present-tense being. It's not advocating that we march into our lives, into the embrace of the world, or open like a flower to its orphic mystery, and everything will be glorious. That too would be a kind of delusion: "soon enough, too soon, momentum just isn't enough." We are offered no way out: our aging is a kind of sickness, and any movement away from that truth would be an illusion, a repudiation, "shocking," "errant." This poem is, in fact, an exercise in mourning: "Our tragedy is to live in a world / that doesn't invite us back."

The weight of mortality, mourning the brevity of summer and human life itself, is a feeling Blair likens to pregnancy: the "fullness of our years, the pull in the gut that's almost sickness." Remembering that the etymological root for nostalgia is homesickness, the wish for retreat is a version of craving what's past, another womb. We all crave a little respite from the intensity and heat of living. Wanting to crawl into the earth, dark and safe from it all. The feeling state of these wavelike returns to the past could be accessed by rounding in and down, opening up the back body and cocooning the vulnerable heart and viscera, perhaps wrapped with internally rotated arms.

But also, you could build yourself a palpable cocoon in your bed. Hang in with me here. If you can find a heavy blanket or a big pillow (or best—a weighted blanket!), lay it on top of you or burrito-wrap yourself. As though encased in a shell, anchored by the weight as though underground, take some time to give yourself over to introspection and darkness, "the color of forgotten things." Give your bones back to gravity. Remember, gravity is actually a force that is embracing you; the planet is literally hugging your body's weight toward its own center. The center of gravity in the physical body is the low belly, just between the hip points. Place your hands there and breathe into your own center. Let your abdomen go soft. The first stage of change is just allowing yourself to return to larva status—soft, pure potential. For now, just give yourself permission to be mush, to return to fetus, to know nothing, to have everything before you.

JULY WEEK 4
HEAT LIGHTNING SPEED

Ted Kooser
"Heat Lightning"

At the horizon, July in heavy boots
paces the hot floor of the darkness.
A bulb in a wobbly lamp jiggles.
Or is that you, my love, approaching
across the firefly hills, swinging
a sloshing pail of moonlight?

Rebecca Wee
"hoop snake"

Any of several snakes, such as the mud snake, said to grasp
the tail in the mouth and move with a rolling, hooplike motion.
—American Heritage Dictionary of the English Language

the second time we met
he told me about the hoop snake

(temporal, exquisite,
a godless man

so I listened)

we weren't sure though
if it could be true

a snake that takes its tail in its mouth
then rolls through the world

but there are reasons to believe in god
and this seems a good one

we brought wine to the porch, spoke
of piety, marriage,

devotion assumed for reasons
that could not sustain it

while lightning took apart the sky
the fields leapt up the stream's

muddy lustre its sinuous length
liminal, lush, the grass black

the unheard melodies and those that catch

the leaves beginning to fret

I don't remember now what he said his eyes
revising that dark

after he left I walked through the grass the rain
asked how do things work?

we are after something miraculous

we open our mouths we believe
we turn
at times

we gather speed

POETIC THEMES

Kooser's poem illustrates a mirage, like the mercury wash blurring some hot July pavement. The reverie of the beloved "approaching / across the firefly hills" is sparked by the heavy-booted sound of summer thunder, pacing "the hot floor of the darkness." Or perhaps the sound of the jiggling lightbulb recalls the creak and sway of her "sloshing pail of moonlight." Some sense experience spurs the mind toward a whole avalanche of associations and storylines. Whether or not the ethereal approach of the lover is a hallucination is a little like the question about heat lightning itself: is it real? From what I gleaned in the most cursory of google searches, the supernatural-seeming glimmer across the horizon line is just a faraway storm. Heat lightning is just regular lightning, perceived at a distance. So the notion of some separate natural phenomenon unique to summer is, itself, a mirage, like the sky reflected on water—moonlight in a pail.

Basho's haiku about heat lighting illustrates a similar domino effect: the flash of heat lightning is made available to our eyes by virtue of the darkness surrounding it and in turn triggers the heron's shriek. Each eerie, Poe-like nighttime effect is triggered by another. If heat lightning is itself a mirage, its beauty or creepiness sets into motion the whirring wheel of associations triggered by—nothing! Just like the workings of the mind, which is always the hidden referent in Basho. Some random flash sparks a reaction, which then causes a reaction and away we go, into the play of the monkey mind. Just like when the lightning takes apart the sky and sets the world in motion, in Rebecca Wee's "hoop snake." This meditation on God, piety, the miraculous functioning of creation ends in wonder. In Wee's description of the stream's "sinuous length," like the mysterious ouroboros rolling through the world, phenomena tumble together, and sky, leaping fields, black grass, and fretting leaves all begin to spin. We open our round mouths in disbelieving belief and "we turn / at times / we gather speed." Oh, the mystery!

The spinning wheel of sense experience flashes across both poems. Kooser, strangely, hears thunder, although heat lightning is typically silent. The scream of the night heron sets Basho's haiku in motion. The leaves catch a melody otherwise unheard in "hoop snake." The visual flash of light relies on darkness, like the fireflies on Kooser's hill, or the whites of the beloved's eyes "revising that dark" in Wee's lush landscape. The sense of touch governs the tremor of a heavy footfall or the slosh of water or the vibratory flitting of sound, or bird wings, or the sensuality of wine or walking through wet grass.

The way our senses distract us into chain reactions of thought is the reason for so many meditative teachings about how to withdraw from them. By eliminating their distraction, we become more aware of our senses' ability to trick us into believing a false appearance that might not be reality, like the beautiful hallucination of the beloved. Fellow lovers, how many summers have led us deep into the sorcery of *that* particular illusion, and would we ever want to give that up? What if beautiful hallucination were at the very heart of human experience and everything in nature calls us to the imaginative world made possible by summer magic? We are, after all, "after something miraculous."

PRACTICE

If, rather than perceiving sense experience as the enemy of clarity, we turn to the senses to transport us into the wisdom mind, the requirement is that we be able to reground ourselves rapidly and solidly in this world, with all its challenges and responsibilities to our fellow humans. It's a tricky gymnastic feat to straddle that line between imagination and the present moment. Building the skill of traveling back and forth between modes is like a muscle we strengthen, a neural pathway we groove more deeply into our minds. One way to practice this is to deliberately shift back and forth between freewheeling inventive associations that riff off sense experience and practices of sense withdrawal that call us back to the moment.

Pratyahara is the yogic practice of controlling a certain kind of hunger (*ahara* translates as "food"). I've heard many teachers—of Zazen, especially—compare the sense mechanisms to a child or a dog that we need to control or discipline. I want to suggest a replacement for that punishing analogy: what if the senses are quite simply *hungry*? When the senses are devouring *us*, we need to feed them to relax *them*. Just as you might need a snack when you're hungry, might consciously feeding the senses help them relax and set you free from their hunger pangs?

To experiment with sense-based grounding, begin by mentally scanning whatever part of the body is making contact with the ground. Then touch in with each of the six senses:

Sight:

Take in the visual plane, including your peripheral vision. Close eyelids, imagine softening the upper lid away from the lower lid without tensing the brow. Cup palms over the eyes to darken the visual plane. Take note of any color or shape or movement behind the lids. Set hands slowly free and notice the shift, doing your best to keep the eyes at rest, suspending the eyeballs instead of directing them.

Sound:

Relax your cheekbones toward the earlobes, and the inner ear will soften. Envision them dilating into your body, rather than opening out. Take note of ambient sounds, starting with the loudest and working your way down to the white noise. Cup your hands over your ears and hear what's inside.

Smell:

If you can't smell the air, smell your hands. First, take the deepest possible inhales through your noise to drink in the subtlety of the scent. Then turn your attention to the bridge of your nose and see if the sense of smell relaxes.

Taste:

Masticate the air, and if you can't catch the residue of toothpaste/coffee/what-have-you, lick your palm or take a sip of water and hold it in the mouth, turn it around and under on the tongue. Then relax the tongue against the teeth and soften the whole muscle way down to its root in the throat. Jaw, lips, teeth, even gums relax.

Touch:

Feel the temperature, textural quality (relative humidity or dryness), and movement of the air on your skin. How is it different on tender spots like the arches of your feet from places more acclimated to the air, like your forearms? How is it different where you are clothed and where the skin is exposed? Find an area of your body that cannot feel the air, and rest the attention there.

Mind:

Patanjali's *Yoga Sutras* teach that when the senses pull away from objects and imitate the nature of the mind, this is *pratyahara*. The mind, in Tibetan thought, is the sixth sense. Try focusing on the mental field as if it were simply one more sense. Any thought is impersonal, floating through, like a scent or a sound. Does this relax the sense of the mind's movements as dangerous distractions and help you enjoy them?

AUGUST WEEK 1

SUMMER AIR

Ellen Bass
"The Thing Is"

to love life, to love it even
when you have no stomach for it
and everything you've held dear
crumbles like burnt paper in your hands,
your throat filled with the silt of it.
When grief sits with you, its tropical heat
thickening the air, heavy as water
more fit for gills than lungs;
when grief weights you down like your own flesh
only more of it, an obesity of grief,
you think, How can a body withstand this?
Then you hold life like a face
between your palms, a plain face,
no charming smile, no violet eyes,
and you say, yes, I will take you
I will love you, again.

Richard Wilbur
"Love Calls Us to the Things of This World"

The eyes open to a cry of pulleys,
And spirited from sleep, the astounded soul
Hangs for a moment bodiless and simple
As false dawn.
               Outside the open window
The morning air is all awash with angels.

       Some are in bed-sheets, some are in blouses,
Some are in smocks: but truly there they are.
Now they are rising together in calm swells
Of halcyon feeling, filling whatever they wear
With the deep joy of their impersonal breathing;
       Now they are flying in place, conveying
The terrible speed of their omnipresence, moving
And staying like white water; and now of a sudden
They swoon down into so rapt a quiet
That nobody seems to be there.
                   The soul shrinks

       From all that it is about to remember,
From the punctual rape of every blessèd day,
And cries,
            "Oh, let there be nothing on earth but laundry,
Nothing but rosy hands in the rising steam
And clear dances done in the sight of heaven."

       Yet, as the sun acknowledges
With a warm look the world's hunks and colors,
The soul descends once more in bitter love
To accept the waking body, saying now
In a changed voice as the man yawns and rises,
       "Bring them down from their ruddy gallows;
Let there be clean linen for the backs of thieves;
Let lovers go fresh and sweet to be undone,
And the heaviest nuns walk in a pure floating
Of dark habits,
            keeping their difficult balance."

POETIC THEMES

As per the commonality in the titles, this week is really about *thingliness*. Humidity and wind are among the few things that makes the air real to us. Like seeing our breath in winter, humid and motile air makes a real, palpable *thing* out of the invisible element that surrounds us always and permeates our being. Like any good anchor for mindfulness, the presence of humidity or breeze makes the familiar more real to us. For whatever reason, the body responds to the thick humidity of August by shortening and shallowing the breath, when we really need to cultivate a deeper and fuller breath to combat the feeling of drowning in water. A friendly way to welcome this breath is to envision ourselves, as Ellen Bass does, like fish with gills, sipping the air easily into our side ribcage as if we were in our natural element. This fishy play is sobered up by the poem's likening of the air's heaviness to the thick oppression of grief, weighting us down "like your own flesh / only more of it, an obesity of grief." Acknowledging the discomfort is a step toward calling it like it is: grief isn't comfortable, but we can learn to live with it, to love the world as is. You can drown in the thick humidity, or you can take life as it comes, "like a face between your palms."

What if truly learning to love the things of this world requires that we forego prettifying them? Wilbur shifts our airy focus from humidity to movement with a spectacular image of a morning "all awash with angels," as laundry moves across the line and in the breeze. Air is likened to breath, as the laundry angels rise "together in calm swells / Of halcyon feeling, filling whatever they wear / With the deep joy of their impersonal breathing." The poem ends with a very different analogy, pulling the clothes from their gallows. In a way, this is the reverse practice of magicking fireflies and heat lightning into some ethereal otherworldly phenomenon. We move away from the tendency to romanticize the natural world. Like laundry off the line, we take our love down to this plane, for nuns and thieves alike.

Both poems explore how the dynamics of air reunite body and soul, by reckoning with this world as it is. Wilbur takes his reader down from the angel dance to harsh reality—"the world's hunks and colors." (Somewhere Wilbur stated that "hunks" is his favorite word here, for its effectiveness is shifting to the real and the quotidian.) With clear, unidealized perception, we fall in love with the things not of heaven but of this world—lovers off to be undone. The soul, in the first stanza, "hangs for a moment bodiless." From this disembodied state, the middle of the poem marks the soul's resistance to heavy, grounded reality: "The soul shrinks / From all that it is about to remember" in a stanza riddled with contrasts between heaven and earth, blessing and rape. But the sun is warm, in the last stanza, looking down on this earth. There are colors among the hunks. The soul's movement is downward, returning to earth: "The soul descends once more in bitter love / To accept the waking body." We come home to this reality, this body, the things in this world of ours.

PRACTICE

To transform August's watery heaviness into some kind of freedom, angel wing movements are clearly a must (lifting and lowering your arms in mock flight). We could also use a little taste of the joy in "impersonal breathing." Liberating the breath in tropical air involves opening and softening the back of the throat to avoid any burning silt feeling. Imagine two bodily points as the ends of the laundry line, and, as though in a breeze, breathe as openly as possibly while waving and undulating the flesh between those points. For example, in many shapes the points might be tailbone and crown; for other movements it might be fingertips and toetips; still others might explore diagonal endpoints like one shoulder to the opposite hip point. When we imagine freedom between those fastened points, how does the breath rise and fill and move-and-stay and swell and swoon and fly and dance and float, to adopt Wilbur's verbs? Inevitably, undulating between these points will involve sidebends—opening the intercostal muscles like bass gills in the humid air— and twists, feeling the skin and viscera crease in one place and stretch open to the breath in another. At the end of the dance, could we take our face in our palms and read its reality like braille

AUGUST WEEK 2
SEA TURTLE HATCHLINGS

Author unknown
"Turtles"

It was the weather that drove us in,
That rainy afternoon in May,
And the weather, I suppose, that drew us out
Cold and shivery, unprotected,
Gulping draughts of salt night air,
Amazed at clouds and the moistness of it all;
Our bare feet rejoiced at pebble and leaf,
Grateful for the grit between our parched toes
And the unmerciful touch of rain.
We knew the sadness of walls,
the cold consistency of ceilings,
the dumb flatness of floors;
We knew the shrill insistence of right angles,
perfect squares, and well drawn lines;
We knew the slow steady sweep of the electric clock,
And we grew quiet.
No small wonder, then, with sense withdrawn,
that beach, and sea, and air at first
were numb and dull to me
Or rather We to them,

Shocked without the shells that encased us blind.
Tumbling as from sleep
We widened at the delicious randomness
Of sea clump, dark sea oat, Lone driftwood
And the unending conversation of surf.
We grew giddy with space,
Toes tracing the sensual curve of ocean's edge,
Skin drunk with salt, wet, and sand,
Until, sea-tossed, wind strewn, and scatterbrained,
We became whole again.
Something in the moon, or wind, or water,
Or none of these, something older
and more removed the sounding waves,
This beaten shore, the hard edged shells
That prick and stab into the present;
Something deep, primordial, an ancient call
She answered, and left her weightless world
For the uncertainty of the shore.
How heavy the burden of herself became,
the massive shell, the tapered limbs
That scratched and clawed
for purchase in the too forgiving sand,
she knew alone,
and alone she bore, amidst the shadowy terrors
Of an alien world seen through eyes already tearing.
We watched her, breathless, perform the rite,
Marveled at her close-lidded patience, her energy,
The thick head that nodded slow acceptance
Of utter exhaustion, the unrelenting will
that rendered her oblivious to all
Save her pearly charges' burial
We fondled her leathery skin,
Gazed into her eyes admired the thickness of her
wrinkled neck, and
thought deeply
of the soft expression on her darkened face.
The deed was done, the sand replaced,
She joined the sea again,
And we waded with her to the edge of our world,
Saw her graceful form retreat into the darkness
In silence, we filled her clumsy tracks,

Erased all trace of what we'd seen,
And dreamed of another cosmic night
When sand shall scatter, and the sea
Shall open up her arms to turtle minions.

Published on chelonian.org with this credit line: Poem obtained by Clay A. Johnson and posted 16 October 1995 on the CTURTLE listserve; original author unknown, no record found through extensive web search.

———

Linda Hogan
"Song for the Turtles in the Gulf"

We had been together so very long,
you willing to swim with me
just last month, myself merely small
in the ocean of splendor and light,
the reflections and distortions of us,
and now when I see the man from British Petroleum
lift you up dead from the plastic
bin of death,
he with a smile, you burned
and covered with red-black oil, torched
and pained, all I can think is that I loved your life,
the very air you exhaled when you rose,
old great mother, the beautiful swimmer,
the mosaic growth of shell
so detailed, no part of you
simple, meaningless,
or able to be created
by any human,
only destroyed.
How can they learn
the secret importance
of your beaten heart,
the eyes of another intelligence
than ours, maybe greater,
with claws, flippers, plastron.

Forgive us for being thrown off true,
for our trespasses,
in the eddies of the water
where we first walked.

———

Margaret Atwood
"Elegy for the Giant Tortoises"

Let others pray for the passenger pigeon
the dodo, the whooping crane, the eskimo:
everyone must specialize

I will confine myself to a meditation
upon the giant tortoises
withering finally on a remote island.

I concentrate in subway stations,
in parks, I can't quite see them,
they move to the peripheries of my eyes

but on the last day they will be there;
already the event
like a wave traveling shapes vision:

on the road where I stand they will materialize,
plodding past me in a straggling line
awkward without water

their small heads pondering
from side to side, their useless armour
sadder than tanks and history,

in their closed gaze ocean and sunlight paralysed,
lumbering up the steps, under the archways

toward the square glass altars

where the brittle gods are kept,
the relics of what we have destroyed,
our holy and obsolete symbols.

———

Margaret Atwood
"Variations on the word Love"

This is a word we use to plug
holes with. It's the right size for those warm
blanks in speech, for those red heart-
shaped vacancies on the page that look nothing
like real hearts. Add lace
and you can sell
it. We insert it also in the one empty
space on the printed form
that comes with no instructions. There are whole
magazines with not much in them
but the word love, you can
rub it all over your body and you
can cook with it too. How do we know
it isn't what goes on at the cool
debaucheries of slugs under damp
pieces of cardboard? As for the weed-
seedlings nosing their tough snouts up
among the lettuces, they shout it.
Love! Love! sing the soldiers, raising
their glittering knives in salute.

Then there's the two
of us. This word
is far too short for us, it has only
four letters, too sparse
to fill those deep bare
vacuums between the stars
that press on us with their deafness.
It's not love we don't wish
to fall into, but that fear.
this word is not enough but it will
have to do. It's a single
vowel in this metallic
silence, a mouth that says
O again and again in wonder
and pain, a breath, a finger
grip on a cliffside. You can
hold on or let go.

POETIC THEMES

It's kind of great that the author of "Turtles" is a mystery, since it is a poem
about mystery. This accessible turtle poem from chelonian.org poses a lovely,
balanced contrast between turtle and human in what counts as home in the
elemental surround: humans, emerging from the shell of our indoor encase-
ments to be set free on the beach, while the tortoise rises from the weightless
water to lumber against gravity, under her huge shell. Maybe August makes us
feel both ways, and maybe tender, too; not just toward freedom in water or
beachy air, but also toward the sweetness of boundaried safety, earthy heaviness. "Minion" here is used in its older sense of something lovable, *sweet*. This
sedimented way of being, this ability to slow down, is perhaps "something
deep, primordial, an ancient call" to us in these slow, sticky last weeks of
summer. The tortoise in this first poem "perform[s] the rite" of continuing her
life-giving with "close-lidded patience." These primordial creatures (one of the
few living species reaching back to the dinosaur age) continue on in their
unlikely ritual of determined, unshakeable survival, in spite of it all.

Even as we focus on the hindbrain with its reptilian wisdom, there's more
to it than that: science has no idea how sea turtles navigate across the ocean to

return to the same microhabitat to nest, typically using experience from the first few years of their long, long lives. Whether they are using olfactory, magnetic, or visual cues, these are complex behaviors normally attributed to mammals. Maybe Western science will figure out the mystery here, as it is beginning to figure out the link between the base of the skull and the nervous system. Different spiritual systems have different ideas about this spot where the spine inserts into the skull; it's alternately the place the soul enters at birth, the center of multiple triangulated sense circuits in the brain, or the sole entryway for outside energy into the body, depending on which tradition. This spot has many names, including the Atlas, the Mouth of God, the Well of Dreams, Zeal Chakra, Jade Pillow Gate, Seat of the Soul, Alta Major 9th chakra; at the risk of TMI, I discovered it organically as a spot that, when stimulated, would open blocked sensation to the sex organs. It's exciting that finally there is some overlap between neurophysiology and energetic physiology, but we can't do justice to these centuries-old maps of the body or even the fifty-some years of biology explaining the whys and wherefores. We can, however, experience certain effects on heart rate, breath, blood pressure, and reflex centers that show stuff is happening—whether it's the reticular activating system in the brain stem or the vagus nerve or the pineal-pituitary-carotid-cerebellum-vagus-foramen magnum-medulla oblongata (feel free to google that stuff). Instead, we will confine ourselves to the experiential effects of stimulating the base of the skull and the whole circumferential orbit of the neck and throat. The goal is just to find our reptilian (or terrapin) self as something cool, compassed, and private to which we can retreat in the heat of August.

As we hunker down into the dark, introspective recesses of the mind and body, the achy feeling of summer's end might be tinged with sadness. If you really want to go there, read Linda Hogan's description of the burned, oil-covered sea turtle being pulled from the Gulf. The speaker, who had just a month before been swimming alongside this "old great mother," wonders at the strange, perhaps superior intelligence. How, she asks with characteristic wordplay, can turtles seemingly intuit the "secret importance / of your beaten heart"? This poem is a plea for forgiveness, Biblical in proportion, for the trespass of covering the perfection and complexity of that shell with "red-black oil." How we could be so "thrown off true," from the ancient path these turtles know?

This question is the theme of Margaret Atwood's "Elegy for the Giant Tortoises." The poem's dirge extends its longing for the actual tortoises withering away somewhere remote to a broader serenity we've lost. This old, sacred wisdom is a relic we have destroyed. And even as the tortoises come to represent something larger, they are brought home to the concrete island of Manhattan. The apocalyptic vision of these tortoises plodding through New

York, with all their "useless armour / sadder than tanks and history," is an elegy for the destruction of reverence and mystery, "our holy and obsolete symbols." I remember my own daughters riding on the back of my mother's pet tortoise, Homer. Homer is gone and so are they, and what world have we given them?

Maybe as some kind of comfort, I want to reference another Atwood poem here, "Variations on the Word Love." Think back to the cosmic night of the first poem, where we witness the tortoise's unrelenting will to answer a primordial call to continue. That's the power of the word love, as Atwood perceives it: a single vowel repeating "again and again / in wonder and in pain"—always a choice whether to persist, to hold on. No creature holds as fast to this world as the turtle. they.are.actual.dinosaurs. We too can hold on, by our fingertips, "in wonder / and pain." What keeps the grip is the capacity to be moved, in T.S. Eliot's haunting phrase in the *Preludes*, by "fancies that are curled / Around these images, and cling:" the straggling line of ancient beasts without water, dead claws and flippers pulled from plastic, the claws scratching for purchase in utter exhaustion. Again, from the end of the *Preludes*: "The notion of some infinitely gentle / infinitely suffering thing." Our humanity relies on being moved, mouth open in the shock of the single vowel O.

PRACTICE

Perhaps you regard the power of the O vowel as part of the OM, which is believed by some to be the seed sound of the universe, promising to return us to creation from the silence following destruction. Or maybe you're more research-cathected and see it as a vehicle for engaging the HPA axis—something about releasing the auricular vagus branch. Manuela Mischke-Reeds, co-director of the Hakomi Insitute, teaches a "Vwooooo" sound for this kind of limbic activation. In any case, its effects are beneficial. Hurray for the stubborn, steadfast, suffering part of us that continues to strive and work and create and love, in spite of it all.

If chanting the sacred word "love" feels unbelievably saccharine and sentimental, all the more reason that you absolutely need to do it, because that means your finger grip is slipping. You could try chanting it in the shape of a turtle, opening the back like a shell and compressing the belly and chest. This might begin to feel cramped and achy by the end, compelling you to progress from there more slowly, extending the limbs and crawling like some ancient arthritic being. To further tone the hindbrain, massage the base of the skull. Massage the tightness from around the ears down to the hinge of the jaw and down the sides of the neck. Extending neck forward and claws out, make your way to a crawl-ready stance, and turn your head slowly over each shoulder, leading from the eyes, until you spontaneously salivate, yawn, swallow, or feel a yielding in the belly to a deeper breath. Engage slow, introspective movements, with deep diaphragmatic breathing. You could close by flipping your turtle-self on its back, limbs loose in the air to drain, before sedimenting supine, knees bent with feet flat as though buried in sand, mentally tracing the imprint of footprints from heel around to each toe and back. The cheesier this kind of stuff feels to us, the more we need to keep love on our lips.

AUGUST WEEK 3
TWO MODELS OF FEMININE POWER

Adrienne Rich
"Planetarium"

Thinking of Caroline Herschel (1750–1848)
astronomer, sister of William; and others.

A woman in the shape of a monster
a monster in the shape of a woman
the skies are full of them

a woman   'in the snow
among the Clocks and instruments
or measuring the ground with poles'

in her 98 years to discover
8 comets

she whom the moon ruled
like us
levitating into the night sky
riding the polished lenses

Galaxies of women, there
doing penance for impetuousness
ribs chilled
in those spaces   of the mind

An eye,

          'virile, precise and absolutely certain'
          from the mad webs of Uranusborg

                    encountering the NOVA

every impulse of light exploding

from the core
as life flies out of us

          Tycho whispering at last
          'Let me not seem to have lived in vain'

What we see, we see
and seeing is changing

the light that shrivels a mountain
and leaves a man alive

Heartbeat of the pulsar
heart sweating through my body

The radio impulse
pouring in from Taurus

          I am bombarded yet   I stand

I have been standing all my life in the
direct path of a battery of signals
the most accurately transmitted most
untranslatable language in the universe
I am a galactic cloud so deep   so involuted that a light wave could take 15

years to travel through me   And has
taken   I am an instrument in the shape
of a woman trying to translate pulsations
into images   for the relief of the body
and the reconstruction of the mind.

———

Adrienne Rich
"August"

Two horses stand in a yellow light
eating windfall apples under a tree

as summer tears apart and the milkweeds stagger
and grasses grow more ragged

They say there are ions in the sun
neutralizing magnetic fields on earth

Some way to explain
what this week has been, and the one before it!

If I am flesh sunning on rock
if I am brain burning in fluorescent light

if I am dream like a wire with fire
throbbing along it

if I am death to man
I have to know it

His mind is too simple, I cannot go on
sharing his nightmares

My own are becoming clearer, they open
into prehistory

which looks like a village lit with blood
where all the fathers are crying: My son is mine!

———

Susan Stewart
"The Forest"

You should lie down now and remember the forest,
for it is disappearing—
no, the truth is it is gone now
and so what details you can bring back
might have a kind of life.

Not the one you had hoped for, but a life
—you should lie down now and remember the forest—
nonetheless, you might call it "in the forest,"
no the truth is, it is gone now,
starting somewhere near the beginning, that edge,

Or instead the first layer, the place you remember
(not the one you had hoped for, but a life)
as if it were firm, underfoot, for that place is a sea,
nonetheless, you might call it "in the forest,"
which we can never drift above, we were there or we were not,

No surface, skimming. And blank in life, too,
or instead the first layer, the place you remember,
as layers fold in time, black humus there,
as if it were firm, underfoot, for that place is a sea,
like a light left hand descending, always on the same keys.

144

The flecked birds of the forest sing behind and before
no surface, skimming. And blank in life, too,
sing without a music where there cannot be an order,
as layers fold in time, black humus there,
where wide swatches of light slice between gray trunks,

Where the air has a texture of drying moss,
the flecked birds of the forest sing behind and before:
a musk from the mushrooms and scalloped molds.
They sing without a music where there cannot be an order,
though high in the dry leaves something does fall,

Nothing comes down to us here.
Where the air has a texture of drying moss,
(in that place where I was raised) the forest was tangled,
a musk from the mushrooms and scalloped molds,
tangled with brambles, soft-starred and moving, ferns

And the marred twines of cinquefoil, false strawberry, sumac—
nothing comes down to us here,
stained. A low branch swinging above a brook
in that place where I was raised, the forest was tangled,
and a cave just the width of shoulder blades.

You can understand what I am doing when I think of the entry—
and the marred twines of cinquefoil, false strawberry, sumac—
as a kind of limit. Sometimes I imagine us walking there
(. . .pokeberry, stained. A low branch swinging above a brook)
in a place that is something like a forest.

But perhaps the other kind, where the ground is covered
(you can understand what I am doing when I think of the entry)
by pliant green needles, there below the piney fronds,
a kind of limit. Sometimes I imagine us walking there.
And quickening below lie the sharp brown blades,

The disfiguring blackness, then the bulbed phosphorescence of the roots.
But perhaps the other kind, where the ground is covered,
so strangely alike and yet singular, too, below
the pliant green needles, the piney fronds.

Once we were lost in the forest, so strangely alike and yet singular, too,
but the truth is, it is, lost to us now.

POETIC THEMES

The month of August is associated astrologically with the sun, and I have
to go personal for a beat here, and not just because Adrienne Rich is my poetic
sun. My dad was in a poetry class with Rich at Harvard, and I remember him
describing how everyone was struck dumb when she first read aloud. I
couldn't get that image out of my head. Rich's story was like mine—an
upbringing pressured by her dad's intellectual ambitions for her—and like my
mom's, marrying a professor. She did divorce him to carve her own path, and
she wrote "August" in the throes of processing his subsequent suicide.

The poem begins with an image of the sun's yellow light illuminating two
horses quietly eating apples under a tree (with all this creature's ancient association with the sun, in Greek myth, Hebrew Scripture, and Vedic lore). But the
poem breaks quickly from this sunny scene, as summer burns itself out in the
solar flare of August, with its staggering milkweeds and ragged grass. The
progress of the poem can only be autobiographical, trying to break from the
nightmare entrapment that opens from her own story to history, or rather a
prehistory, of separations marked by paternal claims and blood. It's not an
exaggeration to say that Rich's departure from traditional marriage was also
her departure from patriarchy, launching her into position as a leader in
second-wave feminist thought. *Diving into the Wreck,* her most famous collection, in which these poems were published (along with others from the three
years following her divorce), established her true voice. Margaret Atwood
described hearing Rich read from it: "It felt as though the top of my head was
being attacked, sometimes with an ice pick, sometimes with a blunter instrument: a hatchet or a hammer." Tantamount to a solar explosion, she blew
everyone away.

We found in my dad's study a note from Rich saying, essentially, "Thanks
for last night." He declined comment. When I met her at a reading and asked
her about the note, a coy grin stretched across her wrinkled face and she said,
"Yep. Sounds like me in college." Maybe my dad reminded her of hers. The
descriptions of her father sure remind me of mine: a literary snob who gave
her daily writing assignments and lauded her poetic achievements especially
when they best replicated Western canonical form. Her departure from her

father's language to find her own brilliant, blinding voice was like Minerva bursting from Zeus's head. I'm still trying to get there. When I can afford it, my plan is to tattoo the final lines of "Planetarium" onto my heart, in some kind of outward-spiraling explosive shape:

"Iamaninstrumentintheshapeofawomantryingtotranslatepulsationsintoim-agesforthereliefoftheboddyandthereconstructionofthemind."

Maybe it will help.

"Planetarium" is dedicated to the famous German astronomer Caroline Herschel, whose biography is a lot like Rich's, struggling with typhus as Rich had struggled with arthritis, relegated to assisting her brother's scientific work and struggling to emerge as an astronomer in her own right all the way until he died, and after his death, busily cataloguing nebulae and star clusters and comets. Herschel's gravestone reads, "The eyes of her who is glorified here below turned to the starry heavens." One might say the same of Adrienne Rich. In "Planetarium," looking up at the night sky, Rich sees "galaxies of women, there / doing penance for impetuousness," until the poem encounters a nova, an astral phenomenon that expels solar masses of material at the speed of light and sends shock waves that can even trigger the formation of new stars. That's a pretty good way to describe Rich's effect on the world. She captures the experience of finding her "untranslatable language" so viscerally: "every impulse of light exploding / from the core / as light flies out of us...." The heart, here, is configured as its own sun, exploding outward.

Compare this vivid description of the effects of heat, light, and blinding sun to the conditional uncertainty of "August." She has yet to truly know her burning brain, throbbing dream "like a wire with fire." She seems to crave the knowledge of how her flesh threatens the patriarchy. The poem's description of the sun's power could be describing the effect of Rich's own, neutralizing the protection of magnetic fields to pierce right through to the bone. And she does. I go back, again and again, to the explosive last stanza of "Planetarium," my future tattoo. Maybe to live in the shadow of the solar event that was Adri-enne Rich is to strive to digest the impulses of this culture and transform them for the liberation of others. To seat feminine power in the solar plexus, reclaiming the sun from its association with masculinity, is to conceptualize feminine power as the capacity for transmutation, the witchlike translation of one thing into another form.

But in the burning heat of summer, perhaps we could marry this with a cooler model. "The Forest" is the perfect mulchy answer to the call to ground down and cool off in the heat of August, beginning with its direct order: "You should lie down now." The language that captures a new quiet in the air, a new stillness and movement toward the end of summer—"disappearing," "gone now," "lost to us"—is joined to the hint of nature's changes in early autumn:

the air's "texture of drying moss," something falling from "high in the dry leaves," and the increasingly covered ground. The forest floor is such a useful and evocative image for the ground floor of our being to which we need so badly to return. We settle down into the poem's musical repetitions, like a chorus returning again and again, "light a light left hand descending." The layers of grounding, going back and back, "fold in time," grounding us in the places we remember. The forest floor as "the first layer" calls up the physical reality of the pelvic floor whose layers are crisscrossed. As the source of life, the pelvic floor issues a call to remember, to go back to beginnings, again and again—root, family, origins, home, tribe. This covered ground is the home turf of Mama Earth, eternally feminized. It is both an entry, a doorway back to our early lived experiences, and a "kind of limit," as we are unable to change or truly inhabit them.

A lovely image for the grounding principle is the left hand on the piano, regardless of what tinkling upper keys the right hand might be playing. This is such a useful way of imagining the two hemispheres of the body. With the heat of this month, its fire and solar flare, we need the balance of the left side, always present, associated in myriad traditions with the moon and the grounding principle. So perhaps Susan Stewart's forest floor is a model of female power that balances Rich's solar flare. The strength of the pelvic floor is in its layering and its multi-directionality, strong enough to hold not just the content of one body but more than one. As a metaphor, this would claim the capacity for holding multiple views, experiences, and truths without having to choose one, sustaining not just one person but guaranteeing the survival of many—a departure from the zero-sum culture of competition and dominance. Perhaps you resonate with one of these models more than the other. In any case, they are not mutually exclusive to our experience: the two can hold hands with one another.

PRACTICE

The two diaphragms, solar plexus and pelvic floor, move together like a dance. Both naturally lift up when we breathe out, and both drop down when we breathe in. If this diaphragmatic tango is new to you, try lying on your belly with a pillow under your abdomen. Gravity accentuates the feeling of the belly pressing into the pillow in the inhale. Picture the diaphragm dropping into the abdomen, stretching the striations of muscle around the solar plexus like sunbeams. This, in turn, helps us ground, as we naturally align the pelvic diaphragm with the abdominal diaphragm, dropping downward on the inhale. If it's elusive, consider placing a hand on the pelvic floor, receiving the added pressure when your belly swells. If possible, spend a little time reflecting on the experience. Does one or the other of these muscle groups feel more familiar, toned, or powerful to you, or do they feel balanced? Do you relate to one or the other as home-base for some material/essential (pun intended) quality of femininity? Are there any recurrent images or thoughts emerging?

AUGUST WEEK 4
SALMON RUN PREP

Elizabeth Bishop
"The Fish"

I caught a tremendous fish
and held him beside the boat
half out of water, with my hook
fast in a corner of his mouth.
He didn't fight.
He hadn't fought at all.
He hung a grunting weight,
battered and venerable
and homely. Here and there
his brown skin hung in strips
like ancient wallpaper,
and its pattern of darker brown
was like wallpaper:
shapes like full-blown roses
stained and lost through age.
He was speckled with barnacles,
fine rosettes of lime,
and infested
with tiny white sea-lice,
and underneath two or three

rags of green weed hung down.
While his gills were breathing in
the terrible oxygen
—the frightening gills,
fresh and crisp with blood,
that can cut so badly—
I thought of the coarse white flesh
packed in like feathers,
the big bones and the little bones,
the dramatic reds and blacks
of his shiny entrails,
and the pink swim-bladder
like a big peony.
I looked into his eyes
which were far larger than mine
but shallower, and yellowed,
the irises backed and packed
with tarnished tinfoil
seen through the lenses
of old scratched isinglass.
They shifted a little, but not
to return my stare.
—It was more like the tipping
of an object toward the light.
I admired his sullen face,
the mechanism of his jaw,
and then I saw
that from his lower lip
—if you could call it a lip—
grim, wet, and weaponlike,
hung five old pieces of fish-line,
or four and a wire leader
with the swivel still attached,
with all their five big hooks
grown firmly in his mouth.
A green line, frayed at the end
where he broke it, two heavier lines,
and a fine black thread
still crimped from the strain and snap
when it broke and he got away.
Like medals with their ribbons

frayed and wavering,
a five-haired beard of wisdom
trailing from his aching jaw.
I stared and stared
and victory filled up
the little rented boat,
from the pool of bilge
where oil had spread a rainbow
around the rusted engine
to the bailer rusted orange,
the sun-cracked thwarts,
the oarlocks on their strings,
the gunnels—until everything
was rainbow, rainbow, rainbow!
And I let the fish go.

———

Kim Addonizio
"Salmon"

In this shallow creek
they flop and writhe forward as the dead
float back toward them. Oh, I know

what I should say: fierce burning in the body
as her eggs burst free, milky cloud
of sperm as he quickens them. I should stand

on the bridge with my camera,
frame the white froth of rapids where one
arcs up for an instant in its final grace.

But I have to go down among
the rocks the glacier left
and squat at the edge of the water

where a stinking pile of them lies,
where one crow balances and sinks
its beak into a gelid eye.

I have to study the small holes
gouged into their skin, their useless gills,
their gowns of black flies. I can't

make them sing. I want to,
but all they do is open
their mouths a little wider

so the water pours in
until I feel like I'm drowning.
On the bridge the tour bus waits

and someone waves, and calls down
It's time, and the current keeps lifting
dirt from the bottom to cover the eggs.

POETIC THEMES

We need to acknowledge the system's shock, facing the sudden, swift uptick in tasks and challenges as September starts. Even for those of us long done with the actual academic calendar, the end of summer marks a return to the demand that we be *productive*. This term is finally being interrogated, blessed be. Here's a back-to-school poem I wrote last August:

Pray, tarry a bit longer, ye aching exhausted mother
Before you slay yourself or your brood
Forsooth, Philadelphia has become subtropical, thy drying laundry is wet
again e'er it dries
And nary a stovetop should be heated for food, so hot methinks thy second
floor becomes.
But hark, there is pizza!
E'en to the last, bitter day of this last, bitter month of summer
The cicadas screaming their death rattle all around thy ears,
Soft, beneath it—another sound!
The whimpering of thy babes, grieving their dying freedom,
Late at night they cry, and after the hour of noon, Because their sleep cycles
are so fucked, sirrah, they sleep till then
Verily thy friends oft post photos of beach vacations
Upon the isle of Thy-ass-cannot-afford
Thy quill has snapped in twain, dispatch thee to find another
For there are still forms, aye, to be filled out on the morrow—
afterschoolactivitybusrequiredboostershotsportsphysicalbaselinetes
tingPSATreviewdramaclub
Untouched summer reading books lie by the doorsill
For they are unrenewable now, thrice as they have been.
The wine doth sing its siren call, thy poor perimenopausal body strains to
resist
But lo, thou wouldst live to see September, angel,
For methinks there is… yoga.

I want to offer the salmon run as an image of "productivity." September,
appropriately, initiates the salmon run season. These strong creatures press
back against the current to return to where they began—and die. Somewhere,
years ago, I heard the term "salmon day," for that familiar day where we do *all*
the adulting; churn through every task in our path, against a strong current.
Then at sunset, we plop down in the riverbed of our couch and zonk out. But
here's a little hopeful note: before they die, the salmon lay eggs! So as much as
returning to the home-base of our work life feels bitter, maybe we could trust
that our efforts are matched by the proverbial riverbed of the world around us.
Each action we take lays the groundwork for the continuance of our vital work
in the world and the life to come that continues beyond us.

Addonizio's "Salmon" must refer back to Elizabeth Bishop's famous poem
"The Fish." Both are unflinching close looks at death and dying. Both poets
dismiss all the heroic dramatization of conquest and passion and what it is to
fight for your life. Unlike Bishop's incredibly detailed depiction of bloody gills,

entrails and sea-lice, barnacles and weed, Addonizio's descriptive mode is broken. The gills are useless, like her strange desire to "make them sing" with the impotent, dangling caesura "I can't." Bishop sees it all and sets it free. Addonizio simply drowns.

But even in "Salmon," there's a tiny, hopeful seed of potential, laid down in the last line. Yes, the poem seems to say, "it's time"; we are called, unwilling, back to our lives. This is clear even before the call to return to the tour bus, in the series of imperatives: "I should say," "I should stand," "But I have to," "I have to," "I can't...." As adults, dying to one version of ourselves to birth the next hurts. It involves a painful surrender of a version of things that we might be willing to let go of—but that may not be willing to let go of us. Mouthing at the water, trying to suck in one last breath, our former selves don't want to die. Change is hard. To attend to this truth isn't just morbid or pessimistic, it's the reality of the natural progress of a life.

We want to capture the glorious salmon leaping against the whitewater caps, but if we want to be true to the process, we "have to go down among the rocks." We must "squat at the edge of the water," to study the stinking pile of what's dying or useless. This honest view actually enables us to focus not on the final triumph of our past, but on the potential for the future. Below the dying salmon with their "gowns of black flies" down in the riverbed, the eggs are laid, and the river is busy burying them so they won't be swept away with the tide. Safe in the dirt, sedimented in their muddy bed, to become something new.

What's lovely about this is that it's not all on us! The riverbed does some of the work; the world helps. I think of David R. Hawkins' juxtaposition between power and force. Dying to the old and allowing space for the new cannot be accomplished through force. Rather it requires a subtraction of will. Which is, paradoxically, super hard to learn! David Whyte, in his "On Being" interview, describes this subtractive mode as "the thousand mile only." He is referring to the famous line of Mary Oliver's "Wild Geese" about allowing the gentle beast of your body to do the loving. Whyte points out that Buddhist monks for centuries have been striving alone in caves for this near-impossible clarity, boiling down the mess of the thinking brain, the buzz of "should." I can still hear the echo of Whyte's lilting low roll, lingering on the words "Only... only...oooonly...."

In a letter to his brother, John Keats described his now-famous notion of Negative Capability, where we are "capable of benign uncertainties, Mysteries, doubt, without any irritable reaching after fact and reason." This capacity comes from the ability "to annul the self." I like to think of this as a soft shift in camera focus when the foregrounded object gives way to the background. Just as Addonizio shifts the focus of her poem from the camera-snap of the arcing salmon to the whole scene—glacier, dead fish, tour bus, waving human, the current burying the eggs. When we can abide with what is, without fixating on solving it, our focus ultimately zooms out to the ambient surround. This shift is like an exhale, like being physically set down to rest, like having a fishing line snipped. When we finally get this reprieve, we can attune to the world around us rather than the barrage of worries, duties, and puzzling banging around in our heads. This is the thousand mile only: stripping away our need to catch, own, analyze, and devour things, so we can simply be free to let the world do its thing.

PRACTICE

In America we are taught to treat the body like a machine whose purpose is exclusively "to get shit done." Common physical symptoms like low-back pain and tight hamstrings stem from socialized habits such as armoring the chest and limiting hip movement and also from exercise habits like aggressive muscle stretching or targeting the "six pack." It's hard to back off overdoing and reaching for things when we learned certain somatic lessons at a young age. These lessons (which obviously relate to gender, race, class, and sexuality) become invisible to us, although and because they permeate most things. The body-as-machine approach has a certain stoicism that accompanies it, a culture of toughness and competition. We learn from this approach the habit of emotionally vacating the premises when faced with pain, encouraged instead to "grin and bear it." These neurobiological patterns are super hard to rewire. All of which is to say: these are not things we can just set free like Bishop's fish.

To practice sedimenting down and letting go, movement should be grounding, low to the earth, and aquatic. Belly down, methodically tense every part of your body in detailed isolation. (Try, for example, tensing one toe at a time.) Build until every part of you is clenched, then set it all free. Can this relax you enough to picture receiving the breath rather than doing it? Could you allow yourself to be breathed? This might soften to yielding, rolling-around actions, as though your half-limp body were being tossed in the river's movement. Then see where the water takes you, perhaps tenting the fingertips on the ground alongside your shoulders and undulating the spine into little backbend rivulets. Let it rebuild into full clenching and repeat the release and half-passive motion. After a few rounds, without any further instruction, free-form experiment with the mental equivalent of what you just did physically.

SEPTEMBER WEEK 1
BACK TO SCHOOL

Brad Aaron Modlin
"What You Missed That Day You Were Absent from Fourth Grade"

Mrs. Nelson explained how to stand still and listen
to the wind, how to find meaning in pumping gas,

how peeling potatoes can be a form of prayer. She took
questions on how not to feel lost in the dark

After lunch she distributed worksheets
that covered ways to remember your grandfather's

voice. Then the class discussed falling asleep
without feeling you had forgotten to do something else—

something important—and how to believe
the house you wake in is your home. This prompted

Mrs. Nelson to draw a chalkboard diagram detailing
how to chant the Psalms during cigarette breaks,

and how not to squirm for sound when your own thoughts
are all you hear; also, that you have enough.

The English lesson was that I am
is a complete sentence.

And just before the afternoon bell, she made the math equation
look easy. The one that proves that hundreds of questions,

and feeling cold, and all those nights spent looking
for whatever it was you lost, and one person

add up to something.

———

Noah Baldino
"Felt Flowers"

The play room's alphabet pattern padding could be pulled apart, then
repositioned; after snack, the older, all-day boys—who tore off,
one by one, the turtles' shells, a hippo's quiet heft, and fed
the bashful ones their heads—huddled around their stockpile of
letters and laid out a dirty word that made the other kids
giggle or gasp and Miss Margaret tap the backs of their hands with
the yellow wooden yardstick. I couldn't read yet.
I wouldn't talk, either;
          my language was the felt
flowers in the clear plastic tub, at the back table by the window, which
looked out at the slide, glistening like a tongue in
the brash noon light. An older boy stole
my poppy, so I assembled a pansy, pre-cut
by Miss Margaret at her house after school. I imagined her
pouring over a private abundance
of patterned scissors for the jaggedness of a lily's leaf, then the sturdy
kitchen shears for a pile of rose petals. Years later, she'd return beneath

the tangled top sheet of dreams, and before I could smooth
the intrusion in me, a muscle-drenched arm—veins like a textbook's
anatomical orchid, dense hair
like my father had—guided her two fingers farther
into the scissor's doubled gape—
       Blistering then in the fully-bloomed heat,
the swings seemed to rock, but within themselves, the way
a lightbulb, untouched for years, holds a spasm
in its tungsten, a self-possessed momentum, awaiting fingers
on the switch. A group of girls, that day, trudged over,
at Miss Margaret's insistence, barrettes wincing above their ears,
the button I'd cut from my best Sunday dress a makeshift bud
atop a glue glob smear. They asked me if I wanted
to play house. I set my pink felt down.
       I didn't know I could be the father, so
I said I'd be the dog. They named me Princess. One girl put on
an apron, white plastic pearls. Two others, fabric dolls in hand,
the daughters. One adhered
       a costume mustache and a voice
absurdly low. We arranged the mats by color for the rooms in our
make-believe home. I played my part; I laid in the yard,
on the green pieces, the letters, an F, an A. My job, I'd decided, was not
to bound into the room, pretend-panting at my family's feet,
with the whimper
       dogs give when they want to be loved, but—
watching Miss Margaret tend to the bullies, our tiny table set,
the family complete, curled up in
my own constant obstinate heat—to guard my made-up post,
on the bladeless lawn, alone, even if anyone called my name.

POETIC THEMES

I love the expression "to get schooled." These days we're all getting collectively schooled, big time. So this back-to-school week maybe we could consider the new lessons we're learning, ones that just might change life on this little imperiled planet and save us all. "What You Missed That Day You

Were Absent From Fourth Grade" is as relatable as its impeccable title. It's not surprising that this poem is popping up all over the place, even recorded as a voiceover to a creepy YouTube video where two towheaded girls move in slow motion through a hallway that looks like something from "The Shining." Missed lesson #1: stay away from abandoned hotels. On the subject of pithy lessons, sometimes when I'm teaching, a somatic cue feels particularly apt for life in general, like, "If you're over-efforting, save some juice for later." I like to then throw in one of two teaching mantras: "T-shirts available after class," or "What if they taught us that in kindergarten?" Brad Aaron Modlin's list of what we coulda shoulda learned in fourth grade could be re-imagined as notes scribbled during the class we actually needed:

-I have enough

-100 questions + feeling cold + nights hunting for what's lost + 1 person = something.

-I am = complete sentence

I really could have used all those t-shirts well before the fourth grade. The long cultural tutorial in scarcity, perfectionism, and individualism started much earlier. The scene of learning in Noah Baldino's "Felt Flowers" rewinds us (is "rewind" a defunct word?) back to kindergarten. I'm picturing myself as a 5-year-old neurodivergent proto-Queer (is *Queer* a defunct word??!) sitting right there on the spongy alphabet-letter padding with him, crisscross-apple-sauce. The titular play on the double meaning of "feeling," given the title of this book, obviously tugged my heart strings, but then Noah immediately wrapped them up in this particular tangle of themes: just for starters there's the ol' vicious power play of normative gender, the x-ray vision that swerves sharply from what's considered "smart," autoeroticism, and the institutional violence that reinforces everyday kindergarten cruelty.

And then, from this crumple, Baldino offers up something origami-beautiful. The poem is a testimony to the powers of imagination that can reinvent one's assigned place—not to play the father of the house, or even Princess the Dog, panting and whimpering for scraps, but a "made-up post" that stakes out a new role. The poem celebrates the obstinate refusal to choose between witness and participation, but rocks between them like the swings outside the classroom window, like the lightbulb with its self-possessed momentum, resistant and tungsten-strong. Companioning Baldino's reading of "Felt Flowers" on Poets.org was a brief explanation about the poem:

"This poem began, as Queer adulthood can begin, by re-animating the play intuited in childhood. What populates my playroom? This speaker's lyric preoccupation is not identity but privacy. Their tension between interiority and interaction. Their resistance stemming not from shame but from a self-possession that, through the quiet heft of its observation, participates. The felt flowers are, after all, present and available in their clear container. Privacy, the poem taught me, does not preclude the world."

Brad Modlin also has spoken in interviews about there being a Queer element in recognizing that one entity can be multiple. Maybe we all used a both/and approach as kids, and to allow tolerance of paradox to spill over into enjoyment is a kind of return to childhood knowing. It's a return that feels good. So here we are, me and Brad and Noah, plopped down on the alphabet padding with our fingers in the felt. Come on over, pop a squat, and choose a color for your flower.

PRACTICE

The swing set from "Felt Flowers" is particularly spicy to me because of early lesbionic play on the swings ('sup Amy and Susie). But don't most kids' limbic systems settle comfortably into the back-and-forth motion? Assuming most of us enjoyed swinging, I'd like to borrow and tweak a practice of "row- ing" I learned from somatics teacher Staci K Haines. Performed seated or standing, practitioners rock forward and back, miming the action of pulling oars. While rowing is designed to train the soma to embody purposeful action, we could reimagine this forward-and-back motion as the less goal-oriented act of swinging. Swinging isn't an attempt to get anywhere; it just mobilizes some- thing stuck, generating a play between elements. Maybe in time we could settle the psyche into embracing a flexible, motile suspension between two spaces, ideas, or forces. The both/and play embraces the interstitial as a queer terrain that is, in itself, powerful and capable of creating ripples of change in the surrounding air.

SEPTEMBER WEEK 2
COOL NIGHTS

Ruth Forman
"On This Day"

this is a day without chairs
a day where all the rooms melt together
and there are only corners / corners and humming
wishes and slight breeze
brushing you like palms
this is a day of prayers
a day of painful breaking / a day of peace beneath
a day of arms
of hands
eyes and quiet windows

i wish you love from your mother backwards

i wish you deep tunnels without fear
i wish you children's laughter
i wish you cactus flowers
i wish you moonlight
i wish you real eyes
i wish you a hand across your back / soft like when you were a child
i wish you tears

i wish you clean
i wish you angels in conference around your bed holding you
so there is no space for me even to touch you/just watch

i wish your mother watching

i wish you abalone dreams
i wish you peace
i wish you doves in your kitchen
moonlight in your bathroom
candles when your eyes close and dawn when they open
i wish you so many arms across your shoulders
so many lips kissing your ears that you smile from the inconvenience
i wish you all your babies' love attacking the center of your heart
just so you know they are there

i wish you banisters, railings, and arms around your waist
i wish you training wheels, i wish you strong shoes
i wish you water o i wish you water
through your feet flowing like a stream
and i wish you hammocks
and melon on your eyes
strawberries in your mouth
and fingers in your hand
fingers in your hand all day
through this house
on this day with no rooms
only corners
and an uncommon breeze

Thomas Lux
"Give it to the Wind"

If the wind touches your cheek
in a manner that pleases you,
then to it give something back.
Give some dollars, a good slice
of bread, a phrase from a woman
who loves you; open an ampule
of joy and wave it, out loud.
If you find a dime, then give two
to a beggar, celebrate

nerve endings, your soup.
If whole minutes exist
when to your left is a river with ducks
and to your right a cathedral slashed
by light, then carry clean bandages
to a battlefront, swab foreheads
in a contagious ward; if a few
cells bloom, a synapse heals,
then stab a thousand tiny flags

into the graves of generals,
then mourn a murderer's childhood.
And if, after furious sleep,
the room is windy
and cool air slides across the blank
dunes of your sheet, then thank
the night for the day
and the day for what
it is: liable to be.

Ama Codjoe
"Slow Drag with Branches of Pine"

Here I am, holding one more
mirror. This time smoke, winding
                    like a river. I close my eyes,
not because the smoke stings—it
does—but because it's a way
to examine myself, like looking
                    at your face in a river certain it is not
          your face. The smoke combs
like a mother through my hair
or like searching the shoreline
for shells unbroken. I sing to myself
and the smoke drags my voice on its back
               just as the breeze heaves it.
                    Here, in my half-singing,
I'm reminded how to slow drag.
I watch the pine trees creak
                    and sway. Here, I am
my own twin. I rest my cheek
against my cheek; I barely move at all.

From *Bluest Nude* by Ama Codjoe (Minneapolis: Milkweed Editions, 2022). Copyright © 2022 by Ama Codjoe. Reprinted with permission from Milkweed Editions. Milkweed.org.

———

Daniel Nester
"Künstlerroman, 1996"

Before I moved to Brooklyn, I hopped
on the L train and, I shit you not,
interviewed the bohemians

of Bedford Avenue, pen and pad
of paper in hand. I asked
if they liked living in Williamsburg.
Most kept walking, ashamed
to be seen with me. Some were nice.
Even the glasses guy from They Might Be Giants
stopped and talked. I lived in a sublet
on Crosby Street, a fifth-floor walk-up frozen in time,
heated from a brick on a stove, rent-controlled
in a building filled with old men.
This was 1995, and Williamsburg
was no SoHo. We had the L Cafe,
Planet (or Planeat?) Thailand, brunch at Oznot's,
open mics at The Charleston,
Styrofoam cups of beer at Turkey's Nest.
And Joe's Busy Corner, where the patriarch
held court outside and cursed through
his artificial larynx. Everyone
in Williamsburg lived on borrowed money.
We walked to the Citibank in Greenpoint
just to use a bank machine. And our landlord
never cashed our rent checks. Like, never.
Months would go by on North Fifth and Havemeyer.
Nothing. I'd watch my checking balance swell
to four digits and start to think, *this is my money,*
not his. So I'd shop at OMG Jeans
or buy new Doc Martens. Then the landlord
would cash the rent checks. A whole year's worth.
All at once. The whole building would shudder.
I can still see myself a year later,
on a summer morning by the East River
with a Strathmore sketch pad, not very humble,
wallet-chained, younger-looking, jaded,
waiting for last night's mushrooms to wear off
and Tops grocery to open. A skinny boy
bums a smoke. I give him a light. I smile.

This week is themed around the astonishing return to cool that marks mid-September. Any seasonal shift sharpens our awareness of what's around us, but especially so when we're talking about suddenly perceiving something formerly invisible. September breezes make manifest an omnipresent force. This is not just the perfect metaphor for how the divine plane sometimes appears to us. (It's no accident that the word *spiritual* is etymologically linked to breath.) It's also a practical, straightforward analogy for mindfulness in general: there's all this life surrounding us, calling us to pay attention.

Being saved from our internal mental churn by awakening to what's around us is, each time, an experience of being refreshed and renewed. Enter Ruth Forman's breathtaking, breathmaking list of uncommon wishes. Riding the wind of our roving attention: humming palm-brushing breeze prayers fingers in your hands all day eyes quiet windows clean abalone dreams strong shoes…. "On this Day" pours blessings, and we are filled to overflow. The waterfall of ways we might experience the "uncommon breeze" of early fall just keeps flowing: like baby hands like tears like lips kissing our ears like moonlight like children's laughter. There are angels in conference around our bed, holding us, and we need only open our eyes to see them.

This feeling of being held safely, wrapped up in the world, reminds me of the final lines to Zora Neale Hurston's *Their Eyes were Watching God*:

Now, in her room, the place tasted fresh again. The wind through the open windows had groomed out all the fetid feeling of absence and nothingness. She closed in and sat down. …Here was peace. She pulled in her horizon like a great fish net. Pulled it from around the waist of the world and draped it over her shoulder. So much of life in its meshes! She called in her soul to come and see.

Catching life in the meshes of our awareness is a form of refreshment and solace. The more we can catch, the more we feel a sense of plenitude, and the more we have to give. This simple mathematics is the premise of "Give it to the Wind," which offers (besides the wonderful line, "Celebrate nerve endings, your soup") an equation for life's give-and-take: if the wind touches your cheek, give something back! Responding to beauty, or luck, or a gift, by giving something back is such an obvious thing. It's simple symmetry. Often gratitude practices can bring about guilt, inadequacy, or a kind of smug self-satisfaction. In contrast, Lux depicts the effortlessness of our natural inclination to give (bread, joy, succor) when we are full. The needs of the world are made known to us in tandem with and as a simple extension of our blessings.

Or, to banish all preciousness and do-goodery, we could pop out for some air with Ama Codjoe. The seductive scene in "Slow Drag with Branches of

Pine" depicts smoking as a form of self-companionship. Like the ragtime jazz and blues dance form referenced in its title, "Slow Drag" is hot—at least it is for anyone who has loved smoking and maybe for many who haven't. Ada Limón, for example, confesses to having always wanted to be a smoker in her commentary on Codjoe's poem for *The Slowdown*. She tells the story of playing Lauren Bacall as a kid with candy cigarettes and later "practicing" at smoking in her twenties, adding that it always made her feel that she needed to go to confession. This naughtydirtysinful vibe is what drags many of us to smoke, but for Limón, the smoke break is enticing as solitary reprieve, a chance to reconnect with self, breath, solitude. All this is currenting through "Slow Drag," but at the same time, Codjoe refuses to jettison what might be considered profane from the realm of the sacred. As much as it's a ritual of elemental rapture—smoke is wind is fire is a river is a mother's touch is shells on the shoreline—it is (or was) also sexy. Cigarettes sting your eyes, which close as you lift your face to the pines, and you sway as the smoke, like a lover, "drags [your] voice on its back / just as the breeze heaves it." Hot dawg.

I have to pause here and linger with this poem from Daniel Nester's larger *künstlerroman, Harsh Realm*. Back in the day, smoking was not only solitary, it was communal. The smile that greets the skinny boy bumming a light at the end of the poem is one of the few smiles in this volume of poetry. Smoking was a tribal observance back then, where rebels and gritty nonconformists could find one another out on the streetcorners of New York. I'm taken back to the seedy bars and coffeehouses where we'd all gather to share poems in not-so-earnest open mics, karaoke sessions, or Mad Libs-style collaborations—Dan, Greg Pardlo, Marion Wrenn, Jason Schneiderman, Kazim Ali. But to approach the poem with less solipsism (and name-dropping), it also captures a truth about smoking that's nostalgic because it just may no longer be true. The owner of Joe's Busy Corner cursing through his artificial larynx is from the same tribe as the guy on his way to buy Doc Martens with borrowed money, extending his lighter to a stranger. We were flipping the bird to responsibility, capitalism, ideas of health, and mortality itself. There are a million reasons that this particular subculture is dead, and nearly all of them are admirable, positive cultural shifts. But this sensual blessing of the breath really was a way of giving thanks for "whole minutes" spent near ducks or pine trees or Tops Grocery. We recognized acutely, and observed ritualistically, the lack of guarantee: each morning is only "liable to be"—a bittersweet, conditional nonpromise.

In whatever way you give thanks to the night for the day—whether it's pulling the horizon from around the waist of the world and wrapping it around you, or watching the breeze rumple the white dunes of your sheets, or lighting up a Marlboro joy ampule, I celebrate your celebration.

But really, I'm not inviting you to become a smoker. Those days are over. In this avalanche of metaphors for September's uncommon breeze, is there one that's dragging you in? How might you give the bodymind a physical experience of, say, Ruth Forman's brush of palms or Codjoe's pine tree sway? One simple way to embody the mathematics of give and take is to lift and lower your arms, deliberately palpating the air as though pressing on a parachute. If this appeals, you might begin by resting your hands in your lap, palms facing up, as though holding something. As you lift the air up on the inhale, try to feel for its temperature and quality. When your arms are fully extended upward, turn the palms to face down, and as you breathe out, soften the hands back down into your lap. As you explore receiving and pouring back out, perhaps add a retention on the inhale with reaching arms, and at the bottom of the exhale, rest for a moment on empty, surrendering upturned hands into your lap. If one of these metaphors come to mind, like doves or wind over dunes, linger with it, as though feeling it with your palms. As your hands receive these prayers, what do they want to give back?

SEPTEMBER WEEK 3
AUTUMN EQUINOX

Joy Harjo
"Eagle Poem"

To pray you open your whole self
To sky, to earth, to sun, to moon
To one whole voice that is you.
And know there is more
That you can't see, can't hear;
Can't know except in moments
Steadily growing, and in languages
That aren't always sound but other
Circles of motion.
Like eagle that Sunday morning
Over Salt River. Circled in blue sky
In wind, swept our hearts clean
With sacred wings.
We see you, see ourselves and know
That we must take the utmost care
And kindness in all things.
Breathe in, knowing we are made of
All this, and breathe, knowing
We are truly blessed because we
Were born, and die soon within a

True circle of motion,
Like eagle rounding out the morning
Inside us.
We pray that it will be done
In beauty.
In beauty.

———

Joy Harjo
"For Anna Mae Pictou Aquash, Whose Spirit Is Present Here and in the Dappled Stars"

(For we remember the story and must tell it again so we may all live)
Beneath a sky blurred with mist and wind,
I am amazed as I watch the violet
heads of crocuses erupt from the stiff earth
after dying for a season,
as I have watched my own dark head
appear each morning after entering
the next world to come back to this one,
amazed.
It is the way in the natural world to understand the place
the ghost dancers named
after the heart breaking destruction.
Anna Mae,
everything and nothing changes.
You are the shimmering young woman
who found her voice,
when you were warned to be silent, or have your body cut away
from you like an elegant weed.
You are the one whose spirit is present in the dappled stars.
(They prance and lope like colored horses who stay with us
through the streets of these steely cities. And I have seen them
nuzzling the frozen bodies of tattered drunks
on the corner.)

This morning when the last star is dimming
and the busses grind toward
the middle of the city, I know it is ten years since they buried you
the second time in Lakota, a language that could
free you.
I heard about it in Oklahoma, or New Mexico,
how the wind howled and pulled everything down
in righteous anger.
(It was the women who told me) and we understood wordlessly
the ripe meaning of your murder.
As I understand ten years later after the slow changing
of the seasons
that we have just begun to touch
the dazzling whirlwind of our anger,
we have just begun to perceive the amazed world the ghost dancers
entered
crazily, beautifully.

POETIC THEMES

The autumn equinox marks the point where the days and nights are nearly of equal length (from the Latin, *aequus nox*). It's a time of balance, where growing things begin to die and, traditionally, harvesting winds down and folks give thanks and take rest. Migrations start. Hibernation plans begin. We accept the movement of nature toward dissolution because we know it is a part of regeneration. There must be death to make way for new life yet to be, like the larva swimming in its own soup before it can grow wings. I think of Mary Oliver's "Lines Written in the Days of Growing Darkness," where our acceptance of death is an expression and extension of our love for the world. I imagine Mary Oliver on her beach walk in the sky, wagging her finger at us for being such babies about death. The invitation to reach past late September decay to intuit the promise of rebirth highlights circles (our movement around the sun), the balance of light and dark, and life and death.

Joy Harjo's "Eagle Poem" is a meditation on these mysteries, insisting on the secret, invisible messages we can't see or hear. Meaning is conveyed through a language of circular motion. I think of this poem as an instruction manual for praying in circles, configuring the cyclical pattern of ruin and renewal as a kind of cleansing. The eagle manifests this cycle, flying in circles and "rounding out the morning inside us," and at the same time is surrounded, "circled in blue sky / in wind." As containers for the world and contained by it, we are asked to open ourselves and breathe, "knowing we are made of all this." We are cleansed by the eagle's circular flight, sweeping our hearts clean. Our perspective, too, is scrubbed clear, and we come to see that we are encircled in something much larger. We glimpse the ultimate truth that our little life is a wee blip in a broader circle of motion.

It seems important to marry Harjo's well-known "Eagle Poem" with the circle of decay and regeneration illustrated in "For Anna Mae Pictou Aquash." Naming and telling the story of the murder of one woman who refused silence is part of a different cycle of continuance in the context of broader cultural genocide. This poem depicts all the same cyclical movements between this world and the next: each spring the crocuses erupt "after dying for a season," each morning the last star dims and we re-enter this world from the spirit world of sleep. But in giving Anna Mae voice, this poem also illustrates a darker ghost dance, performed ritually to connect the living and the dead. The howling winds of this poem's "righteous anger" pull everything down to the grinding buses in steely cities where "tattered drunks" lie frozen on street corners. This "dazzling whirlwind" of anger is an important corollary to the soft wind carrying the eagle through its blue sky circles. Harjo's "own dark head" echoes not just the "heads of crocuses" but also the ghost dancers who "prance and lope like colored horses." "For Anna Mae" performs another kind of ghost dance: giving voice to the heartbreaking destruction of a people is part of keeping that culture alive.

PRACTICE

Perhaps you could source your movement practice back to circular dance forms from your own ancestry. It's not only Native American dance that manifests in flesh the way we orbit around a spiritual core, even as we move within broader circles of motion. Many other movement traditions sequence in circles, both within specific gestures and in the broader structure that turns the practitioner in a complete 360. The only circle dance I studied in any significant depth was a technique by Rudolf Laban, the Austro-Hungarian dance theorist. Laban devised a circular, spiraling sequences inspired by Sufi circling, where the body moves in a deliberate spatial polygon, on the vertical, lateral, and sagittal dimensions. Mary Anthony, a contemporary of Martha Graham and Merce Cunningham, taught me the traditional Laban circle, which I'll simplify here into an accessible exercise. Imagine a figure 8 on the floor, and take eight steps to trace one circle back to the center of the figure 8, then change directions to trace the complementary circle. Keep your eyes at the spot where the circles merge, and do your best to make each step precisely even in length, so as to divide each circle of steps into a perfect, symmetrical octagon. Slow your pace. Begin to rhythm your breathing with your steps. As your concentration transitions to an effortless zone where you begin to move spontaneously, stay with the practice just a little longer. What is the feeling-state rounding out inside of you?

SEPTEMBER WEEK 4

SEASON OF MELANCHOLY

W.S. Merwin
"To the Light of September"

When you are already here
you appear to be only
a name that tells of you
whether you are present or not

and for now it seems as though
you are still summer
still the high familiar
endless summer
yet with a glint
of bronze in the chill mornings
and the late yellow petals
of the mullein fluttering
on the stalks that lean
over their broken
shadows across the cracked ground

but they all know
that you have come
the seed heads of the sage
the whispering birds
with nowhere to hide you
to keep you for later

you
who fly with them

you who are neither
before nor after
you who arrive
with blue plums
that have fallen through the night

perfect in the dew

———

Marge Piercy
"The Late Year"

I like Rosh Hashonah late,
when the leaves are half burnt
umber and scarlet, when sunset
marks the horizon with slow fire
and the black silhouettes
of migrating birds perch
on the wires davening.

I like Rosh Hashonah late
when all living are counting
their days toward death
or sleep or the putting by
of what will sustain them—

when the cold whose tendrils
translucent as a jellyfish

and with a hidden sting
just brush our faces
at twilight. The threat
of frost, a premonition
a warning, a whisper
whose words we cannot
yet decipher but will.

I repent better in the waning
season when the blood
runs swiftly and all creatures
look keenly about them
for quickening danger.
Then I study the rockface
of my life, its granite pitted

and pocked and pickaxed
eroded, discolored by sun
and wind and rain—
my rock emerging
from the veil of greenery
to be mapped, to be
examined, to be judged.

John of Milano
excerpt from "Humors," Part III of *Regimen Sanitatis Salernitanum*

But if that dangerous humour ouer-raigne,
Of Melancholy, sometime making mad,
These tokens then will be appearing plaine,
The pulse beat hard, the colour darke and bad:
The water thin, a weake fantasticke braine,
False-grounded ioy, or else perpetuall sad,
Affrighted oftentimes with dreames like visions,
Presenting to the thought ill apparitions,
Of bitter belches from the stomacke comming,
His eare (the left especiall) euer humming.

Regimen Sanitatis Salernitanum (ca. 11th c.) commonly attributed to John of Milano. English translation (1608) by Sir John Harington. This poem is in the public domain.

POETIC THEMES

If we call autumn "fall," maybe we could call this fifth season "lean." Late summer, so replete it can't even hold up its own fullness, is yearning downward for earthy rest. According to Chinese medicine, the fifth season is associated with the stomach and especially the spleen, which is not only part of digesting the ripe harvest, but also controls blood vessels, keeps the organs upright, and governs clear thinking. Medieval medicine in the West shares the view that the spleen is the center of physical imbalance in September. According to the system of the four humors, the autumnal season of melancholy can cause imbalances of stomach and spleen, whose symptoms are described in the *Regimen Sanitatis*. Even if your left ear isn't humming, if your pulse is not beating hard (as Marge Piercy puts it, "in the waning / season when the blood runs swiftly"), the tendency toward pensive introspection as the light shifts at the end of September might be familiar.

If this sounds hypothetical rather than experiential, try listening to Arvo Pärt's "*Spiegel Im Spiegel*" as you read Merwin's direct address "To the Light of September." In that violin croon, I find all the sweet melancholy of the golden lengthening light, with its morning glint of bronze. But that might be because I listened to it a lot when I was hospicing my dad into the next world. The days still feel like "the high familiar endless summer," marking September as an interstitial realm, seasonally, "neither before nor after." Something precious is slipping through our fingers as we reach out to hold the last of summer. We have nowhere to hide it to keep it for later. The cacophony of springtime birds has died down to a whisper. The sage is in seed. The ground is cracked, and the shadows are broken. The plums are falling. Perhaps so are your spirits.

While this downward, inward pull is almost Buddhist for Merwin (Is it too much to read an implied theology in his existential-ish riddle of a first stanza?), Piercy's "The Late Year" adds a sense of reverential dread appropriate for the Days of Awe, counting the days toward "death / or sleep or the putting by / of what will sustain." The sense of impending doom in early autumn refigures chill mornings into stinging twilight. The frost is a premonition and the creatures are alert to danger. Merwin's birds are whispering, whereas Piercy's are davening. Rosh Hashanah's call to repentance gives a very different feel to this season and to the sense of bowing down, leaning in to perceive our life's granite rock face with frank reckoning.

PRACTICE

The grace and sadness of sidebends! In the fifth season of "lean," we might explore the relishing extension of the limbs and the arcing ribcage in a sideways bow, a drop of an ear toward a shoulder, a downward turn of the chest that isn't fully frontal. Even as we turn in and down, there's the feeling of reaching, yearning, for something. Anatomically, we are growing the girth of the ribcage to allow for a bigger breath, but simultaneously squeezing the organs. Our focus—not just the gaze, but the tonal focus—can be upward, looking up to relish the light, or downward, like the yellow stalks bowing to the cracked ground. As you engage these stretches and pressure points, note the subtleties of emotional tone—for me it bends between sadness and bittersweet nostalgia.

Try sitting with one leg extended in a straddle and the other knee bent out to the side, leaning toward the straight leg. Rest your head on one hand (if the elbow doesn't reach your leg or the ground, bring the earth up to you with a big pillow). Flop the other arm loosely over your head in a way that doesn't require muscular effort, or rest the hand on your bent knee. Breathe into the top ribs for one or two minutes, then switch sides.

Or, if you are more inclined to move, engage a supine whole-body side stretch, with arms extended on the ground overhead, creating a crescent moon with your whole body. Perhaps cross your ankles and bracelet one wrist with the other hand. Or you could start in a fetal position on one side, open the body through center (with feet together and knees apart, while windmilling the arms on the ground overhead), and close the body back to fetal on the second side.

However you come into the side ribs, close by stimulating the acupressure point for the spleen. Bring one hand, flat-palmed, just below your armpit, and use the other hand to feel around just under your pinky finger and a few inches below for a sensitive spot. Spend just a few moments gently tapping or massaging this point. You might go medieval in this practice by imagining black bile draining from your side waist, down the side of your hip, and into the earth, taking the melancholia with it and bringing you into balance.

OCTOBER WEEK 1
SELF-BLESSING

Galway Kinnell
"St. Francis and the Sow"

The bud
stands for all things,
even for those things that don't flower,
for everything flowers, from within, of self-blessing;
though sometimes it is necessary
to reteach a thing its loveliness,
to put a hand on its brow
of the flower
and retell it in words and in touch
it is lovely
until it flowers again from within, of self-blessing;
as Saint Francis
put his hand on the creased forehead
of the sow, and told her in words and in touch
blessings of earth on the sow, and the sow
began remembering all down her thick length,
from the earthen snout all the way
through the fodder and slops to the spiritual curl of the tail,
from the hard spininess spiked out from the spine
down through the great broken heart

to the sheer blue milken dreaminess spurting and shuddering
from the fourteen teats into the fourteen mouths sucking and blowing
    beneath them:
the long, perfect loveliness of sow.

————

Jennifer Rahim,
"Saint Francis and the Douen"
After reading Galway Kinnell

The head
sheltered by a great mushroom hat
holds the secret of all things beginning
and the wisdom of all their endings.
Hidden there
is the knowledge of mysteries unbaptised,
tiny, faceless creatures—
those knots of possibility are the dread
beneath the hat.
Hidden there
is a mouth crying in the forests,
calling the living to step
beyond the boundary of their seeing;

but sometimes it is necessary
to reach out and cradle the child,
and tell again in touch and sweet lullaby
of its loveliness and wonderful promise;
as Saint Francis did
when he followed the small voice
that beckoned him from the darkness,
then stooped low to where the infant sat
naked on a wet riverbank,
swaddled in the mud of all things beginning;

and reaching to take the child into his arms
he saw a face look back at him,
right there, from the water's surface,
and in that moment's recognition
found again the gift of self-blessing—
for all things rise to life again, from within,
in the waters of self-blessing;
so that Saint gently removed the hat
in a sun-bathed spot witnessed by the river,
the earth, the trees and the passing breeze,
and with healing touch and soft song
sang of the infant's perfect loveliness;
from the tender head and troubled brow,
the shy, half-formed face
and the small wounded heart,
he blessed the whole length of the body;
from the upstretched arms
to the strange, backward turn of the feet,
he blessed their high intelligence
to brave the abandoned places
only to save what was theirs alone to give,
blessed again and again that perfect beauty
until the child became sunlight,
forever shining within—
of self-blessing.

POETIC THEMES

Yom Kippur marks a return to innate goodness, casting off whatever detracts from that natural state. Many synagogues mark this time of purification with the blessing of animals, as with the concurrent (and much less important) Christian holiday of St. Francis Day. Galway Kinnell's "St. Francis and the Sow" re-minds us of the bud of goodness in all things, the opportunity for flowering at any point, and the potential for self-blessing that is only impeded when we forget our true nature. He intentionally mishmashes the wrinkled brow of a pig with the more enigmatic "brow" of a flower-bud—one that "stands for all things." The pure physicality of every earthy blessing is one hundred percent *that of God*, as Quakers say—even the curl of the tail is spiritual! The celebration of fleshiness in fodder and slops and earthen snout and spurting teats offers a nice balance to the practice of fasting this week. At the same time, the poem takes us in through the flesh to the center of our core, dropping through "the hard spininess spiked out from the spine / down through the great broken heart." Blessings of earth are told through these touching words. At the center of each of us is the great broken heart we share with Kinnell's sweet, lovely sow. And if we can touch it, the promise is that we will remember our loveliness and the world will come back to color. Blessings of earth indeed.

Jennifer Rahim's haunting rendering of the poem is not so simple. The Douen, a mythological figure from Trinidad and Tobego folklore, is a creepy figure with backward feet and knees, no distinguishable facial features except for a mouth, and a big, floppy hat. Said to embody the wandering souls of children that were not christened before death, they lure unsuspecting children deep into the forest until they are lost. These liminal creatures are figured as more mischievous than evil—they are, after all, innocent—but they double as a warning to kids not to wander after strangers and to parents to be sure to baptize their children. This lends something more sinister to the poem's act of blessing, as part of a colonial history of control, domination, and cultural genocide. These slip-slidey nuances extend our sense of who and what these creatures really represent, with their "high intelligence / to brave the abandoned places / only to save what was theirs alone to give." The celebration of resistance to imperialism seemingly implied here lends a fuller scope and thrust to the poem, "calling the living to step / beyond the boundary of their seeing." I mean, who is redeemed here, after all? Rahim troubles the waters in the scene of baptism: surely the face the Saint perceives at the riverbank is his own? The pronouns get, so to speak, muddy: "reaching to take the child into his arms, / he saw his face look back at him, / right there, from the water's surface." This is a "moment of recognition," not the discovery of an "other"—and what Saint Francis "found again" is a gift of *self* blessing. Even so, the child is the focus of the poem, from the first lines describing its head and the secrets, knowledge, and wisdom held there, to the last lines bursting into sunlight. Rahim lures us into the wilderness with these uncertainties, which is maybe the only place from which to begin to see things differently.

When we return, the familiar is suddenly layered with deeper, fuller meaning. Perceiving the postcolonial undercurrent in this poem doesn't undermine its ability to touch us and gives nuance to what, precisely, is being recuperated in the blessing. In this sun-bathed spot by the river, with its breeze and trees and earth, we witness the transformation of a banished, exiled creature, who is changed into actual sunlight. The poem touches this child so gently, sings the song of healing so softly, that we can almost feel the infant's "tender head and troubled brow / the shy, half-formed face / and the small wounded heart." Yom Kippur, the day of atonement, is where we see all our wrongdoings, back for generations, and heal them. Blessings of earth on sow, and Saint, and Douen, and us all.

PRACTICE

The progress of touch in both poems, from the brow down the length of the body, lends itself to a physical practice that can be approached (like Yom Kippur) as penance or as self-forgiveness. You could begin by just holding a fingertip to the "troubled brow," behind which churn all the horrors in your personal and ancestral history. If that sensitive spot between the eyebrows awakens you to feeling, you might, like the Douen, reach your "upstretched arms" overhead (perhaps with palms touching, if it feels organic to you), and draw them in slow motion down to the crown of the head, micromillimeter by micromillimeter. When your prayer hands hover just over your "tender head," you'll feel the warmth of the scalp and the tickle of hair, and you might have the impression of the head lifting toward the hands. Spend some time perching the hands on the crown before moving down to the addled forehead, then the "small wounded heart," and then down the "whole length of the body" with a lingering touch anywhere along the central axis of the torso that feels especially tender or resonant. To emphasize your grounding in earth, "swaddled in the mud of all things beginning," you might close each pass by folding forward. (Full prostration is only practiced, in Jewish tradition, on Yom Kippur).

OCTOBER WEEK 2
MIGRATORY PATTERNS

Joy Harjo
"Map to the Next World"

for Desiray Kierra Chee

In the last days of the fourth world I wished to make a map for those who would climb through the hole in the sky.

My only tools were the desires of humans as they emerged from the killing fields, from the bedrooms and the kitchens.

For the soul is a wanderer with many hands and feet.

The map must be of sand and can't be read by ordinary light. It must carry fire to the next tribal town, for renewal of spirit.

In the legend are instructions on the language of the land, how it was we forgot to acknowledge the gift, as if we were not in it or of it.

Take note of the proliferation of supermarkets and malls, the altars of money. They best describe the detour from grace.

Keep track of the errors of our forgetfulness; the fog steals our children while we sleep.

Flowers of rage spring up in the depression. Monsters are born there of nuclear anger.

Trees of ashes wave good-bye to good-bye and the map appears to disappear.

We no longer know the names of the birds here, how to speak to them by their personal names.

Once we knew everything in this lush promise.

What I am telling you is real and is printed in a warning on the map. Our for-getfulness stalks us, walks the earth behind us, leaving a trail of paper diapers, needles, and wasted blood.

An imperfect map will have to do, little one.

The place of entry is the sea of your mother's blood, your father's small death as he longs to know himself in another.

There is no exit.

The map can be interpreted through the wall of the intestine—a spiral on the road of knowledge.

You will travel through the membrane of death, smell cooking from the en-campment where our relatives make a feast of fresh deer meat and corn soup, in the Milky Way.

They have never left us; we abandoned them for science.

And when you take your next breath as we enter the fifth world there will be no X, no guidebook with words you can carry.

You will have to navigate by your mother's voice, renew the song she is singing.

Fresh courage glimmers from planets.

And lights the map printed with the blood of history, a map you will have to know by your intention, by the language of suns.

When you emerge note the tracks of the monster slayers where they entered the cities of artificial light and killed what was killing us.

You will see red cliffs. They are the heart, contain the ladder.

A white deer will greet you when the last human climbs from the destruction.

Remember the hole of shame marking the act of abandoning our tribal grounds.

We were never perfect.

Yet, the journey we make together is perfect on this earth who was once a star and made the same mistakes as humans.

We might make them again, she said.

Crucial to finding the way is this: there is no beginning or end.

You must make your own map.

Wendell Berry
"The Wild Geese"

Horseback on Sunday morning,
harvest over, we taste persimmon
and wild grape, sharp sweet
of summer's end. In time's maze
over fall fields, we name names
that went west from here, names
that rest on graves. We open
a persimmon seed to find the tree
that stands in promise,
pale, in the seed's marrow.
Geese appear high over us,
pass, and the sky closes. Abandon,
as in love or sleep, holds
them to their way, clear,
in the ancient faith: what we need
is here. And we pray, not
for new earth or heaven, but to be
quiet in heart, and in eye
clear. What we need is here.

———

David Whyte
"The Journey"

Above the mountains
the geese turn into
the light again

Painting their
black silhouettes
on an open sky.

Sometimes everything
has to be
inscribed across
the heavens

so you can find
the one line
already written
inside you.

Sometimes it takes
a great sky
to find that

first, bright
and indescribable
wedge of freedom
in your own heart.

Sometimes with
the bones of the black
sticks left when the fire
has gone out

someone has written
something new
in the ashes of your life.

You are not leaving.
Even as the light fades quickly now,
you are arriving.

Evie Shockley
"anti-immigration"

the black people left, and took with them their furious
          hurricanes and their fire-breathing rap songs melting
the polar ice caps. they left behind the mining jobs,
          but took that nasty black lung disease and the insurance
regulations that loop around everything concerning
          health and care, giant holes of text that all the coverage
falls through. the brown people left, and took with
          them the pesticides collecting like a sheen on the skins
of fruit. they went packing, and packed off with them
          went all the miserable low-paying gigs, the pre-dawn
commutes, the children with expensive special needs
          and the hard-up public schools that tried to meet them.
the brown people left, railroaded into carting off those
          tests that keep your average bright young student outside
the leagues of ivy-lined classrooms, and also hauled off
          their concentrated campuses, their great expectations, their
invasive technology, and the outrageous pay gap between
          a company's c.e.o. and its not-quite-full-time workers. they
took their fragile endangered pandas and species extinction
          and got the hell outta dodge. the black people left and took
hiv / aids, the rest of their plagues, and all that deviant
          sexuality with them. they took their beat-down matriarchies
and endless teen pregnancies, too. those monster-sized
          extended families, the brown people took those. the brown
people boxed up their turbans and suspicious sheet-like
          coverings, their terrifying gun violence, cluster bombs,
and drones, and took the whole bloody mess with them,
          they took war and religious brow-beating tucked under
their robes. they took theocracy and their cruel, unusual
          punishments right back where they came from. finally,
the white people left, as serenely unburdened as when
          they arrived, sailing off from plymouth rock with nothing
in their hands but a recipe for cranberry sauce, a bit
          of corn seed, and the dream of a better life. there were
only certain kinds of people here, after the exodus, left
          to wander the underdeveloped wilderness in search
of buffalo, tobacco, and potable water, following old

migratory patterns that would have been better left alone.

POETIC THEMES

Changing this week's holiday from Columbus Day to Indigenous Peoples' Day marks a clear redirecting of America's energy and intention. Evie Shockley imagines a more extreme redirection, in "anti-immigration." Fed up with the discourse about immigration policy and who gets to quality as authentically American, Shockley wryly portrays a mass exodus of unamerican Americans right on out of this country. The last stragglers are left to wander—and here the poetic tone is no longer edged, but earnest—and follow the old ways, "that would have been better left alone."

These old migratory patterns have been scattered and destroyed, and the "gift of reading the land" nearly forgotten, as Joy Harjo tells her "little one." A map, one made of sand that "can't be read by ordinary light" must be drawn from scratch, in order to "climb through the hole in the sky." The few suggestions the poem is able to give for beginning this process are all deeply physical—rooted in mother's blood and voice and song, father's semen, the wall of intestine, the membrane of death, red cliffs, corn soup, deer meat. "Once," she writes wistfully, "we knew everything in this lush promise." The atrocities of the decimation of a people slice through this poem. The maps that need to be drawn after a genocide cannot be compared to the way that children of imperialists might find their way, on sacred stolen ground. It seems presumptuous to co-opt Harjo's recipe for building a world map out of entrails and landscape, even or especially since most of our awareness of the patterns of nature are sourced from Indigenous wisdom.

So in the interest of staying in my lane, I want to offer a "way-finding" practice that's closer to home. It's kind of a stretch to find Quaker themes in Wendell Berry. But one internet search reported that Berry's love for sacred silence led him to confess, "maybe I'm a Quaker of sorts." I'll take it. He certainly shares the conviction among Friends that divinity exists in all of nature, "God's second book." Quaker modes of discernment rely on a quiet heart and a clear eye to listen intuitively for direction. In this season of quickly fading sun and ash, and the closing sky, there's a sense of urgency to the discernment process. The light is dying. But what we need, he reassures us, is here.

Perhaps Whyte thought of "The Wild Geese" when he wrote "The Journey," importing Berry's awareness of a twilight now-ness. The final line—"you are arriving"—similarly presses us to re-direct our focus to what is here and now, to discern our path. Both Berry and Whyte promise new life after loss—the taste of persimmon after the harvest's end, and the "something new" to be found in the ashes of our lives. Both poets coax us urgently to *find our way*, to intuit our natural path like the wild geese. Whether we continue in our clear V and the sky closes, or we turn around into the light and the sky opens, we need to figure out where, individually and collectively, we are being called to move.

Both poems incite us to look within for a small, secret message reflecting the broader changing natural world around us. Berry finds the macrocosmic tree's imprint in the marrow of a seed—as above, so below. Whyte perceives a mysterious message about openness and freedom written in the heavens but promises that we can find it mirrored in our hearts. The bones of black sticks, according to David Whyte, carry an inscription written by—*someone*. We don't need to know where the message comes from, we just need to be willing to drop down into the ashes of our lives to look for it. Berry's theology is more explicit: we can only perceive the message from the universe when we surrender to the divine, which is a process as natural—and sometimes as hard—as abandoning ourselves to love or sleep. In discerning our steps, we will make mistakes. We were never perfect. We must make our own map.

PRACTICE

These broad themes of finding direction, intuitive listening, and reading the secret messages in nature open all kinds of possibilities for physical practice. Dancers might crave graceful, open-armed balances. The feeling of air in expansive, floating movements with lots of airtime in the transitions can mimic flight. Big geometric shapes with limbs extended can help evoke the silhouette of dark bird wings against light. The skeletal shape of the future tree in the seed could be expressed splayed out with bird wings spread, looking for the message written in the "wedge of freedom" under the line of the sternum.

Here's another way to awaken our awareness to secret signs. I'm not sure who began transposing the monastic practice of *Lectio Divina* into the worship of nature, "God's other book." My mother first taught it to me, and she learned it from Quaker teacher Nancy Bieber. Traditionally, *Lectio Divina* referred to scriptural reading, meditation, and prayer to promote communion with the divine. It does not treat scripture as texts to be studied, but as the living word. It takes in the word in four separate steps: read (bite); meditate (taste); pray (savor); contemplate (digest). In answering Oliver's call to love this world through devoted, reverential attention, stop whatever you are doing and look, feel, smell, taste, listen. Allow your attention to be called to something beautiful (the word beauty is, after all, etymologically related to "calling"). Try not to penetrate or study what's around you, instead try to adopt a passive role where you receive the call of beauty.

Chew on it:

Approach what calls you, BE with that bark, blade of grass, bug, or crack in the cement. Touch it if you can.

Savor it:

Suspend any preconceived idea of what it might have to tell you. Try to free yourself from composing an idea in your mind, and instead truly listen with a mental blank slate.

Digest it:

What is the nutrient-rich, life-giving message or substance this phenomenon relays to you? In contemplative stillness, consider: what is the line written there, and how does it speak to something in your own heart?

OCTOBER WEEK 3
LEAV-ING

Linda Pastan
"October"

Who can mediate
between the body and its undoing?
At night in each of my limbs
I feel the skeletal tree ache,
and I dream of leaves
in their feverish colors, floating
through the small streams
and tributaries of the blood.
At noon in the smoldering woods
I gather black grapes
that purse and caress the mouth,
I gather thistles and burrs—
whole armfuls of dissolution,
while from a branch
the chuck-will's widow calls
forgive, forgive

Marie Ponsot
"End of October"

Leaves wait as the reversal of wind
comes to a stop. The stopped woods
are seized of quiet; waiting for rain
bird & bug conversations stutter to a
stop.
Between the road
and the car in the road and me in the car,
and the woods
and the forms standing tall and the broken
forms and the small forms that crawl there,
the rain begins to fall. Rain-strands,
thin slips of vertical rivers, roll
the shredded waters out of the cloud
and dump them puddling to the ground.
Like sticks half-drowned the trees
lean so my eyes snap some into
lightning shapes, bent & bent.
I leave the car to wee where, lower,
the leaves of the shrubs beaten goldleaf
huddle together. In some spaces
nothing but rain appears.

Whatever crosses over
through the wall of rain
changes; old leaves are
now gold. The wall is
continuous, doorless. True,
to get past this wall
there's no need for a door
since it closes around me
as I go through.

Czeslow Milosz
"This Only"

A valley and above it forests in autumn colors.
A voyager arrives, a map leads him there.
Or perhaps memory. Once long ago in the sun,
When snow first fell, riding this way
He felt joy, strong, without reason,
Joy of the eyes. Everything was the rhythm
Of shifting trees, of a bird in flight,
Of a train on the viaduct, a feast in motion.
He returns years later, has no demands.
He wants only one, most precious thing:
To see, purely and simply, without name,
Without expectations, fears, or hopes,
At the edge where there is no I or not-I.

POETIC THEMES

Last October I fell in love with a meme on Facebook—an image of a tree in its full glory with the message, "The trees are about to show us how beautiful letting go can be." This year I saw it again and, for some reason, it made me furious! Something between Covid or my dog dying or my kid leaving for college or maybe perimenopause—who knows—calls bullshit on the beauty of letting go. It's not beautiful. It's just plain HARD. In a poem entitled "In a Northern Country," Linda Pastan confesses, "I'm tired of the way the seasons keep changing, / mimicking the seasons of the flesh which are real / and finite." Amen, sister. There's a fatigue that I recognize in Pastan that keeps me company. It's an exhaustion with the deterioration of the flesh. In "End of October" she wonders, "Perhaps beauty / is the mother of death, / not the other way around." There's a kind of crone-wisdom in perceiving that truth can be toothed, arresting and still tender. Nothing can mediate the ache of undoing as we watch our colorful leaves float on down the river. Buh-bye youth and prettiness! Living is an exercise in loss, as we break down to skeleton. Still, the grapes that purse the mouth also caress it. Knowing as we do that we can't hold the world forever, our "armfuls of dissolution" are spiky, bristled —not pussy-willows but thistles and burrs.

In the autumn of our lives, not only do we experience minute by minute the dissolution of the body, but also an increased feeling of urgency to give up the ghosts. The rolling call of the nocturnal chuck-will widow, with all the implication of loss implied in its name, is beautiful until it is crazy-making, persisting as it does all. night. long. The cadenced onomatopoeia haunts us with its insistent repetition to forgive, forgive, before it's too late. The hard work of forgiving is not, in fact, about someone else's behavior, but about surrendering to our own past. What has been will be, and we need to decide what we're going to do with it. There's nothing complacent about forgiving; it's about *making peace,* in the sense of actively forging something out of nothing.

Marie Ponsot's "End of October" is another dissolution poem, where the leaves are low to the ground. The skeletal trees are in lightning shapes; all that is left are the leaves of the shrubs, huddled low and beaten gold. The transformation of old leaves turned gold gives a sense-based experience of the liminal, in the spaces between raindrops, between car and woods, between the witnesser and the autumn leaves, between human and animal. To enter this rain-drenched scene is not to pass through it but to become different in it—the doorless wall partitioning stages of change is continuous, and it closes around us as we move through. We huddle together, bent.

A depiction of this transformation, "This Only" enacts a distillation of our needs as we age, redefining what is precious. The poem looks backward and forward at once, to a past winter when a traveler visited a valley down in the forest. In this first visit, some epiphanic moment dissolved him into the natural world. But the poem is set in autumn, with winter still to come. When the traveler returns years later, there's no sublime epiphany. It's more of a streamlining of need. "He wants only one, most precious thing / To see, purely and simply." With age we discover a kind of pure dissipation of self into our surround, the dissolving of ego that enables pure witness. At this edge, beyond and yet definitive of self, there is no fear or hope, only rhythm and joy and reasonlessness. From the perspective of the autumn of our lives, that time of year where leaves, or none, or few do hang, we can look forward to our winter crone wisdom that privileges presence—only. We are whittled down.

In an episode of "On Being" with Krista Tippett, John O'Donohue describes this process of distilling and streamlining, in the etymology of the word "threshold." Coming from the verb to thresh, to separate the grain from the husk, he describes the threshold as a line that separates "two territories of spirit." As we transition from one way of being to another, O'Donohue draws our attention to the question of *how* we cross over. To cross "worthily," he says, is to heal certain patterns of behavior that had us stuck or caught. He concludes,

"It's a kind of homecoming for the enriched memory of your unfolding life." The kerfuffled verb tense of this last line recalls Milosz's: we are returning home to a memory of our future as we always knew it. The word "worthy" is an interesting choice, Biblical as it is and the root of the word "worship." What is it, then, to cross worthily? Perhaps it is to attend to every micro-detail, each worthy of our attention, so that we may dissolve what is and join with whatever future thing awaits. To worship every autumn leaf is to fully inhabit this threshold of change, this period of crossing over that promises the dissolution of ego and the discovery of true presence.

PRACTICE

Expressing the "skeletal tree ache" in movement is to find the sway inside stillness, the certain sadness in the extension of limbs. We could express longing and limit by reaching out our arms and gathering them back in, like Pastan's "armfuls of dissolution." I teach a kind of threshold play in a physical exercise exploring boundaries: bringing your hands to the center of your chest, interlace your fingers, flip your palms to face away from you, and as you push the hands away, round your back and drop your head. It's sometimes nice to linger in this extension. Then turn the palms to face inward and gather the interlaced hands back to the chest, lingering again as you receive the warm imprint of the palms on your chest. Go slowly, so you might check in with the space between letting go and longing and receiving and releasing again. Whatever crosses over changes. Notice the shifts in the streams and tributaries that flood from the heart center. Tune in to the flow of blood and energy from the trunk to the branched tips of fingers. Could you drop in deep enough to find Milosz's "edge where there is no I or not-I"? What does that zone feel like and how does it relate to forgiveness?

OCTOBER WEEK 4

SUKKOT, ALL HALLOWS EVE, DAY OF THE DEAD

John Paul Martinez
"To Offer Sweet Fruit to the Ghost"
for Lolo

Ma says not to swat at the housefly
chirring in our headspace

for the past two hours
because it just might be you.

Ma shows me the flimsy browned pictures
of you & me in your workshop,

a scored-leather tool belt strapped across
your chest like a bandolier.

My whole body smaller still
than a durian, than a jackfruit.

Ma asks if I remember you. I tell her:

I don't even remember myself.

I have now lived over ten times
the years that I have known you.

All my life, I have known you
only through unknowing.

Each year, Ma collects more and more
superstitions. On your death anniversaries,

she reminds me & Ate & Ading to not be
so heavy-footed around your annual shrine.

The tame light of a fat candle splashes
on the bowl brimmed with your favorites:

plantains, mangoes, and the plumpest grapes.
How odd it feels to celebrate your passing.

To offer sweet fruit to the ghost

of a ghost.

Because it is all I am ever able to offer,
I practice a few reminding beliefs.

I walk lightly
around candles.

I leave sugar out
for flies.

"To Offer Sweet Fruit to the Ghost" by John Paul Martinez. Originally published in The Slowdown on September 29, 2021. Reprinted by permission of the poet.

Kasey Jueds
"The Bat"

First dark, then more dark
smoothed over it.
First sleep, then eyes
open to the ceiling
where something circles. For a moment,
you can't name it. And for a moment
you're not afraid. Remember
Blake's angels, how they leaned
toward each other, and balanced
by touching only the tips of their wings?
Between their bodies, a space
like the one just after rain begins, when rain
isn't rain, but the smell
of dust lifted, something silent and clean.

POETIC THEMES

This week is all about the in-between, halfway between the autumnal equinox (life) and the winter solstice (death), where the veil between worlds is said to grow thin. Sukkot marks the fragility of our existence, the temporary worldly dwellings that house our spirits, the fleeting harvest that feeds us. Halloween, like Samhain before it, is all about the mysterious Bardo between our conscious and our unconscious minds—the underworld of our pasts, lost ones, and ancestors. Less solemn is the Day of the Dead: bright *cempazúchitl* are everywhere, temporary altars hold a ghost's favorite food (or more commonly, their favorite cigar or booze), and people write irreverent mock epitaphs for one another. Morbid? Maybe. Wicked? Certainly. *Dia de los Muertos* expresses a kind of collective ease in handling death and dying. Death pervades all of life and does not disturb it. In this liminal time, *we* are the disturbance, running the risk of agitating the ghosts, who could arrive in any form, like John Paul Martinez's housefly spirit, "chirring in our headspace." So our job is to walk lightly, make offerings, and practice "reminding beliefs." If we were to "collect more and more superstitions," how might we be different, more loving and reverential toward the world surrounding us?

The first poem in the first book of poetry by Kasey Jueds, "The Bat," ventures a guess. When the otherworldly is apprehended outside the boundaries of fear, all our ghosts become angels. Like the housefly, something is chirring overhead in this poem, but this time it's dark, with "more dark / smoothed down over it." Jueds compares the purity of witness to how we might perceive the rain before actual raindrops fall, as "the smell / of dust lifted, something silent and clean." But it's not the actual scent that grounds the clean perception, it is the pre-rain *space*. She compares this to the space between the bodies of Blake's angels, wingtips touching in the watercolor darkness. They form a kind of protective umbrella of prayer hands, in a sepulcher about to yawn open, above the corpse of a saint who was never quite human, never quite dead. The interstitial mode of not-this-anymore, not-yet-that, is the realm of the Bardo to which we have access this week. How does superstition relate to this modality of witnessing the beyond, untainted by fear? Both have an imaginative range that bypasses the rational, the logical. All our ghosts become angels.

PRACTICE

So, so simple: walk lightly for ghosts! Employ the lightest, barest footfall, as though walking on snow without footprints. Employ a profound delicacy of hand in whatever you do, as though the fragile membrane of whatever you touch could rupture at any time. Tiptoe through your next half hour, imagining that any phenomenon, natural or manmade, could be the incarnation of someone you have lost. If you discover the ghost of a beloved somewhere, pause and consider making an offering. The grandest offering might be a playful *Calaveras*, imaginatively written in your lost love one's voice, for *you*!

NOVEMBER WEEK 1
WANDERING LIGHT

W.S. Merwin
"The Love for October"

A child looking at ruins grows younger
but cold
and wants to wake to a new name
I have been younger in October
than in all the months of spring
walnut and may leaves the color
of shoulders at the end of summer
a month that has been to the mountain
and become light there
the long grass lies pointing uphill
even in death for a reason
that none of us knows
and the wren laughs in the early shade now
come again shining glance in your good time
naked air late morning
my love is for lightness
of touch foot feather
the day is yet one more yellow leaf
and without turning I kiss the light
by an old well on the last of the month

gathering wild rose hips
in the sun

———

W.S. Merwin
"December Morning"

How did I come to this late happiness
as I wake into my remaining days
another morning in my life with Paula
taking me by surprise like the first one
I know it is rash to speak about happiness
with the Fates so near that I can hear
them but this morning even the old regrets
seem to have lost their rancor
and to harbor shy hopes like the first grass
of spring appearing between paving stones
when I was a small child and I see
that each step has been leading me
to the present morning that I recognize
before daylight and I forget that
I am almost blind and I see the piles
of books I was going to read next
there they wait like statues of sitting dogs
faithful to someone they used to know
but happiness has a shape made of air
it was never owned by anyone
it comes when it will in its own time

Rainer Maria Rilke
"A Walk"

Already my gaze is on the hill, that sunlit one,
up ahead on the path I've scarcely started.
In the same way, what we couldn't grasp grasps us:
blazingly visible, there in the distance—

and changes us, even if we don't reach it,
into what we, scarcely sensing it, already are;
a gesture signals, answering our gesture...
But we feel only the opposing wind.

Rainer Maria Rilke, "A Walk" from *The Book of Images: A Bilingual Edition* by Rainer Maria Rilke, translated by Edward Snow. Reprinted with the permission of Farrar, Straus and Giroux.

POETIC THEMES

W.S. Merwin's season-specific poems, riddled as they are with the theme of light, trace the shifts made painfully clear at this time of year. We can begin by circling back a few weeks to the golden lengthening light, with its morning glint of bronze, in "To the Light of September." In October, visual light plays on lightness of being—touch foot feather—as we pare down to skeletal. "The Love for October" reaches toward a light that is always already gone: the poem looks up past the wren to the sky, to pray for the sun god's return. "Come again shining glance," written by a translator of Greek, can only be a nod to Phoebus, for whom "Shining One" is a common address (thanks for this, Sue Wells!). The first two inscrutable lines of the poem indicate this play of time where past and future, youth and age, get mussed. In the autumn, like children witnessing something ancient, we watch the trees stripped to ruin. Could we feel the potential for our new self-to-be, our "new name," in the dying of one year? I dunno, y'all. But the next lines are so super straightforward, so familiar and just plain true—"I have been younger in October than in all the months of spring"—we just know this feeling of vitality when we are drenched in beauty. The grammar play of "walnut and may leaves the color of shoulders at the end of summer," is still legible even with its noun and verb scramble. And the upward movement is a lovely way to think about the process of wisening; the literal en-lighten-ment of a hermit climbing the mountain is also the grass

213

lying uphill even in death. We climb toward kissing the light and gathering wild rose hips in the sun, marking the golden leaf of each day… until November, and suddenly the light is gone mid-afternoon!

The movement of autumn light in Merwin's poetry arrives at completion in "December Morning." Here the poet awakens into the pre-dawn of one of his few "remaining days," beyond old regrets and rancor. He is "almost blind," in the pre-dawn dark, barely perceiving "the books I was going to read next." The sense of sight yields to sound—"with the Fates so near that I can hear / them" —signaling the arrival of a different God, a "late happiness." Gone is the climb, the crawl, the need for supplication—we have moved altogether beyond sense experience: "happiness has a shape made of air / it was never owned by anyone / it comes when it will in its own time." Active seeking gives way to passively receiving the kind of happiness that can't be rushed or hunted. What more could we ask from aging?

If Merwin's poems carry us through all kinds of possibilities for how sense experience relates to spiritual seeking, perhaps we could find a steadier hand in the paradigmatic poetic scene of the mountain climb toward divine light: Rilke's "A Walk." Maybe the role of sense experience in the uphill climb toward source is clearer in the original; it's hard to pin down in translation. It might be of interest to examine Snow's rendering, reprinted here, through the lens of some other translations. Robert Bly takes liberal choices in service of poetic "feel" (how he manages to find "inner light" in the German I'll never know). He massages out an extraordinary number of references to the sense of touch. We touch the hill with our eyes, we are grasped, we are reachingsensingwaving in this uphill journey. Then *POW* the last line: "But what we feel is the wind in our faces." Bly plays the deeply sensual touch of *gegenwind* (headwind) by taking it literally—wind on our head! In Crego's translation, in place of eyes touching the hill we have a gaze that just kind of… is. The visual component of what we're reaching for—inner light—is replaced by "manifest" as a noun, not an action verb. We are waving gesturally in Bly, as opposed to the oblique "sign" in Crego. Most notably, Crego renders the final line in a total abstraction: "what we sense is the falling wind." This is a kind of wonderful truism: if you're going uphill, the headwind will be falling. While Crego's last line captures the poem's gravity (scientifically and in terms of gravitas), the concrete feeling of wind in our faces is undone: the verb "sense" is robbed of its very sensuality, used instead to signal apprehension.

To say it more simply: these two translations capture two interpretations of the relationship of body and spirit. Bly's choices portray a sense-based experience, whereas Crego presents the experience as metaphysical—literally, above or beyond the physical plane. I feel like Bly gets it right. The title, "A Walk," is no accident—physically moving in space is a change at the level of lived, human-fleshy experience. The poem's meditation on transformation lives inside the play of body in contact with sun and wind, distance and always-already-changedness. We are becoming what we have always known our future self has always been: rich and strange. We are real-izing ourselves changed; true knowing is only fully realized with an actual physical change of place, state, being. Even if our transformation is incomplete, it is concrete. Felt. This is like being physically dragged into newness, uphill, intuiting its truth and power and draw. We can't even really see it clearly, not just for its distance but also because we are so blinded by the brightness of what's ahead. And yet in spite of its brilliance and its distance, we feel it, it reaches us in touch. I think of two cousin quotes, one from the Rig Veda—"The Sun receive thine eye, the Wind thy *prana* (breath/spirit)" [10:16]—and one from the Gospels: "The eye is the lamp of the body. When the eye is clear, the whole body is full of light" (Luke 11:34). The whole body, full of light.

PRACTICE

Mindful wandering is different from mindful walking, both in the direction of our focus and the quality of mind we are cultivating. I have found that Friends prefer mindful wandering. Walking meditation, the way it's taught in the Zen tradition, involves not just a strict hand *mudra*, but also a pinprick concentration on the actual physical details of walking. Typically, the instruction begins with a lesson in shifting the weight from heel to toe in slow motion —which is surprisingly challenging for our balance—noticing the ripple effects on the entire muscle system of the body. Most mindful wandering practices, in contrast, spend just a few moments on the physicality of walking and then turn to focus on the interaction of the practitioner's attention with the surround. The focus is less on the action of walking and more on cultivating a quality of mind that is receptive, rather than self-directed. Useful to the practice of mindful wandering is the metaphor of the "sacred compass within," as described by Quaker theologian J. Brent Bill. A compass literally cannot function when we are constantly in motion, so too we must slow down to let the direction needle point North. Weaving our way in the world while following the needle requires a slow pace and times of stillness, etymologically expressing winding, turning, and weaving.

Basically, it's Bly vs. Crego, folks. How do you wind *your* way toward the metaphysical light? Zen walking meditation, in the Zendo where I learned it, is practiced with the hands held in the shape of an oval in front of the solar plexus. The four fingers of the left hand rest in the four fingers of the right hand, thumbs touching. Slow, measured steps need to be small enough to enable a focus on the deliberate distribution of weight rolling along the bottom of the feet. Mindful wandering, it has been taught in my Quaker lineage, is an undirected walk responsive to the pull of something outside the self, stopping periodically to make space for noticing. To engage a more Rilkean experience, you could wander uphill or turn your face up to catch the sun, imagining you are being pulled forward.

Whichever practice you engage, allow time to check in with soma and gauge where the play of active and passive takes place in the body. Are you initiating movement or being pulled, as a passive recipient of some external force? Are you reaching or being grasped? How, for you, is spiritual sensibility related to sense-ability?

NOVEMBER WEEK 2
VETERANS DAY

Yehuda Amichai
"Wildpeace"

Not the peace of a cease-fire,
not even the vision of the wolf and the lamb,
but rather
as in the heart when the excitement is over
and you can talk only about a great weariness.
I know that I know how to kill,
that makes me an adult.
And my son plays with a toy gun that knows
how to open and close its eyes and say Mama.
A peace
without the big noise of beating swords into ploughshares,
without words, without
the thud of the heavy rubber stamp: let it be
light, floating, like lazy white foam.
A little rest for the wounds—
who speaks of healing?
(And the howl of the orphans is passed from one generation
to the next, as in a relay race:
the baton never falls.)

Let it come
like wildflowers,
suddenly, because the field
must have it: wildpeace.

POETIC THEMES

I don't have a lot to say about Veterans Day. It gives me the same feeling I had in middle school when I encountered Randall Jarrell's gut-punch poem, "The Death of the Ball Turret Gunner." Like the wind is knocked out of me and I can't say much. Like when I threw up after watching "Gallipoli" with my dad (who was in the military). Maybe wartime losses *should* feel like that: nightmare and black flak. Animal. And Jarrell's decimating last line that washes out the body with a hose.

But the thing is, the jolt and shock of violence that America feeds on all day, every day has dulled us to the point of inaction. It serves to bolster Empire. So instead of rolling around in violent imagery all day, we could try for a little reparation. Amichai survived the 1948 Arab-Israeli war, then World War II, only to face his country's future—endless violence with no promise of a ceasefire. Amichai's perspective is the wisdom of a "great weariness," when face to face with no aftermath, no healing for wounds. "Wildpeace" instead just hopes for some kind of rest, rest from the exhaustion of running a race where the baton passed from generation to generation is an *orphan*—an orphan whose baby doll is a talking toy gun. And isn't exhaustion one way peace finally graces the body? Suddenly the fight goes out of us, and with no drama, no "big noise," a sense of exhausted surrender descends "like lazy white foam." Maybe instead of celebrating war heroes today, we might instead, "as in the heart when the excitement is over," let our psychic field lie fallow to make a space for peace. "Let it come / like wildflowers."

PRACTICE

It feels apt to embody the attrition of "Wildpeace" by fatiguing the fight-or-flight muscle (the psoas) until it releases. The psoas is more than the connection between upper and lower body; it actually *becomes* the diaphragm, which is in turn tethered to the adrenals, all functioning as a whole system to rev up the violence. In order to catch a moment of reprieve from the flood of stress hormones that amp up the nervous system, we'll try to soothe the psoas by wearing it out. Stand next to a wall and rest one hand on it for a sense of orientation, support, and solidity. Place the foot proximal to the wall on a large book (or step on a staircase or yoga block). Swing the outside leg forward and back in a modest arc for a minimum of three minutes on each leg. Use minimal muscular effort, allowing the weight of the leg to provide the required momentum. Be sure to keep the hip points level and allow the rocking motion to tip the pelvis in its anterior/posterior plane.

When you've pooped out the psoas, and hopefully its connection to the fight reflex, come to sit quietly and witness the mental field. One way to welcome the wildflowers is the practice of *Tonglen*, which is typically a kind of reversal of violence. Picture someone you know who is suffering. Holding their image very concretely in your mind, envision taking in all of their pain and darkness on the inhalation and sending them all your light, joy, and power on the exhalation.

NOVEMBER WEEK 3

SCORPIO SEASON

Dion Lissner O'Reilly
"Scavenged"

> *what becomes*
> *of us once we've been torn apart*
> *and returned to our future…*
>> Dorianne Laux

When I was nineteen, a flame clung to my back,
ate me to the spine. Torch-lit and alone,
I ran through the house, a contagion
cindering couches and carpets.
Flayed, my fingertips peeled back
to the nail beds. My spongy tissues touched air,
light, and the steel cot where they took me.

Each day, they peeled me
like Velcro from my sheets,
left bits of my meat there.
Lowered me into Betadine,
scrubbed me to screams—
that became my history. Scavenged
by the curious. They see my twisted fingers

and are hungry for the tale.

I've done the same, stared
at a leg's nubbed end, wanted to touch it,
feel the cut bone under the knob,
hear its shrapnel story. I wanted to know
how that man was alive, arms glistening
playing basketball from a high-tech chair,
making his shots.

The body's scarred terrain becomes
consecrated field. We gather to pick
through the pieces that remain—
an ear hanging from its hinge of skin,
diamond stud in the lobe, ring finger
shining with its promise-band of gold.

———

Marion Wrenn
"Firebird"

I'm the girl who smelled of kerosene

& candy, who, once   supine in a treefort

& already forgetting   the damp magazines

slick with women   the jinxed shag carpet

under bucket seats pried from a junked Camaro,

boys watching the boy on top of me,

was unthinking   breath that would be kisses,

222

the pressure of a body & mine

a fulcrum: of course—   of course

I can still feel a finger on my philtrum.

An angel whispers plunk & I keep quiet,

cleaving   & knowing   not to ask or tell,

unwilling to risk   turning my mother to ash,

trusting only   my strength   to hold tight.

———

Robin Coste Lewis
"On the Road to Sri Bhuvaneshwari"

v.
Thick coat. Black fur. Two russet horns
twisted to stone. One night
          I was stuck on a narrow road,
                panting.
I was pregnant.
I was dead.
          I was a fetus.
                I was just born.
(Most days
I don't know what I am).
          I am a photograph
                of a saint, smiling.
For years, my whole body ran
away from me. When I flew—charred—
          through the air, my ankles and toes fell off
                onto the peaks of impassable mountains.

I have to go back
to that wet black thing
        dead in the road. I have to turn around.
      I must put my face in it.
It is my first time.
I would not have it any other way.
     I am a valley of repeating
       verdant balconies.

POETIC THEMES

I'm no astrology master, but as a Scorpio Rising, I feel I can say the attributes of this sign are uncomfortably intense. Scorpios like to get right down to the bottom of things, without necessarily driving at the speed of trust. I've never felt from the inside the watery aspects of Scorpios; hanging out with one is like being held to a flame, and being one is like... well... it's like *being* fire. So I'd like to issue a trigger warning for these poems, which touch wounds that many of you may prefer not to poke and prod. But as the #MeToo movement showed, spitting out the stories we were all taught to choke down and swallow does hold potential for transforming the culture at large. If we want change, now is the moment to hold ourselves and one another to the fire. Maybe we can burn off what doesn't serve.

The progress of O'Reilly's brutal poem "Scavenged" is as straightforward as it is generous. The first half is about the excruciating pain of being, essentially, burned alive. The second half hinges this unusual personal story to the shared morbid curiosity we all feel about other human wounds, our shared hunger for one another's darkest stories. And the poem arrives, finally, by declaring all of us, our scarred living remains, sacred: our flesh is depicted as a "consecrated field" spangled in diamonds and gold.

The kerosene girl of "Firebird" endures a more metaphorical, and more common, manner of scorching. The setting is like a movie rendition of '80s Americana: a kid's tree fort, damp magazines (*ew*) dating back to a pre-digital age, bucket seats pried from a Camaro, and the shag carpet, jinxed. The superstitions of the scene reflect the times, when we used to play with Ouija boards and ceremoniously lift one another's as-if-dead bodies in the game "Light as a Feather, Stiff as a Board." The plunk-whispering angel and the near-beatific Firebird (almost identical to a Camaro) wrap in dark magic the unspoken rule "not to ask or tell." Here the code of silence ensures that the speaker's mother won't be turned to ash, kind of like "step on a crack, break your mother's back." This is a telling reversal of the phoenix theme: nobody is going to rise from the ash in a circle of horny onlookers. The only thing to be trusted is the survivor's "strength to hold tight," minimizing the orbit of harm to a tight circle of one. Like you do with a fire.

So, returning to the question from O'Reilly's epigraph: "…what becomes / of us once we've been torn apart?" I think of the "torch-lit" girl in O'Reilly's poem, "cindering couches and carpets," the bits of her meat left on the sheets. A nightmare inverse of the phoenix is the myth of Parvati, a goddess whose punishment for immodesty is to be charred, dismembered, and scattered across the valley that bears her name. One of the purported sites where Parvati's charred body parts fell from the sky is the setting for Robin Coste Lewis' long poem "On the Road to Sri Bhuvaneshwari." Zinging around this poem are the subtle crosscurrents of power and violence at work in South Asian tourism, not only in the scarred aftermath of British colonial conquest, but in Indian culture and mythology itself.

The poem depicts an African American woman and a group of American college students traveling down the dark mountain, where they encounter a nomadic clan with a herd of water buffalo, one of which is giving birth. This is all taking place, we have to remember, at the very site of the self-immolation of the goddess of fertility. When the baby turns out to be stillborn, the tribe ropes the mother buffalo, holding her down until she looks directly at the dark fur of her dead offspring. She finally gives up and stops bucking, to put her nose down in the "folded and wet black nothing." The buffalo's suffering overlaps associatively with the speaker's own childbirth experience, and she describes feeling drawn back to the corpse: "I have to turn around. / I must put my face in it." By the end of the poem, the speaker has a kind of clarity born from clear witness—of the bereaved mother animal, the charred goddess falling in pieces, the fetus, death, the smiling saint, the valley itself. The shadow work of Scorpio season beckons us all past the surface to dive down into our own darkness and history, put our face in the hard thing. It's a form of consecration.

PRACTICE

If you're down for some down-and-dirty shadow work, this is the week for it. If you are a menstruating woman, you could dive into the Parvati theme and scatter your blood as an earth offering. Or, if it's your thing, you could make art out of it or ritual marks on your skin. You could study roadkill if you happen to pass it; that's an ancient meditation. But maybe the true Scorpio practice would be to go back to a time you were wounded, if and only if you feel you can trust your strength to hold tight. Dr. Sarà King teaches a practice of holding pain. Nothing could be simpler: the practitioner simply holds their cupped hands, like a little bowl or container, in front of their chest. Could you hold your wound in this way or hold your body where it has been wounded, as a way of giving it a place that's separate from you and also as a way of caring for it and, symbiotically, caring for *you*? What is the associative web of thoughts and feelings?

NOVEMBER WEEK 4

LAMP DAY

Matthew Zapruder
"Lamp Day"

All day I've felt today is a holiday,
but the calendar is blank.
Maybe it's Lamp Day. There is
one very small one I love
so much I have taken it everywhere,
even with its loose switch.
On its porcelain shade are painted
tiny red flowers, clearly
by someone whose careful
hand we will never know.
Because it's Lamp Day I'm trying
to remember where I got it,
maybe it was waiting for me
in the house on Summer Street
I moved into almost exactly
17 years ago. I think
without thinking I just picked it
up from the floor and put it
on my desk and plugged
it into the socket and already

I was working. So much
since that moment has happened.
On Lamp Day we try
not dreamily but systematically
to remember it all. I do it
by thinking about the hidden
reasons I love something
small. When you take
a series of careful steps
to solve a complex problem,
mathematicians call it an algorithm.
It's like moving through
a series of rooms, each with
two doors, you must choose one,
you can't go back. I begin
by sitting on a bench in the sun
on September 21st thinking
all the walks I have taken
in all the cities I have chosen
to live in or visit with loved ones
and alone make a sunlit
and rainy map no one
will ever be able to hold.
Is this important? Yes and no.
Now I am staring
at clean metal girders.
People keep walking past
a hotel, its bright
glass calmly reflecting
everything bad and good.
Blue boots. Bright glass.
Guests in this moment. A child
through the puddles steps
exuberant, clearly feeling the power.
I am plugged in. I am calm.
Lamp Day has a name.
Just like this cup
that has somehow drifted
into my life, and towards which
sometimes for its own reasons
my hand drifts in turn.

Upon it is written the single
word Omaha.

———

Roger Robinson
"A Portable Paradise"

And if I speak of Paradise,
then I'm speaking of my grandmother
who told me to carry it always
on my person, concealed, so
no one else would know but me.
That way they can't steal it, she'd say.
And if life puts you under pressure,
trace its ridges in your pocket,
smell its piney scent on your handkerchief,
hum its anthem under your breath.
And if your stresses are sustained and daily,
get yourself to an empty room—be it hotel,
hostel or hovel—find a lamp
and empty your paradise onto a desk:
your white sands, green hills and fresh fish.
Shine the lamp on it like the fresh hope
of morning, and keep staring at it till you sleep.

Welp, here we are in the week of Thanksgiving, the one day America devotes to gratitude. This week crosses us over from autumn to holiday season, America's celebration of family and cheer and… nuclear-sized greed. I'm gonna go all Quaker on you for a moment. Friends learn as children in "First Day School" that every day is a sabbath; we name the days of the week by number (first day, second day, and so on) as a way of observing that each day is as holy as the next. How would this reframe the idea of a holiday for gratitude? What if every blank calendar day were considered sacred? Matthew Zapruder's wonderful "Lamp Day" presses the re-set button on gratitude practices. We could arbitrarily pick a memento, or person, or place, and reconstruct its history. It's not, Zapruder tells us, a sentimental or mawkish activity, but rather a scientific study: "On Lamp Day we try / not dreamily but systematically / to remember it all." Zapruder is proposing an earnest celebration of the objects of our affection, rather than a celebration of our own gratefulness, which is kind of what Thanksgiving feels like.

This practice is an invitation to take something, anything, and trace its contours with our consciousness, revering its place in our lives. We "do it by thinking about the hidden reasons [we] love something small." Zapruder leaves the question of its importance unanswered but makes clear that thinking about why we love things is not about their exchange value. Surrounding an object with our attention is an internal process, not for show: we *alone* "make a sunlit / and rainy map no one / will ever be able to hold." Like the hotel window, we begin to reflect the history all around us, each object in its wholeness, "calmly reflecting / everything bad and good." I connect this mode of perception with the Tibetan concept of *shiné*, as I've understood it from Pema Chodron's teaching: the quality of mind that sees everything from a place of calm but at the same time with crisp, accurate clarity. As if under bright lamplight. "I am plugged in. I am calm. / Lamp Day has a name." As if to bring home the poem's focus not on itself, but on the stories of objects, this seeming finale of the poem drifts off into an awareness of the speaker's coffee cup, inscribed with the story of its origin: the word Omaha.

Gratitude lamplight is sharper and more edged in Robinson's "Portable Paradise." The references to island beauty suggest, half-ironically, a reprieve from sustained and daily stresses. As a Trinidadian living in England, Robinson knows life under pressure and also knows all about the orientalist fantasy of an island utopia. So this poem sticks a knife in it. Staring at whatever is precious in your memory bank is a way to stay hopeful, a way to sleep at night. The speaker has been taught to conceal his happy place, its white sands and fresh fish, like a weapon against the dominant culture lest it be stolen. Here, if you sing the song of peace, you'd better hum it under your breath. To combat the "sustained and daily" stress, this poem recommends finding a safe, private space to pour out any remnant of calm, like shards of shrapnel, and comb through it under the mind's lamplight. The message here is to keep your Omaha safe in your pocket.

PRACTICE

"Plugging in" to this mode of clear, accurate perception requires that we include, rather than dismiss, our emotional response to the phenomena around us. Zapruder's window reflects everything, bad and good. We are challenged to take in the objects around us with attention to their history, their function, their story, their feel. Perhaps you could glance around your room, taking stock of the objects that catch your gaze. This does not have to be a sentimental acknowledgment of stuff you like; as the edge in Robinson's poem implies. It's a witnessing of your world with fearless precision, inclusive of feelings of threat, or rage, or sorrow. Choose an object and linger with it. If possible, hold it in your hands, feeling its shape as you would a worry stone. Turn in the palm of your mind its round, full-bodied history. What is its resonance for you, its lesson for you, its role in defining you?

DECEMBER WEEK 1
HEART HISTORIES

Robert Pinsky
"History of My Heart"

One Christmastime Fats Waller in a fur coat
Rolled beaming from a taxicab with two pretty girls
Each at an arm as he led them in a thick downy snowfall

Across Thirty-Fourth Street into the busy crowd
Shopping at Macy's: perfume, holly, snowflake displays.
Chimes rang for change. In Toys, where my mother worked

Over her school vacation, the crowd swelled and stood
Filling the aisles, whispered at the fringes, listening
To the sounds of the large, gorgeously dressed man,

His smile bemused and exalted, lips boom-booming a bold
Bass line as he improvised on an expensive, tinkly
Piano the size of a lady's jewel box or a wedding cake.

She put into my heart this scene from the romance of Joy,
Co-authored by her and the movies, like her others—
My father making the winning basket at the buzzer

And punching the enraged gambler who came onto the court—
The brilliant black and white of the movies, texture
Of wet snowy fur, the taxi's windshield, piano keys,

Reflections that slid over the thick brass baton
That worked the elevator. Happiness needs a setting:
Shepherds and shepherdesses in the grass, kids in a store,

The back room of Carly's parents' shop, record-player
And paper streamers twisted in two colors: what I felt
Dancing close one afternoon with a thin blonde girl

Was my amazing good luck, the pleased erection
Stretching and stretching at the idea *She likes me,*
She likes it, the thought of legs under a woolen skirt,

To see eyes "melting" so I could think *This is it,*
They're melting! Mutual arousal of suddenly feeling
Desired: *This is it: "desire"!* When we came out

Into the street we saw it had begun, the firm flakes
Sticking, coating the tops of cars, melting on the wet
Black street that reflected storelights, soft

Separate crystals clinging intact on the nap of collar
And cuff, swarms of them stalling in the wind to plunge
Sideways and cluster in spangles on our hair and lashes,

Melting to a fresh glaze on the bloodwarm porcelain
Of our faces, Hey nonny-nonny boom-boom, the cold graceful
Manna, heartfelt, falling and gathering copious

As the air itself in the small-town main street
As it fell over my mother's imaginary and remembered
Macy's in New York years before I was even born,

II

And the little white piano, tinkling away like crazy—
My unconceived heart in a way waiting somewhere like
Wherever it goes in sleep. Later, my eyes opened

And I woke up glad to feel the sunlight warm
High up in the window, a brighter blue striping
Blue folds of curtain, and glad to hear the house

Was still sleeping. I didn't call, but climbed up
To balance my chest on the top rail, cheek
Pressed close where I had grooved the rail's varnish

With sets of double tooth-lines. Clinging
With both arms, I grunted, pulled one leg over
And stretched it as my weight started to slip down

With some panic till my toes found the bottom rail,
Then let my weight slide more till I was over—
Thrilled, half-scared, still hanging high up

With both hands from the spindles. Then lower
Slipping down until I could fall to the floor
With a thud but not hurt, and out, free in the house.

Then softly down the hall to the other bedroom
To push against the door; and when it came open
More light came in, opening out like a fan

So they woke up and laughed, as she lifted me
Up in between them under the dark red blanket,
We all three laughing there because I climbed out myself.

Earlier still, she held me curled in close
With everyone around saying my name, and hovering,
After my grandpa's cigarette burned me on the neck

As he held me up for the camera, and the pain buzzed
Scaring me because it twisted right inside me;
So when she took me and held me and I curled up, sucking,

It was as if she had put me back together again
So sweetly I was glad the hurt had torn me.
She wanted to have made the whole world up,

So that it could be hers to give. So she opened
A letter I wrote my sister, who was having trouble
Getting on with her, and read some things about herself

That made her go to the telephone and call me up:
"You shouldn't open other people's letters," I said
And she said "Yes—*who taught you that?*"

—As if she owned the copyright on good and bad,
Or having followed pain inside she owned her children
From the inside out, or made us when she named us,

III

Made me Robert. She took me with her to a print-shop
Where the man struck a slug: a five-inch strip of lead
With the twelve letters of my name, reversed,

Raised along one edge, that for her sake he made
For me, so I could take it home with me to keep
And hold the letters up close to a mirror

Or press their shapes into clay, or inked from a pad
Onto all kinds of paper surfaces, onto walls and shirts,
Lengthwise on a Band-Aid, or even on my own skin—

The little characters fading from my arm, the gift
Always ready to be used again. Gifts from the heart:
Her giving me her breast milk or my name, Waller

Showing off in a store, for free, giving them
A thrill as someone might give someone an erection,
For the thrill of it—or you come back salty from a swim:

Eighteen shucked fresh oysters and the cold bottle
Sweating in its ribbon, surprise, happy birthday!
So what if the giver also takes, is after something?

So what if with guile she strove to color
Everything she gave with herself, the lady's favor
A scarf or bit of sleeve of her favorite color

Fluttering on the horseman's bloodflecked armor
Just over the heart—how presume to forgive the breast
Or sudden jazz for becoming what we want? I want

Presents I can't picture until they come,
The generator flashlight Italo gave me one Christmas:
One squeeze and the gears visibly churning in the amber

Pistol-shaped handle hummed for half a minute
In my palm, the spare bulb in its chamber under my thumb,
Secret; or, the knife and basswood Ellen gave me to whittle.

And until the gift of desire, the heart is a titular,

IV

Toward war, new forms of worship or migration.
I went out from my mother's kitchen, across the yard
Of the little two-family house, and into the Woods:

Guns, chevrons, swordplay, a scarf of sooty smoke
Rolled upwards from a little cratewood fire
Under the low tent of a Winesap fallen

With fingers rooting in the dirt, the old orchard
Smothered among the brush of wild cherry, sumac,
Sassafras and the stifling shade of oak

In the strip of overgrown terrain running
East from the train tracks to the ocean, woods
Of demarcation, where boys went like newly-converted

Christian kings with angels on helmet and breastplate,
Bent on blood or poaching. *There are a mountain and a woods
Between us*–a male covenant, longbows, headlocks. A pack

Of four stayed half-aware it was past dark
In a crude hut roasting meat stolen from the A&P
Until someone's annoyed father hailed us from the tracks

And scared us home to catch hell: We were worried,
Where have you been? In the Woods. With snakes and tramps.
An actual hobo knocked at our back door

One morning, declining food, to get hot water.
He shaved on our steps from an enamel basin with brush
And cut-throat razor, the gray hair on his chest

Armorial in the sunlight–then back to the woods,
And the otherlife of snakes, poison oak, boxcars.
Were the trees cleared first for the trains or the orchard?

Walking home by the street because it was dark,
That night, the smoke-smell in my clothes was like a bearskin.
Where the lone hunter and late bird have seen us

Pass and repass, the mountain and the woods seem
To stand darker than before—words of sexual nostalgia
In a song or poem seemed cloaked laments

For the woods when Indians made lodges from the skin
Of birch or deer. When the mysterious lighted room
Of a bus glided past in the mist, the faces

Passing me in the yellow light inside
Were a half-heard story or a song. And my heart
Moved, restless and empty as a scrap of something

Blowing in wide spirals on the wind carrying
The sound of breakers clearly to me through the pass
Between the blocks of houses. The horn of Roland

V

But what was it I was too young for? On moonless
Nights, water and sand are one shade of black,
And the creamy foam rising with moaning noises

Charges like a spectral army in a poem toward the bluffs
Before it subsides dreamily to gather again.
I thought of going down there to watch it a while,

Feeling as though it could turn me into fog,
Or that the wind would start to speak a language
And change me—as if I knocked where I saw a light

Burning in some certain misted window I passed,
A house or store or tap-room where the strangers inside
Would recognize me, locus of a new life like a woods

Or orchard that waxed and vanished into cloud
Like the moon, under a spell. Shrill flutes,
Oboes and cymbals of doom. My poor mother fell,

And after the accident loud noises and bright lights
Hurt her. And heights. She went down stairs backwards,
Sometimes with one arm on my small brother's shoulder.

Over the years, she got better. But I was lost in music;
The cold brazen bow of the saxophone, its weight
At thumb, neck and lip, came to a bloodwarm life

Like Italo's flashlight in the hand. In a white
Jacket and pants with a satin stripe I aspired
To the roughneck elegance of my Grandfather Dave.

Sometimes, playing in a bar or at a high school dance, I felt
My heart following after a capacious form,
Sexual and abstract, in the thunk, thrum,

Thrum, come-wallow and then a little screen
Of quicker notes goosing to a fifth higher, winging
To clang-whomp of a major seventh: listen to me

Listen to me, the heart says in reprise until sometimes
In the course of giving itself it flows out of itself
All the way across the air, in a music piercing

As the kids at the beach calling from the water Look,
Look at me, to their mothers, but out of itself, into
The listener the way feeling pretty or full of erotic revery

Makes the one who feels seem beautiful to the beholder
Witnessing the idea of the giving of desire—nothing more wanted
Than the little singing notes of wanting—the heart

Yearning further into giving itself into the air, breath
Strained into song emptying the golden bell it comes from,
The pure source poured altogether out and away.

POETIC THEMES

I had a thing for Advent calendars as a kid. Even if it wasn't one of those
plastic ones that held chocolates behind each box, there was always a surprise
behind the little cardboard door. The month of December can feel like that,
and not always in a good way. *PING* you get that dreaded text that asks
about your holiday plans. You wander into the stupid, sweltering CVS just to
get some stupid tampons, and you're met with your *least favorite* Christmas
song. Even your annoyance can open into surprise: you hear the song and
you're transported back to you and your mom cracking up together, imagining
it sung really angrily, by carolers screaming into your front door, "SILVER
BELLS SWEET SILVER BELLS SONGS OF GOOD CHEER CHRISTMAS IS
HERE"! Then suddenly, you're crying in the Jiffy Lube because someone has
the same little menorah paperweight that you put on the napkins when you
were still trying to win over your Jewish stepsons. Anyway. Enough about me.

The point is, if these midwinter days are riddled by cultural stimuli that
only come around once a year, you never know when you're going to be hit by
some *je ne sais quoi* that stabs you with pinprick sweetness, irritation, the
passing of time, or loss. So in this oldest month of the year, when we are meant
to turn in and down, we are turned around like something stuck in a dryer,
tumbled in the confusion of family memories. Pinsky's poem renders history
like this. Like the unexpected object behind the cardboard door, memories pop
out line by line. Now Grandpa's cigarette! Now tooth marks on a crib! Now a
brazen saxophone! Or they are tumbling, a chaotic jumble of interleaving
sleeves and tangled drawstrings: the armorial chest hair touches the spectral
meta-poetic army, the blue-on-blue spirals of the curtains echo the twisted
colors on the paper streamers. The self-referential themes in the poem spill out
of someone "lost in music." We could trace each of the poem's five parts as a

musical piece: "thrum, come-wallow and then a little screen / of quicker notes goosing to a fifth higher, / winging to clang-whomp of a major seventh." But for folks like me who are not musicians or music scholars, it might be more accessible to read the poem's form according to the general attributes of jazz music.

After all, jazz isn't like blues, formally speaking: although jazz can employ formal structure, there is no strict structural template to the genre itself. So while the poem resists the clear formal breakdown of, say, a sonnet or a haiku, we can trace its basic contours in terms of improvisational form. Each of the poem's parts carries over the theme of the prior section in its first line and then takes it in a new direction; just as each new instrument would riff on what has been laid down by the musician(s) who came before. Part of the demonstration of virtuosity is to incorporate as many references as possible and also to display the most imaginative, technically impressive improvisation possible. And the poem does.

The first sections lay down a narrative illustrating a theme: his mother's memory of Fats Waller playing in Macy's defines "Joy." "Happiness" is dancing wrapped up with another person, like two colors twisted in a streamer, and emerging outside where snowflakes "cluster in spangles." A little backward sweep to Macy's, before moving on to the third long memory of climbing out of the crib, linked to a scene of being comforted after a cigarette burn. The gorgeous line, "she wanted to have made the whole world up / so that it could be hers to give" turns dark when his mother opens a private letter, then defends her action with a remark that seems to declare "the copyright on good and bad." The claim to ethics, like the claim to her children's identities based on having named them, makes explicit what has been a tacit through-line: his mother gifted him the world, which he can never then experience separately from her. Joy has been "co-authored by her and the movies." The speaker's private experiences, like snowflakes falling, just seem to refer back to some "imaginary and remembered" scene from his mother's life. The name claim gets picked up in the first line of Part III, a long section that zigzags between display and desire, with references to the prior scenes and meta-reflections on tainted modes of giving. The heart configured as an "insane king," impossible to satisfy and tyrannical, sparks the scene of Part IV, in which a boy finally busts out of his mother's kitchen and into the woods, where he and his friends pretend to be kings. Still, his heart is not quite his own, only able to perceive the faces in the bus windows vaguely, distantly, like a "half-heard story or song." The heart just gets swept around, "restless and empty as a scrap of something / Blowing in wide spirals on the wind."

The final section of the poem abandons the long, scenic descriptions, instead tumbling quick references to prior memories inside reflections on them: what was the speaker too young for? What could change him; turn him into something else; help him be recognized? He picks up the saxophone in the poem's final lines for himself, although he admits to being derivative, imitating something "sexual and abstract." This mimicry merits more reflection, and not only because it's a poem by a white man, and the speaker follows after the "capacious form" of Fats Waller in a fur coat. The speaker tries to claim some kind of expression for himself—"listen to *me* / listen to *me*"—reaching for a pure note that isn't complicated by ricochet and endless regress. Could the heart, instead of being just a pump—an organ in a self-contained system that never really generates or relays feeling, but just circulates it around and around—actually draw from "pure source" and "flow out of itself / all the way across the air"? Unclear. It's hard to parse the threads of final lines, comparing the heart's "little singing notes of wanting" to kids at the beach calling out to their mamas for witness. In this tangle, erotic feeling makes the beholder perceive not just beauty, but the desire to transmit desire.

Perhaps the purest response to this poem is to pick up the riff and continue the practice on our own. Do any of this poem's "little singing notes of wanting" seem to call out to you? Do they transmit any desire to dig down into your own reservoir for some December memories to pour back out?

PRACTICE

To embody the poem's form of jazz-style riffing, we might borrow from improvisational movement technique. In the modern dance world, Bill T. Jones (or "Bill T," as he sometimes refers to himself) is one of the great improv masters. He starts a dance with small units of choreography, from which he begins to compose longer choreographic phrases. Sometimes he numbers them, other times he verbalizes them descriptively, breaking their movements down for the audience. Then he combines and recombines them like film clips to build a whole narrative. Classical dance forms like dips and leaps and pirouettes co-exist with pedestrian movements like scrubbing the floor. He might drop a colloquial or overtly sexual gesture like a pelvic thrust or an outstretched tongue. His glossary of hybrid moves is alternately funny ("19: special effects action hero"), lyrical ("21: Celestial Maiden"), playfully colloquial ("22: Steven Spielberg"), or jokingly self-aggrandizing ("6: The Money Shot"). He works the audience between the medium of movement and that of verbal free association, as his spoken text accretes from phrases to sentences to revelatory, often decimating narrative. I could go on and on about Bill T., but particularly relevant is a practice he calls "Floating the Tongue," borrowing from a Buddhist meditation practice of suspending the tongue in the middle of the mouth. Sometimes he invites audiences to practice this, with closed eyes, to share a physical experience of "dropping in" and experiencing the effortlessness that improvisation requires. This pedagogical moment gives the audience a lived experience of the starting place for all genuine play: releasing willed control to allow larger and more subconscious forces to take over. True to Bill T.'s pun, alongside the movement but distinct from it, the dancer's tongue floats free, composing its own narrative.

So maybe you could practice a minute or two of floating your tongue before trying Bill T-style choreographic improvisation. This might awaken a little thrum-thrum of desire to experience memories in motion. You could start by highlighting a few of Pinsky's phrases that draw your attention, numbering, naming them, and giving them a movement: 1: The Actual Hobo shaving; 2: The Crib Climb, hanging by the hands; 3: The Name Stamp, pressing lettered blocks into clay. Play with repeating and recombining these units, allowing free association to manifest until verbal riffing or motion happens organically. Maybe a flow or a storyline or a new feeling state will emerge. Instead of or after toying with Pinsky's memories, you might list three childhood memories of your own and let an embodied heart history unfold.

DECEMBER WEEK 2
NEOPLATONIC MATERIALISM

Carl Dennis
"To Plato"

I'm writing this for a friend, a painter,
Who wants to thank you for the contrast you've drawn
Between the frail beauty at hand and the beauty enduring eternally
    elsewhere.
It's helped her to give a name to the challenge she feels
In confining herself to the facts before her.

To thank you and then to suggest a correction
To your attempt to connect the two
By calling the beauty at hand a shadowy copy
Of a bright, timeless original.

To her it's clear that they're wholly separate,
One class containing no example she knows about,
The other containing them all;
One indifferent to whatever she thinks of it,
The other relying on her to protect it,
For a moment at least, from oblivion.

She wants to thank you for explaining the impulse
To climb the ladder from particular instances
To general truth. Can you thank her
For practicing the vocation of climbing down
To dwell among entities local and doomed?

Step close and look at her painting of peonies
In a Chinese vase on a cherry table.
Try to imagine why she considers this subject
Worth the effort, why she's given these items
The time required to catch the light
As it falls on glaze and petal, water and wood,
So that each surface looks cherished.

Open yourself to musing awhile on the difference
Between a longing for the eternal and a longing
To hold what vanishes in a grip that time,
However patient it proves, has trouble loosening.

———

Eve Kosofsky Sedgwick
"Bathroom Song"

I was only one year old;
I could tinkle in the loo,
such was my precocity.
Letting go of Number Two
in my potty, not pajama,
was a wee bit more forbidding
—and I feared the ravening flush.
So my clever folks appealed
to my generosity:
"What a masterpiece, Evita!
Look! We'll send it off to Grandma!"

. . .

Under the river, under the woods,
off to Brooklyn and the breathing
cavern of Mnemosyne
from the fleshpotties of Dayton—
what could be more kind or lucky?

From the issue of my bowels
straight to God's ear—or to Frieda's,
to the presence of my Grandma,
to the anxious chuckling
of her flushed and handsome face
that was so much like my daddy's,
to her agitated jowls,
Off! Away! To Grandma's place!

As, in Sanskrit, who should say
of the clinging scenes of karma,
"Gaté, gaté, paragaté"
(gone, gone, forever gone),
"parasamgaté; bodhi; Svaha!"
(utterly gone—enlightenment—
svaha! Whatever svaha means),
Send the sucker off to Grandma.
Gaté, gaté, paragaté;
parasamgaté; bodhi; svaha!

Reprinted with Hal's permission (smooches).

POETIC THEMES

If like me you're allergic to this month's hedonistic thrall to "stuff," maybe we could look at our perception of materialism and tweak it a bit. Philosophically speaking, materialism is a physicalist orientation uninterested in the spiritual plane, which corresponds to the yuck of December's focus on objects during a time that's supposed to be sacred. The opposite of materialism, in this sense, might be the kind of ungrounded, escapist spirituality that refuses to acknowledge or reckon with the real world; what many of us think of as "woo-woo" spiritual bypassing. Might we find a more nuanced way of thinking about the relationship of material and spiritual planes?

We could start with Plato. Carl Dennis writes his direct address "To Plato" to re-imagine the relationship between matter and what matters. This elegant defense of artistic and intellectual work is an act of generosity—a kind of gift—upholding the vocation of his friend, a painter. Representing worldly phenomena on paper is a way of preserving the "frail beauty at hand." Time's grip won't loosen, he explains, so everything in its clutches can only be saved by our witness and our care for it. The work of an artist is not to climb up toward the Eternal but downward into the cave of this world's fleeting, earthly objects, "To dwell among entities local and doomed." The poem argues for a shift in perspective away from an orientation upward to the spiritual plane of which our reality is merely a copy, and toward a celebration of human efforts that bring divinity down to earth.

Perhaps Dennis shares Eve Sedgwick's preoccupation with Neoplatonism, which is all about this shift. It wouldn't be a stretch to read obscure philosophical influences into poetry by a guy who has written about Nietzsche and Hegel. And Dennis' take on rebirth, like Eve's, is also pretty Neoplatonic (in poems like "Former Lives," "Eternal Life," and "The God Who Loves You"). In any case, this school of philosophy is a useful one for reframing the aims of holiday shopping. From the thrall to high art in early thinkers like Plotinus, to the later, weirder rituals incorporating physical tokens, it's all about pulling the divine down to our earthly gifts.

Might we give new life to gift-giving by adopting a Neoplatonic view? What happens when we relate to concrete objects as talismans, elemental nature as manipulatable substance for ritual, and language as incantation? I want to borrow a word from Dennis, who argues that we save the material plane from oblivion by cherishing it: the paintbrush catches the light "So that each object looks cherished." I'd like to linger with that word for a moment. My parents joked that they couldn't figure out why the marriage vow would include both "to love" and "to cherish." Redundant, no? In searching for a distinct meaning for cherishing, my mother decided it must mean that whenever the cat brought some gross, dead rodent to the door, it was my dad's job to pick it up. And so small, furry corpses became "cherishes"—as in, "Sherman, there's a cherish on the back porch!" There's wisdom in this joke, as in most of their weird marital rituals: in learning to cherish our nearest and dearest, it's helpful to practice on small things like fallen leaves and coffee cups. And half-eaten mice. In the place of grand expressions of art or thought, we can build our cherishing muscles through small, local actions, rituals, and practices that enact our care and concern in ways that make them real to us and to our beloveds. The low grounds the high: a 4-inch corpse stands in for a sacred vow. And according to the laws of symmetry in the Neoplatonic system of correspondences (as above so below), the lower the low, the higher the high.

It makes sense, then, that Eve's "Bathroom Song" uses potty training as a metaphor for the release of our mortal coil(s). This is a poem about dying. Convincing toddler Evita to surrender to the U.S. Mail her miraculous creation of "Number Two" required the perfect recipient on the other side: Grandma, the paradigmatic (Proustian) figure of the infinitely adoring, invested, tolerant fan. Its final lines borrow from the Heart Sutra, recalling the parable of crossing the ocean of ignorance to reach the banks of Nirvana. Jason Edwards, a British Queer Theorist and my favorite Facebook friend, gives a brilliant reading of the Buddhism of this poem in a book entitled *Bathroom Songs*. I'd like to add that this reference to Nirvana's far shore ties back to Eve's early mention of Mnemosyne, not only the Greek goddess of memory but also the name of another body of water to be crossed in the afterlife. This metaphysical sprawl reflects the 19th-century European mishmash of traditions that fascinated Eve, with its proliferation of deities from Asia, Greece, Rome, and Egypt. The Neoplatonic brushstrokes on this poem's Buddhist canvas are part of Eve's distinct way of drawing correspondences between complex psychological processes and the material plane. Poop, low on the manifest totem pole, relates to enlightenment, the top rung on the ladder of spiritual ideals. "Why would it be a scandal," Eve asks, if the work of dying and toilet training were "not so different—were, so to speak, molded of the same odorous, biomorphic clay?" Just as with potty training, in order to let go of this world, Eve needed something intellect alone couldn't provide her. Her "very hungry" hands found in silk cords and shibori dye what she couldn't find in theory-making or even poetry. She called it a convergence between "making and unmaking." Her interest in fabric art dated back to childhood, and it's unclear (I join Jonathan Goldberg in wondering, as he does in his recent book *Come as You Are*) if Grandma Frieda was the same grandmother who taught Eve to weave. In any case, these later textile practices were a form of rendering thought in 3D. Jason Edwards notes the continuity between her poetic flare (for enjambment, parenthetical sentences, and strings of clauses or dangling ones) and her experiments with textile practices like marbling and enfoldment. I have written elsewhere about the profound transformations of self that couldn't be enacted through thought alone, but instead had to be fondled and woven and stained and sculpted. Rather than focusing on Eve's cognitive habits and elemental intimacies, we might instead borrow her process of transforming abstraction into real artifacts and experiment with what needs of our own might be met by "making stuff."

PRACTICE

One Christmas Eve, still inside the post-divorce shock of being without my children, I decided to make stuff. I cobbled together a Christmas tree ornament

249

out of glitter and cardboard: a miniature package wrapped in parchment leaf, complete with a silver bow, inside of which I glued a kidney-bean sized stone wrapped in metallic wire, like a little silver Evita poo. It helped me reckon with letting go of the nuclear-family-holiday scene I'd always had to make way for whatever divorced Christmas looked like.

If material objects can stand in for subtle forms of human experience and connection, how might you craft, however crudely, some kind of talismanic gift? It might be for someone important, concretizing your connection, or it might represent a psychological task for transition, serving a more abstract function (like my ornament on the family tree, which prompts lots of questions). If the end of the calendar year resonates as a time of release, you might in fact work with excrement. And by that I mean, of course, silk, because, in the words of Eve's therapist: "the silk and the shit go together." I remember when I was writing about Eve's obsession with silk, I fell into a fascinating abyss, down deep in the bowels of the Columbia library where I combed through factoids about mulberry silkworms and salivary enzymes and molting and stuffing and boiling and harvesting.... Here I'll just say that if you want to work in the ur-medium of strange and otherworldly elemental transformation, work with silk. You could look into slow stitching, or if you need a straightforward idea, you might create an eye pillow, sewing a piece of silk (or silky cloth) into a sleeve for filler, which could also be symbolic (like pebbles from the creek behind your mom's house, or sand from your favorite beach, or rice from your friend's wedding). Whatever you craft, what different faculties are recruited in this kind of play? Remember, this is not painterly high art, but process-driven work that's serving a ritual function. Resist the drive toward perfection and stay down here with the idiosyncratic, flawed entities of this realm, local and doomed.

DECEMBER WEEK 3

WINTER SOLSTICE

James Wright
"The Jewel"

> There is this cave
> In the air behind my body
> That nobody is going to touch:
> A cloister, a silence
> Closing around a blossom of fire.
> When I stand upright in the wind,
> My bones turn to dark emeralds.

James Wright "The Jewel" from *Above the River: The Complete Poems and Selected Prose.* Copyright © 1990 by James Wright. Reprinted by permission of Wesleyan University Press.

James Wright
"Trying to Pray"

This time, I have left my body behind me, crying
In its dark thorns.
Still,
There are good things in this world.
It is dusk.
It is the good darkness
Of women's hands that touch loaves.
The spirit of a tree begins to move.
I touch leaves.
I close my eyes and think of water.

———

James Wright
"A Blessing"

Just off the highway to Rochester, Minnesota,
Twilight bounds softly forth on the grass.
And the eyes of those two Indian ponies
Darken with kindness.
They have come gladly out of the willows
To welcome my friend and me.
We step over the barbed wire into the pasture
Where they have been grazing all day, alone.
They ripple tensely, they can hardly contain their happiness
That we have come.
They bow shyly as wet swans. They love each other.
There is no loneliness like theirs.
At home once more,
They begin munching the young tufts of spring in the darkness.
I would like to hold the slenderer one in my arms,

For she has walked over to me
And nuzzled my left hand.
She is black and white,
Her mane falls wild on her forehead,
And the light breeze moves me to caress her long ear
That is delicate as the skin over a girl's wrist.
Suddenly I realize
That if I stepped out of my body I would break
Into blossom.

———

Theodore Roethke
"In a Dark Time"

In a dark time, the eye begins to see,
I meet my shadow in the deepening shade;
I hear my echo in the echoing wood—
A lord of nature weeping to a tree.
I live between the heron and the wren,
Beasts of the hill and serpents of the den.

What's madness but nobility of soul
At odds with circumstance? The day's on fire!
I know the purity of pure despair,
My shadow pinned against a sweating wall.
That place among the rocks—is it a cave,
Or winding path? The edge is what I have.

A steady storm of correspondences!
A night flowing with birds, a ragged moon,
And in broad day the midnight come again!
A man goes far to find out what he is—
Death of the self in a long, tearless night,
All natural shapes blazing unnatural light.

Dark, dark my light, and darker my desire.
My soul, like some heat-maddened summer fly,
Keeps buzzing at the sill. Which I is I?
A fallen man, I climb out of my fear.
The mind enters itself, and God the mind,
And one is One, free in the tearing wind.

POETIC THEMES

At the darkest time of the year, we can reorient toward light, or we can delve into the transformative power of darkness. Pagan traditions hold midwinter as the most sacred time of the year, with the most potential for mysterious, secret processes of spiritual change. I love the gem-like precision of these tiny poems of Wright's, which condense their ingredients into crystal form, like the pressurizing force in metamorphism. In "The Jewel," the wind turns our bones to emerald. The air behind our body is a cave. A cloister. A closing silence. A fire blossom. Wright goes spelunking around in a sensual underworld menagerie, all murk and glorious riddle.

I want to reference "A Blessing" mostly for contrast. This poem, probably Wright's most famous, is atypical in its all-over sweetness. Barely a pinky finger is dipped into the darkness that most of his work swims in. Hanging out with a couple of lonely ponies by the highway, something becomes real to him: "Suddenly I realize / That if I stepped out of my body I would break / Into blossom." Those final lines are a barebones layout of one view of body and spirit: one must be transcended to reach the other.

Nowhere in his other work do you find that kind of facile reading of the body's place in the realm of spirit. These two shorter poems are in many ways more challenging. Both are working through something more complicated than body transcendence. In "Trying to Pray," Wright proclaims, "I have left my body behind me, crying / in its dark thorns." But then he lifts the poem from despair with a list of Good Things, all sense-based: good darkness, women's hands kneading bread, the leaves of a tree being touched. In Wright's poetry, the amalgam of our senses interacting with the mysteries of nature sparks a kind of transformation. Sense experience nudges our conceptual faculties toward the mystical. Wright's focus, as per "The Jewel," isn't in what we can see with our eyes, the clear, controlled space in front of us, but in the mysterious zone behind or inside our body, which we can never see but always follows us. And the recognition of the mysteries one can't quite see releases a kind of epiphanic clarity. Wind touches not skin, but bone. We have felt this—the wind down in our bones like the crystalized cold of emerald.

This dark, mysterious, sensual tone is one Wright shares with Theodore Roethke (who was in fact his professor). Roethke's hard-earned rendering of Immanence isn't to be found in his most-anthologized poems, like "The Waking," but in the deep dive of a poem like "In a Dark Time." Roethke's poetry is a relentless, inward probing, an introspection that picks at the scabs of the psyche's machinations until they bleed again. Living just this side of madness may have thrown this poet in and out of the sanatorium, but arguably this threshold state is transformed into a "nobility of soul" by his art. It's noble because it's healing. At least it has been for me, having taken so much comfort in his companioning darkness. In my own dark times, I had someone to hold my hand, even "pinned against a sweating wall" or dying to myself in the "long, tearless night." Living on the edge of what the mind can withstand isn't so much a choice as a temperament—"The edge is what I have." Those of us who resonate with the line "Dark, dark my light, and darker my desire" do, in fact, see better "in the deepening shade." But the involuted process of compression in Roethke's poetry gives hope because it eventually goes so deep as to spin us free of the poem with a glimpse of the sparkling sublime. "The mind enters itself, and God the mind, / And one is One, free in the tearing wind." It's lines like this that help us climb out of our fear.

PRACTICE

Could you spend a half an hour in darkness? There is a summer program that leads clusters of people with blindfolds and canes along my block in Philadelphia. This is a simulation exercise to train people to work with the visually impaired by walking a mile in their shoes. I tried this out while walking the dog and decided it was better to leave the dog at home (sorry, Skunky). On my own, it was still brutally difficult, even without an enthusiastic fluffy thing tugging me around. It involves mentally projecting a parallel line to the movement of traffic, navigating uneven sidewalk, and using sensory cues to inwardly construct the geometry of an intersection to cross a street. I found that I was focused more on the practical challenges of being blind, as opposed to the psychology of darkness.

So instead, you might simply try a half an hour feeling your way down the stairs, to the coffee machine, to your toothbrush. You can expect that few practical tasks will get done. What is the psychology of darkness for you? Does deprivation of one sensory pathway heighten others, and which? Is there any shift in your experience of the relationship between sense and spirit? You might even free-write from your own "steady storm of correspondences," by keeping pen to paper, resisting the urge to pause. If you get stuck, you can always simply write one word over and over until your mind unclogs. Or, consider a blind drawing of any object or face you encountered in the darkness, without looking at the page and without lifting the mark of the pen from paper. This one-touch technique often alleviates any perfectionism or interest in reproducing reality, instead making manifest an impressionistic picture of something as it exists within you.

DECEMBER WEEK 4
CLOSETS AND CAGES

Louise Erdrich
"Advice to Myself"

Leave the dishes.
Let the celery rot in the bottom drawer of the refrigerator
and an earthen scum harden on the kitchen floor.
Leave the black crumbs in the bottom of the toaster.
Throw the cracked bowl out and don't patch the cup.
Don't patch anything. Don't mend. Buy safety pins.
Don't even sew on a button.
Let the wind have its way, then the earth
that invades as dust and then the dead
foaming up in gray rolls underneath the couch.
Talk to them. Tell them they are welcome.
Don't keep all the pieces of the puzzles
or the doll's tiny shoes in pairs, don't worry
who uses whose toothbrush or if anything
matches, at all.
Except one word to another. Or a thought.
Pursue the authentic-decide first
what is authentic,
then go after it with all your heart.

Your heart, that place
you don't even think of cleaning out.
That closet stuffed with savage mementos.
Don't sort the paper clips from screws from saved baby teeth
or worry if we're all eating cereal for dinner
again. Don't answer the telephone, ever,
or weep over anything at all that breaks.
Pink molds will grow within those sealed cartons
in the refrigerator. Accept new forms of life
and talk to the dead
who drift in through the screened windows, who collect
patiently on the tops of food jars and books.
Recycle the mail, don't read it, don't read anything
except what destroys
the insulation between yourself and your experience
or what pulls down or what strikes at or what shatters
this ruse you call necessity.

———

Ellen Skilton
"New Fridge, Old Song"

This morning, lemon seltzer cans all line up in the new refrigerator door preening for the cameras. Oh, the sweet joy of new beginnings in refrigeration! Soon enough though, spills, half-eaten burritos, and partial cat food cans will take over again, lurking in the back corners, hiding in hard-to-reach spots. Its stainless-steel skin shimmers in afternoon light, but the sheen of this cooling wonder is already dulled by a weekend of fingers opening its doors. And yet, even when bread and cheese turn moldy and milk transforms from liquid to a smelly solid mass, a white-throated sparrow's welcome song can still reach your aging ears from its perch on the back gate.

Smudged, dinged and damaged
by the long slog of it all.
Then daybreak again.

———

W. S. Di Piero
"Chicago and December"

Trying to find my roost
one lidded, late afternoon,
the consolation of color
worked up like neediness,
like craving chocolate,
I'm at Art Institute favorites:
Velasquez's "Servant,"
her bashful attention fixed
to place things just right,
Beckmann's "Self-Portrait,"
whose fishy fingers seem
never to do a day's work,
the great stone lions outside
monumentally pissed
by jumbo wreaths and ribbons
municipal good cheer
yoked around their heads.
Mealy mist. Furred air.
I walk north across
the river, Christmas lights
crushed on skyscraper glass,
bling stringing Michigan Ave.,
sunlight's last-gasp sighing
through the artless fog.
Vague fatigued promise hangs
in the low darkened sky
when bunched scrawny starlings
rattle up from trees,
switchback and snag
like tossed rags dressing

the bare wintering branches,
black-on-black shining,
and I'm in a moment
more like a fore-moment:
from the sidewalk, watching them
poised without purpose,
I feel lifted inside the common
hazards and orders of things
when from their stillness,
the formal, aimless, not-waiting birds
erupt again, clap, elated weather-
making wing-clouds changing,
smithereened back and forth,
now already gone to follow
the river's running course.

POETIC THEMES

Just as the natural world is dialing down to darkness, this week we're asked to rev up for the holidays. This can mean only one thing, sooner or later: whole body exhaustion. If you are a ball of goo on the couch, it's not just social expectations this week; there's a special kind of emotional fatigue at work too, especially for those of us for whom cultural and family traditions can be triggering. Setting limits on output isn't easy. A somatic approach to the psyche insists that we don't really have a choice about those limits. We can't "construct" boundaries based on a cognitive construct or willpower; there are limitations that we quite simply *have*, and ultimately they will find a way to stop us. The choices we make about energy output have consequences because we have predetermined, finite resources.

The "spoon model" of energy output, observed by those with chronic illness, is useful for all of us: each daily activity is measured by how many spoonfuls of energy it requires, and careful priorities must be set since we have only so much juice in the tank. To discern how much we have to give, we must go beyond what the dominant culture says we *should* give (since we are embedded in systems that are designed to exploit our resources to benefit the few. Disproportionally. Yay, Nap Ministry!). If we are to heal the damage done by compulsive patterns of mismanaging our energy, we must reexamine the toxic habits our culture has inculcated in us that teach blatant disregard for the needs of the body and psyche. Over time, as the messages from within are continually drowned out and silenced, we can lose touch with our own needs entirely. To repair this rift, we need to tap into physical feeling as we would attend to hunger or thirst so that we can sense again, and honor, the signals our body is sending.

These poems offer different prescriptions for treating ho-ho-holiday exhaustion. We can allow for stillness, even stagnancy, or we can escape! Erdrich's advice is to stop organizing, stop fixing, stop *doing*, as is epitomized in the poem's mantra-like first line, "leave the dishes." This principle is not just about repairing our culture's tendency to overdo, it actually breaks down the "insulation" between the daily grind and who we really are. Beyond the ruse of necessity, according to this poem, lies our truth. But this poem's specific strategy for touching truth is to toggle between depth and humor. The prescribed reaction to mold in the fridge: accept new life! And her irreverence helps us . . . well . . . *relax*.

The instructions to welcome the dead who collect on kitchen jars might be dark and intense if they didn't follow on the heels of her instructions to let everybody eat cereal for dinner. Some of us sink into this blend of morbidity and humor like a comfortable couch. The poem shifts us from "doing" verbs— throw patch mend buy sew invade worry pursue go after stuff sort answer weep break grow recycle read destroy pull strike shatter—to "non-doing" verbs: leave. let. drift. grow. And arguably: don't? "Let the wind have its way" is such a lovely articulation of the ethic of allowing, which respects dust as a precious manifestation of the earth element. Each instantiation of rot, crumb, and crack is a holy testament to natural processes of death and decay. As a defense for non-doing, we are called to imagine the heart as a memento-stuffed closet we'd never want to clean. We're invited into this inner chamber, away from the ruse of necessity and toward all that is authentic, genuine, gritty, true. Spending some time in stillness, we can sift through the dusty stuff tucked away in the corners of our heart. Allowing natural processes to have their way is a kind of unflinching esteem for the whole of creation as holy.

And I just had to include a variation on the theme in Ellen Skilton's *haibun*, a poetic form of prose interspersed with haiku that was originally used for travel narratives. And truly, there's the promise of change that moves this poem along, from the pristine, cool wonder of now and the half-empty cat food cans to come. The old slogsong of awakening to newness each morning, only to watch the mold and milkcurdle take over, is the story of aging. And yet —yet! The white-throated sparrow still breaks through the "hard-to-reach" spots in our heart, like a haiku breaking up the prose.

In contrast, "Chicago and December" insists that to escape all that is damaged, insincere, and affected, we need to fly toward whatever ragged, authentic form of beauty we can find. For those of us staggering through the end of the year "one-lidded," the craving for something colorful in the gray Chicago fog is so like the way we hunger, viscerally, for something real inside aaaaall the cultural bullshit around us. Di Piero, an art critic herself, uses the art world to represent what is true. Looking out on the bling of Christmas lights all across the skyscrapers, we feel, more than see, the two museum lions guarding the world of art, wild and proud as pyramid sphinxes. We feel, more than see, their proud heads yoked with wreaths, ribbons, and "municipal good cheer." From this "mealy mist," our desire for escape, "worked up like neediness," is granted by an explosion of starlings. Not pretty or nice birds, but "bunched scrawny" things. Real things.

The pace of the poem picks up to a staccato rhythm, like wings flapping, till we as readers, as movers moved, feel galvanized. We too crave release from all the holiday ribbons and baubles; want instead to be "lifted inside the common hazards and orders of things." Nothing strung with lights, just the rattling dance of nature "smithereened back and forth." The snare-drum rhythm of movements is cadenced by unexpected rhymes: "switchback and snag / like tossed rags." Enjambments both condense and stretch out a moment: "elated weather- / making wing-clouds changing." It's a relief to be for a moment "already gone" with them, following the river's course, lifted out of the whole scene of bling and jumbo wreath and crushed Christmas lights. And so we pray: move us, lift us from out of it all, give us our wings back, our proud lion manes.

PRACTICE

The explosion of starlings, wrought physical, might inspire you to go for a run. If so: HUZZAH! YOU ROCK! Lift yourself out of the sleepy fog and awaken fire and flight and freedom.

Or, your couch-huggin' brownie-poundin' booze-guzzlin' body might have a whole lot to say about the prospect of a jog. In that case, you could instead explore Erdrich's evocative models for non-doing: how might you experience physically the feeling of dust bunnies forming, the buildup of earth, new forms of life growing, old things drifting in through the windows of the mind? Find a weighted object to place on your chest and consider adding a source of heat, like a hot pad. Best of all is a "laundry bath." I like to dump all the laundry hot from the dryer onto whichever kid happens to be prone on the couch, feeling low. With or without heat, allow yourself to recline on your back with your legs extended up the wall, or furniture, and relish the warmth of thoracic cavity, imagining your ribcage as a dark receptacle stuffed with sacred-to-you people or things, stuff you'd never throw away. The imprint of life lived, like the sticky fingers dirtying the fridge door with sacred smudges. Take yourself out of the long slog, and wait for daybreak.

JANUARY WEEK 1
THE AULDE NEW YEAR

Naomi Shihab Nye
"Burning the Old Year"

Letters swallow themselves in seconds.
Notes friends tied to the doorknob,
transparent scarlet paper,
sizzle like moth wings,
marry the air.

So much of any year is flammable,
lists of vegetables, partial poems.
Orange swirling flame of days,
so little is a stone.

Where there was something and suddenly isn't,
an absence shouts, celebrates, leaves a space.
I begin again with the smallest numbers.

Quick dance, shuffle of losses and leaves,
only the things I didn't do
crackle after the blazing dies.

––––––

Tracy K. Smith
"An Old Story"

We were made to understand it would be
Terrible. Every small want, every niggling urge,
Every hate swollen to a kind of epic wind.

Livid, the land, and ravaged, like a rageful
Dream. The worst in us having taken over
And broken the rest utterly down.

                              A long age
Passed. When at last we knew how little
Would survive us—how little we had mended

Or built that was not now lost—something
Large and old awoke. And then our singing
Brought on a different manner of weather.

Then animals long believed gone crept down
From trees. We took new stock of one another.
We wept to be reminded of such color.

Ah, New Year's Day: Lucy with the football. All of us experience at times a sense of staleness in the routines of our daily life, the monotony of our psychological issues, the desire to wake up as new. January first, even if it's a fake-out, marks at least the hope for renewal. If you're hunting around for a poetic reflection of the earnest, hopeful resolutions we make each January, you might go back to the wild and wooly list of "what you shall do" in Whitman's preface to *Leaves of Grass*. But now that I'm mentioning dead white guys, I'm thinking instead of the sober ending of Eliot's "Little Gidding," set in this dark time of year: "A condition of complete simplicity / (Costing not less than everything.)" This might be more in keeping with the reality of a pandemic age. The tortured five sections show a man haunted by virtue misunderstood, bungling action, folly, mistaken humor, and harm done. By the end of the poem the midwinter fire has refined all of it, burning the speaker down to simple. Part of our own refining process is the collapse of time back to source, and the ouroboros of future and past in coming to know presence: "What we call the beginning is often the end / And to make an end is to make a beginning. / The end is where we start from." To honor this week as the meeting place of beginnings and endings, let's abandon the old and turn to some more current poems on how past and future intermingle. Maybe we could find a new way to explore the simple, somewhat broken hope of the New Year: that we could be different.

In Naomi Shihab Nye's "Burning the Old Year" the old and the new are like two sticks that, when rubbed together, create a kind of burning friction. We are called closer to the flames to reconsider loss, regret, and what simple elemental truths stay around. Turning something material into sheer air is not just subtraction—beginning again "with the smallest numbers"—but distillation, separating the flammable from the enduring (and sparse) stone. It reframes what kinds of things we can celebrate, teaching us to reimagine even the most devastating loss as capable of creating a new open space for potential. When we are contracted in on ourselves, burdened, crowded in, there's a need for mental/psychological space to breathe. With so much flammable material in the course of a year, we are invited to distill our lives down to what's most real. And something else remains: the ominous crackling that also hangs around "after the blazing dies" is what we have *not* done. Regret lingers.

Tracy K. Smith's meditation is about something slower. The rebirth of old phenomena in a new form is like the reappearance of a soul in a Garcia Marquez novel. The slow undergrowth of invisible things eventually emerges. Sea changes over decades and centuries can soften even the most "rageful dream." We need something "large and old" to handle what we've been handed. Smith's epic, livid, broken land seems more like a description of Sumerian or Egyptian myth than a modern-day city. And with plagues, fires, and tornados, these days we actually seem to be in some kind of Biblical old story. So can we stagger dazed through the heart of winter, anticipating the possibility of green again? The concluding line—"We wept to be reminded of such color"—leaves us with a reminder of how we can be moved by all that is familiar, as it courses through new beginnings. Humanity has made it through plagues before; how can we be changed after this time of destruction? Ours is a fragile, urgent kind of hope.

PRACTICE

One popular lesson in teaching Sanskrit is to place *dukkha,* or suffering, in relationship to *sukha,* which translates to mean not just sweetness, but also space. Yogic practices offer some ways to approach the turning of the calendar year as purification—burning up what's stale and ready for release to make space for the new. But also there's the potential reincarnation of the old in new form. These themes give us plenty of work to do physically, although not necessarily the easiest or most relaxing work. Targeting the solar plexus, the seat of digestive fire in the body, might help us channel the element's purifying properties. A *kriya,* or cleansing technique, called "Breath of Fire" by yoga practitioners (at least in America) builds heat in the solar plexus and then disperses it to create new spaciousness. A way of stoking the fire is to add a challenge to big muscles like quadriceps and "glutes" (your butt). You could stand in "chair pose," with knees bent and torso angled forward on the high diagonal or place your back against a wall as though sitting in a chair, with knees bent as close to 90 degrees as possible. Depending on the intensity appropriate for your body (google counter-indications if you're unsure, but best to listen to and honor your body's responses), you might practice pumping air in a punctuated rhythm in and out of the nostrils, feeling the solar plexus snap back toward the spine with each exhalation. To up the challenge, you could amp up to a quicker pace.

Notice, when focusing on what you're ready to burn up, which moments, people, actions, or qualities come to mind. Heat is considered a somatic expression of anger, so keep tabs on your internal temperature: if swollen hate rises like Smith's "epic wind," take a break. Pause to listen to anger's message, often a wise part of you requesting some kind of change. Based on the associations that rise to mind, discern whether to fan the flames or to squelch the fire. You can do the latter by straightening your legs and imaginatively saturating the chest cavity with the greenest of greens. Imagine a coloring book, and you're filling in all the tubular branches of your lungs with your very favorite shade of green.

When you feel well-cooked but not burned out, slow down your breath practice and fold forward at the waist, flooding the brain. I like to imagine (to mix my metaphors) cleaning a dirty fish tank: after the breath practice churns the stale water, the forward fold feels like dumping out all the gunky, swirling algae into the earth. Observe any imagery sparked by this inversion practice, and be sure to stretch out your quadriceps or any other "hot spot" before coming to relax and allow the breath and pulse to regulate. Is there any renewed sense of internal space? If so, what parts of you remain after the fire? Metaphorically speaking, wait for the soft little animals in your psyche to come back out, perhaps welcoming them with names.

JANUARY WEEK 2
EPIPHANY STRIP

Jane Kenyon
"Taking Down the Tree"

"Give me some light!" cries Hamlet's
uncle midway through the murder
of Gonzago. "Light! Light!" cry scattering
courtesans. Here, as in Denmark,
it's dark at four, and even the moon
shines with only half a heart.

The ornaments go down into the box:
the silver spaniel, *My Darling*
on its collar, from Mother's childhood
in Illinois; the balsa jumping jack
my brother and I fought over,
pulling limb from limb. Mother
drew it together again with thread
while I watched, feeling depraved
at the age of ten.

With something more than caution
I handle them, and the lights, with their

tin star-shaped reflectors, brought along
from house to house, their pasteboard
toy suitcases increasingly flimsy.
Tick, tick, the desiccated needles drop.

By suppertime all that remains is the scent
of balsam fir. If it's darkness
we're having, let it be extravagant.

———

Wallace Stevens
"The Snow Man"

One must have a mind of winter
To regard the frost and the boughs
Of the pine-trees crusted with snow;

And have been cold a long time
To behold the junipers shagged with ice,
The spruces rough in the distant glitter

Of the January sun; and not to think
Of any misery in the sound of the wind,
In the sound of a few leaves,

Which is the sound of the land
Full of the same wind
That is blowing in the same bare place

For the listener, who listens in the snow,
And, nothing himself, beholds
Nothing that is not there and the nothing that is.

Christmas wraps up somewhere between January 6th and 19th, depending on where you are. Some places celebrate Three Kings Day, marking the visitation of the Magi; others focus on Jesus' baptism. Even though most Americans don't observe Epiphany, in the second week of January any small American town will be littered with mangy discarded trees by the side of the road: not-so-evergreen needles, residual tinsel or none. Something about this speaks to the psychological moment of the season. Earnest New Year resolutions clash against the holiday hangover. We dip into the leftover spice cake, reencountering the annual defeat of sudden transformations based on a randomly designated date on the calendar. After and in spite of all the shiny wrapping paper and blinky lights, we are faced with stark, barren reality: cold, darkness, solitude, and nature's death. Acknowledging these winter realities requires a different spiritual skill set. For some of us, it feels like permission to release. We can let go of the ruse, among other things, and quiet the clamor toward something that is simply not there—at least not right now, in the dead of winter.

Hamlet's Denmark offers an apt psychological setting for early January. Jane Kenyon nails it. "Taking Down the Tree" takes us down into the Shakespearean closed world: maddening mental solitude, excruciating bereavement, cold betrayal, loss after loss, and a darkness where "even the moon / shines with only half a heart." We are, for sure, taken down. The "closed world" is the term my father coined for the tragic corollary to Northrop Frye's "green world." These two paradigms are so user-friendly as to have been employed to describe contemporary phenomena as diverse as Cold War political discourse (in Paul Edwards' book *The Closed World*) and digital bot taxonomies (in Mark Sample's blog, samplereality). What's recognizable, aside from any religious framework, is the closed world's inward spiral imploding toward oblivion, a nightmarish perversion of cozy winter *hygge*. The movement of Kenyon's poem from a desperation for light to the delicious ending—having extravagant darkness for dinner—is like the release of the insistent, exhausting cultural expectation for an optimistic holiday disposition. Slowly, piece by piece, like the "tick tick tick" soundscape of needles falling off the tree, we let our need for light fall off our shoulders and fingers and feet. I like to reverse the syllables of the word, and think of needles backward, as "less-need." Dropping my need. To do, to change, to strive, to shine.

At the same time, Jane Kenyon's whole poetic oeuvre is a fight for optimism. Kenyon's brand of depression is a furious, doomed hunt for light, especially in her late poems, which scour reality for any tiny quotidian detail with the potential to fend off despair. In "Notes from the Other Side," she describes

God as "mercy clothed in light." "In the Grove: The Poet at 10" depicts a kid so worked up by the battle between the sun and a cloud as to feel a violent joy "hard to distinguish from pain." That's a pretty good description of the feeling state of Kenyon's poetry. In a section of "Having it Out with Melancholy" entitled "Once There was Light," Kenyon visualizes herself as part of the human family in the form of a "speck of light in the great / river of light that undulates through time." But melancholy descends on her and yanks her out of the "glowing stream." After this, she weeps for days. Sometimes divine light only appears in Kenyon's poem as some kind of joke, as in "Dutch Interiors," where the Holy Ghost only appears on gleaming cutlery or pewter beakers of beer, leading the poet to decide sourly that "Christ has been done to death / in the cold reaches of northern Europe."

And so we return to the frozen north of "Taking Down the Tree." Our own desperation for light and change in midwinter is as fragile as the flimsy pasteboard case that holds the Christmas ornaments. And yet, in spite of their delicacy, the tin-reflected lights and ornaments reappear each year: the spaniel marked "*My Darling*," older than its owner, and the jumping jack that survived dismemberment. They are testimonies to the durability of the memories we move "from house to house." We handle them "with something more than caution"—perhaps we could call it reverence—then tuck them safely away again till next December. The tin-reflected lights and idiosyncratic, storied hanging objects are just markers—symbols of our stubborn, renewable hope. Christmas is made of our longing, and the echo of it remains like the residual scent of balsam fir, the actual earthy substance from which the little jumping jack was made.

The ornament never falls far from the tree. I inherited from my mother a worldview I find in Kenyon's poetry, characterized by a simple and definitional state of yearning. Some might call it depressive, particularly if they were fond of Melanie Klein. The first real theological battle with my father, at the dining room table when I was a tween, was about Milton. Not yet thirteen, just tasting the fruits of independent thinking, I wanted to defend the choice to pick the fruit. I argued that humanity only fully became human when we acquired separation from the divine. At thirteen, I probably didn't reference Michael's promise of a "paradise within thee, happier far" in Book 12 (12.587), but I think of it now. I still think that longing for contact with the divine creates the internal ethical and spiritual compass that defines our humanity. The human condition is literally woven out of yearning, a truth I could feel in my bones, even (and especially?) at that age. My dad countered with some very Christian interpretation and stormed away, which was anathema to his so-very-sanguine character.

But what's remarkable to me is that the next day my father, knowing that his green world was not mine, gave me Wallace Stevens' "The Idea of Order at Key West." I can't afford to reprint this poem, but man oh man, the extravagance of its theology! It's not an existential declaration about human potential in a godless world. It's not about humanity bowing to a higher power, be it God or Nature, or reflecting its power through art. The "plungings of water" are meaningless in and of themselves, Stevens tells us, and the "high horizons" with their mountainous distances are merely theatrical. The poem's scope is wider, encompassing a merging and a transcendence "beyond the genius of the sea," beyond "the outer voice of sky and cloud," beyond "the heaving speech of air." It's about the alchemy of longing, the melding of "the ever-hooded, tragic-gestured sea" with the person singing to it, creating a sublime universe larger than both. The (feminine, my father would point out) mortal not only expresses but creates a whole world out of longing, spoken in "the dark voice of the sea." The poem not only asks, but self-referentially remarks on its repeated asking, "Whose spirit is this?" The woman singing fuses with the originary Word of creation, as the chaos of ocean and deepening night organize themselves to become "the self that was her song." I remember how my father would watch my mom saunter off alone to walk by the sea. He wasn't part of it, this union, and he watched from the beach with a version of Stevens' reverential wonder: "As we beheld her striding there alone, / Knew that there never was a world for her / Except the one she sang and, singing, made."

Stevens' complement to this seascape of a woman entering the heart of longing is "The Snow Man," a man entering the emptiness of cold. This poem is a celebration of "a mind of winter," a perfect illustration of Stevens' trademark stance on the role of art ("Not Ideas About the Thing but the Thing Itself"). Instead of superimposing human notions of misery onto the cold or the sound of wind, we are encouraged to practice being "the listener who listens in the snow, / And, nothing himself, beholds / Nothing that is not there and nothing that is." This decimation of the self, of imagination, and of our personification of nature relates to Stevens' negation of transcendence in "Sunday Morning," which places Jesus within "the heavenly fellowship / of men that perish." There is no beyond. Stevens' winter mind finds expression this second week of January, exploring the porous line between pain and violent joy: in the cold reaches of Hamlet's Northern Europe, folk celebrate Epiphany with ice swimming.

Wim Hoff, known as "The Ice Man," used cold exposure as a remedy for grief as his wife spiraled deeper into depression. As the darkness permeated her psyche, he says in his book, he moved his four children closer to her family to get parenting support. He was leading a trip in the canyons when she threw herself from the eighth story—freeing her from her demons, he writes. Hoff is not sure whether he was healed by his children or by the cold water that led his mind to stillness and functioned as a mirror to face himself. Anyway, that's the context in which Wim Hoff's school of cold exposure was born.

I was born into a family whose genetics are riddled with depression and whose New Year tradition is ice swimming. Each January my daughters and I choose whether to join the ice swimming contingency. I've always felt torn. As someone who finds a way into spirit via the senses, I want to celebrate this gritty and stoical approach to pain and mortality. I do think, as Hoff claims, that the experience helps us enter deep parts of the mind. The cleansing rush, the feeling of total renewal, the symbolism of starting fresh in a culture sorely lacking in rituals with a physiological component—how can one resist? And it does seem logical that sensory extremes train us to withstand suffering. But might they teach us, instead, to transcend it? Is this alleged entry into the belly of what-it-is-to-be-mortal just one more version of spiritual escapism?

As my teenage daughters wrestle with the epigenetic demons I gave them, it seems more courageous to prioritize quieter, humbler holiday traditions. We find new lights at CVS to replace the broken ones, then we pull from the flimsy cardboard the three matching red balls with our names written in gold glitter script, knowing that the fourth is hanging at their dad's house. The glitter catches the light from the replacement strand, and inevitably I cry, and nowadays they know I'm crying. There is sorrow in the hanging of stockings, and we hold each other through it. This is grit.

PRACTICE

Maybe we should just end with the fact of the sun's return. We could simply remind ourselves that the light is increasing, a few minutes a day. Maybe what's required to keep falling in love with life is out there. And for those we love, for the world that's such a mess, we have to keep looking for it. What brightens us from the inside so that we might better help each other through the dark? I want to make an argument for a cold shower. Don't close the book—just hear me out! I'm not asking you to Wim Hoff your way up Mount Everest in your small clothes. But the benefits of graduated cold exposure are not just scientifically proven, they are palpable with just one taste. If, part way through your next shower, you turn the water cold for just a few moments and then try it again after just a couple minutes, the second time feels so much easier. Compare this to most meditation strategies, which are for many people torturous for a significant period of time before sitting begins to actually feel good. Or the excruciating time it takes for foam rolling and

276

massage ball mushing and Bengay burning to create any change at all. But in just one shower you can feel the changes in physiological processes like circulation and cortisol level. There is a palpable letting go, which seems to be the theme of January. Google the benefits of a cold shower, and just consider it, okay?

JANUARY WEEK 3
THREE BRAINS AND MLK

Audre Lorde
"Coal"

I
Is the total black, being spoken
From the earth's inside.
There are many kinds of open.
How a diamond comes into a knot of flame
How a sound comes into a word, coloured
By who pays what for speaking.

Some words are open
Like a diamond on glass windows
Singing out within the crash of passing sun
Then there are words like stapled wagers
In a perforated book—buy and sign and tear apart—
And come whatever wills all chances
The stub remains
An ill-pulled tooth with a ragged edge.
Some words live in my throat
Breeding like adders. Others know sun
Seeking like gypsies over my tongue
To explode through my lips

Like young sparrows bursting from shell.
Some words
Bedevil me.

Love is a word another kind of open—
As a diamond comes into a knot of flame
I am black because I come from the earth's inside
Take my word for jewel in your open light.

————

"This is poetry as illumination, for it is through poetry that we give name to those ideas which are, until the poem, nameless and formless—about to be birthed, but already felt.

...For each of us as women, there is a dark place within where hidden and growing our true spirit rises.... These places of possibility within ourselves are dark because they are ancient and hidden; they have survived and grown strong through darkness. Within these deep places, each one of us holds an incredible reserve of creativity and power, of unexamined and unrecorded emotion and feeling. The woman's place of power within each of us is neither white nor surface; it is dark, it is ancient, and it is deep. When we view living, in the European mode, only as a problem to be solved, we then rely solely upon our ideas to make us free, for these were what the white fathers told us were precious.

But as we become more in touch with our own ancient, black, non-European view of living as a situation to be experienced and interacted with, we learn more and more to cherish our feelings, and to respect those hidden sources of power from where true knowledge and therefore lasting action comes. At this point in time, I believe that women carry within ourselves the possibility for fusion of these two approaches as keystone for survival, and we come closest to this combination in our poetry.

...For women, then, poetry is not a luxury. It is a vital necessity of our existence. It forms the quality of light within which we predicate our hopes and dreams toward survival and change, first made into language, then into idea, then into more tangible action. Poetry is the way we help give name to the nameless so it can be thought."

From the essay <u>Poetry is not a Luxury</u>, published in the collection *Sister Outsider*, Penguin Random House/the Crossing Press; 1984, 2007 by Audre Lorde.

POETIC THEMES

In a book about language and embodiment, it seems right to celebrate Martin Luther King Jr.'s powerhouse poetic style by examining the revolutionary function of language. In Lorde's turn of phrase, "poetry of illumination" transforms our dark, formless reserves of power into tangible ideas and actions. I'd like to lift Lorde's alchemical process from its material feminist frame and examine it through new formulations in the field of Embodied Social Justice. Resmaa Menakem completely transformed diversity activism by introducing a trauma-informed lens, insisting that the perpetuation of racism in our culture can only be healed through a somatic approach.

We all need, Menakem teaches, to metabolize the poisons of white supremacist culture that we have introjected into our bodies. This intervention imports into race relations the current shift in psychology from exclusively cognitive approaches like talk therapy toward body-centric healing modalities. It bears mentioning that the discovery of physiological centers with which we can retrain the nervous system predates the field of psychology. The West discovered the "wandering nerve" just like Columbus discovered America. In any case, a new body of race equity activism, like progressive psychology, now acknowledges that if we truly want to change, we need to work with more than the brain in our skull, but also other conscious domains of the body.

The field of somatics has been developing practical applications for working with the seats of consciousness outside the brain, like the psoas, the diaphragm, the endocrine glands, and the gut. Leaning into change requires that we listen to the intuitive wisdom of other equally aware body systems. Here I want to borrow an approach I learned from Susan Raffo, which she calls the "three brain system" (not so very different from Aristotle's rational, nutritive, and appetitive parts of the soul). The head brain focuses on executive function and individual knowledge. The heart brain focuses on connection, and the gut brain, on nourishment. Embryologically, these three brains were linked, and it's worth speculating on how we each, individually, might put them back in conversation with one another.

An elemental approach to the three primary seats of consciousness configures the low body as earth, the core as fire, and the head as air. A model for how the three systems collaborate in speaking truth to power is Audre Lorde's poem, "Coal." Doing what it describes, the poem is performative. The first stanza functions like a little microcosm of the poem's big world: speech is compared to the process of taking the earth element and firing it deep within the earth's core until it emerges as a diamond. The poem's form begins with one letter in its first line: the element that is being fired is the "I." Even as the first-person singular gains further definition in the second line as black, Lorde identifies the poetic/alchemical process as speech, originating in "the earth's inside." The earth element moves through the fire of glinting, gorgeous variations of what speech can look like in one long middle stanza about language. Words are tongue-roving gypsies. They sing out or breed like adders or break at the stub or burst from shells, knowing sun and seeking explosion. Word gems.

And the earth-to-jewel process of the poem itself feeds us into the final stanza, whose subject is love. But not woo-woo huggybear love, but the deep internal fire of giving a shit, inside this unbelievably pressurized environment, until that which we care about explodes and our thoughts come out in the open. But lest things get whitewashed, Lorde hammers home the centrality of race; she states bluntly, "I am black because I come from the earth's inside," and reminds us that speaking up is "coloured by who pays what for speaking." The level of risk required to speak up correlates directly to our responsibility to do so. So on this MLK Day, the only holiday celebrated through political action, what message is your gut, heart, and head gestating?

PRACTICE

To answer the injunction to speak truth to power, we might experiment with Lorde's earth-to-gem alchemy. We linger with a query while placing our awareness sequentially on body's three brains to listen for their wisdom. Could we practice, somatically, moving up through our roots through the fire of what we've been through and what we care about, in order that we might air our truth?

It might be useful to preface the practice itself with some insight borrowed from Tema Okun about freeing *our process* from white supremacy cultural norms—like perfectionism and defensiveness. In our discernment, we might instead honor the slow and complicated processes of working through conflict. We need to prioritize how we do the work over any specific outcome. In keeping with the grace of a more compassionate approach, be gentle with your expectations. This practice will not necessarily generate a letter to your senator, although it might! What's key is that you come closer to capturing a truth, your truth, the word-adders breeding in your throat.

Part of the work for white folk is metabolizing our reactivity to race-related stimuli, to stay in the fight and continue to act as allies. But the queries below might show up really differently for people of color. Nkem Ndefo teaches a process of slowly building resources for facing adversity that she calls

"Alchemical Resilience." Rather than expecting folk to simply "bounce back," those who have not historically had access to pleasure, ease, or joy have a chance to build their capacity slowly, over time. Integral to respecting the different needs of justifiably vigilant nervous systems in building agency is observing the right to recognize your own discomfort and decline any given practice. For marginalized people who have not had access to this right to stop, defending it is revolutionary. So I encourage you to tailor this practice in any way that feels protective of your boundaries and gentle with your wounds.

The invitation is to begin at the root, with movements and postures that create sensation in the feet and legs, belly, and pelvis. Whether it's sitting with one ankle on one knee or kneading the arches of your feet, find an intense but safe level of sensation in the area of your body that today seems to evoke foundations, origins, a sense of home base. As you make contact with gut feeling, consider: What was your first awakening to your own race identity? Stay with the feeling in your lower body as you paint the scene. Does this recollection bring about a change in pelvic tone, facial expression, or some other zone of muscle tension? How many different emotions are associated with this moment, and can you dip your toes into each of them without drowning? What is the tone, the color, the texture of your gut response?

As you move to the feeling in the core, place your body in shapes that center your awareness here. Be with the rhythm of your heartbeat, admire the fancy tango of diaphragm and lungs, feel for the subtle burn of the digestive fire. Hone your attention on all the interactions of inner and outer worlds— blood going in and out of the heart chambers, the shifts in temperature and humidity taking place in the lungs, all the magical transformations you might intuit in the organs of purification and detoxification. Then call to mind an experience that shifted your thinking from one understanding about race to another. This could be a scene from later in childhood or it could be yesterday. What were the interactions at play, who was a part of it, what was the feeling state in this moment of change? Could you associate a color or type of weather or a musical tone with the time before and the time after?

Bring your attention to the neck and head (especially the throat). Explore movements that close and compress the larynx, and then reopen and stretch it. Just be with the question of what you need to say, without any expectation that it be articulate or elegant. Typically, body wisdom emerges as something very, very simple. Take some time to listen, rather than sculpting or forcing a message. If you feel stuck, return to either of these two primary scenes and see if there is something you wish you had said. Try to speak it out loud, or if that feels hard, write it down. After a few minutes, whatever comes or doesn't, let it go. Release it, take rest, chill, do something comforting and familiar and nurturing.

JANUARY WEEK 4

HAPPY BIRTHDAY, TREES!

Yehuda Amichai
"A Pace Like That"

I'm looking at the lemon tree I planted.
A year ago. I need a different pace, a slower one,
To observe the growth of its branches, its leaves as they open.
I want a pace like that.
Not like reading a newspaper
But the way a child learns to read,
Or the way you quietly decipher the inscription
On an ancient tombstone.
And what a Torah scroll takes an entire year to do
as it rolls its way from Genesis to the death of Moses,
I do each day in haste
or in sleepless nights, rolling over from side to side.
The longer you live, the more people there are
who comment on your actions. Like a worker
in a manhole: at the opening above him
people stand around giving free advice
and yelling instructions,
but he's all alone down there in his depths.

———

Joy Harjo
"Speaking Tree"

I had a beautiful dream I was dancing with a tree.
                                    —Sandra Cisneros

Some things on this earth are unspeakable:
Genealogy of the broken—
A shy wind threading leaves after a massacre,
Or the smell of coffee and no one there—

Some humans say trees are not sentient beings,
But they do not understand poetry—

Nor can they hear the singing of trees when they are fed by
Wind, or water music—
Or hear their cries of anguish when they are broken and bereft—

Now I am a woman longing to be a tree, planted in a moist, dark earth
Between sunrise and sunset—

I cannot walk through all realms—
I carry a yearning I cannot bear alone in the dark—

What shall I do with all this heartache?

The deepest-rooted dream of a tree is to walk
Even just a little ways, from the place next to the doorway—
To the edge of the river of life, and drink—

I have heard trees talking, long after the sun has gone down:

Imagine what would it be like to dance close together
In this land of water and knowledge. . .

To drink deep what is undrinkable.

———

Danusha Laméris
"What Trees Dream Of"

This one thinks, let me be the slender bow
of the violin. Another, the body of the instrument,
burnished, the color of amber.
One imagines life as a narrow boat
crossing water,
a light mist of salt on the prow.
And still another— planed down to planks,
then hammered into shelter
toices vibrating through the rafters.
We do not notice their pleasure,
the slight hum of the banister
beneath our palms,
The satisfaction of the desk
as we tap our pens, impatiently,
upon its weathered surface.
They have ferried us
across rough seas
to lands that smelled of cinnamon
housed our senators,
who pace the creaky floors, debating,
carried arrowheads to pierce our enemies.
We have boiled their pulp, pressed it
into thin, white sheets of paper
on which we describe all of the above in great detail.
And when we die
they hold our empty forms
in bare cedar

until the moment—and how they long for this,
when we meet again in the blackened soil
and they take us back
in their embrace, carry us
up the length of their bodies
into the glittery, trembling movement of the leaves.

POETIC THEMES

The Jewish New Year of the Trees marks the revival of nature in Israel, falling on the Hebrew calendar somewhere between late January and early February. The reason I've chosen it for our focus this week—besides the fact that there ain't too much happening in the long, cold soup of January—is because we would do well to take our cue from an ancient faith that has managed to enliven a holiday to match our current ecological crisis. To be clear, nobody said Tu Bishvat is a major Jewish holiday. And its origins are kind of suspect, arguably a Zionist creation crafted as a nationalist tool for justifying an attachment to the land and expanding it through reforestation. But the holiday has created an environmentalist buzz globally, adopted across the diaspora as a day of agricultural awareness and tree planting. So huzzah! The needs of our planet beg us all to resist capitalism's extractive approach to the earth and rehabilitate our intimacy with and reverence for nature.

These three tree poems offer a range of modes of imagining the interrelationship between humans and the natural sphere. Although Yehuda Amichai is perhaps the most celebrated Israeli poet globally, "A Pace Like That" is hardly the most obvious choice for a reverential poem about a tree. Its frank, un-precious style underscores that Amichai is very much a secular poet. Nature here provides a practical model for human behavior: the speaker simply wishes to mimic the slower pace of his lemon tree. But there's a slip-slide between the sacred and the profane: trees model a way of being whose slow deliberation is likened to the care we take with sacred things. Not the perfunctory daily flip of the newspaper, but the deciphering of an inscription on a tombstone. Not the troubled movement of rolling from side to side in our sleep, but the deliberate slow unraveling of a Torah scroll over the course of a full year.

Then Amichai flips the script with his final metonymic link: the secret underground force of renewal and vitality coursing through the tree's roots is like… a worker in a manhole. He fuses the quotidian—the people above him who "stand around giving free advice / and yelling instructions"—with the profundity and solitude of the final line: "he's all alone down there in his depths." In a glorious upset of our expectations for attributing soul wisdom to natural forces, the mysterious workings of nature are compared to the methodical, practical, skilled industriousness of a manual laborer.

Compare this way of modeling human behavior after the livelihood of a tree to the mutual push me/pull you of Joy Harjo's "Speaking Tree." To speak the language of tree (which for Harjo is related to poetic language) is to understand the longing not only to root down but also to move. To hear the singing of trees is to understand yearning. But the human "longing to be a tree, planted in a moist, dark earth" first appears as the inverse of what trees long for: "The deepest-rooted dream of a tree / is to walk." This dream, as Harjo translates from tree speech, is to walk not as a human walks, but away from the human: "even just a little ways, from the place next to the doorway— / to the edge of the river of life, and drink." So the animism expressed here doesn't show nature mirroring human emotion, but instead longing for independence from the realm of people to get closer to some primordial source. Unlike the human longing for tree-ness, conveyed in the epigraph quoting Cisneros—"I had a beautiful dream I was dancing with a tree"—the trees dream of dancing with one another: "Imagine what it would be like to dance close together." Free.

According to Danusha Laméris, trees dream of something different. "What Trees Dream Of" is the very opposite of Harjo's animism, where the natural realm craves its freedom from humanity. Laméris' trees dream of nothing *but* humanity. They want to be our musical instruments, our boats, the beams that construct our shelter. The desk is satisfied with our tapping pens, the banister loves our sliding palms. In the form of benevolent protectors, they ferry us around and provide the material on which we write our histories. This comforting view of parentified nature reaches its apex in the poem's glorious ending, about endings. Trees, in their afterlife as coffins, embrace the human corpse until there's an elemental co-mingling: "and how they long for this, / when we meet again in the blackened soil." These lines bring humanity into a deeply corporeal union with nature that is also transcendent, as the trees take us back, embrace us, and "carry us / up the length of their bodies / into the glittery, trembling movement of the leaves." Here in the dead of winter, I like this tree dream of becoming a kind of posthumous human humus.

Perhaps to find our own animistic intimacy with the natural surround, we could revisit our broken genealogies for older ritual systems that regard trees with reverence. Are there approaches to trees as bearers of the numinous? Tree ceremonies for quarrel settling. Divining rods. Hearts planted in acorns. Griots in baobabs. The shunned oak. Perhaps we could all dip into a little research on how animism shows up in our ancestral histories and devise our own tree ritual this week!

Alternately, you might revisit your personal history and call to mind your very favorite tree. What were the contours of your relationship to it? The birch tree grown from the spot you buried your first dog denotes one set of relational properties and powers, the huge pine whose branches held the tire swing another. Still another set of powers are to be found in the protective dark of the Japanese maple screening your windows from the world. Whatever you value in and draw from your tree friend is a good place to begin building your personal version of the numinous. In meditating on this, you could jot down a word description of the tree, or write your tree's history, or a fairy tale where the tree is the protagonist.

Or perhaps try to embody this tree, envisioning the central axis of your trunk, the rising sap, the symmetrical explosion of roots below and branches above. If you were to breathe like a tree, would you inhale from the foundation of the body that's rooted to the ground, upward to the glittery, trembling leaves of uplifted fingertips, with the exhalation drifting down all around you? Or would the inhale pull from the skin of the scalp to feed some central ring deep in your trunk and then radiate out in every direction?

Whichever exercise helps you concretize what you value in nature, what would integrating those needs into your daily life look like, and how can you commit to establishing a practice around it?

FEBRUARY WEEK 1
LIFE PRINCIPLE

Margaret Atwood
"February"

Winter. Time to eat fat
and watch hockey. In the pewter mornings, the cat,
a black fur sausage with yellow
Houdini eyes, jumps up on the bed and tries
to get onto my head. It's his
way of telling whether or not I'm dead.
If I'm not, he wants to be scratched; if I am
He'll think of something. He settles
on my chest, breathing his breath
of burped-up meat and musty sofas,
purring like a washboard. Some other tomcat,
not yet a capon, has been spraying our front door,
declaring war. It's all about sex and territory,
which are what will finish us off
in the long run. Some cat owners around here
should snip a few testicles. If we wise
hominids were sensible, we'd do that too,
or eat our young, like sharks.
But it's love that does us in. Over and over
again, *He shoots, he scores!* and famine

crouches in the bedsheets, ambushing the pulsing
eiderdown, and the windchill factor hits
thirty below, and pollution pours
out of our chimneys to keep us warm.
February, month of despair,
with a skewered heart in the centre.
I think dire thoughts, and lust for French fries
with a splash of vinegar.
Cat, enough of your greedy whining
and your small pink bumhole.
Off my face! You're the life principle,
more or less, so get going
on a little optimism around here.
Get rid of death. Celebrate increase. Make it be spring.

———

Tamiko Beyer
"February"

I'm climbing out of this season, fingernails ragged, belly soft. I tuck a stem of
dried mint behind my ear to remind myself.

Once, I bared my shoulders. The bottom of my feet roughed up the dirt with
their hard calluses. When I harvested arugula, it smelled of green spice—
alchemical veins pulsing sun and dirt and water. I do remember this. I
pinned summer light up in my hair and made no apologies for the space I
took up—barely clothed and sun-bound.

Now, a ball of twine in the grey sky. The sun rolls low on the horizon. Hangs.
Then dips back down again, wind howling us into night.

Inside the erratic rhythm of this wavering flame, I conjure the potent sky of the longest day. Seeds with a whole galaxy inside them. Cicadas vibrating in the alders.

But the sensation of joy slips too quickly into simulacra. Song on repeat. I never meant to find myself in such a cold place, my hair thinning against winter.

Once, red clover grew thick where today's rabbit tracks pattern the snow. Clover said flow, clover said nourish, clover said we've got this.

I reel the memory out, let it linger on the horizon, then reel it back in. I play it out and reel it back in. Some kind of fishing, some kind of flying—again and again. I loosen the buckles of my mind. I take up space in the precision of my breath. I call us all back in.

POETIC THEMES

This is a big turning point! Halfway through winter, this week marks the very beginning of spring renewal. Neo-paganism, claiming to draw from traditions reaching back as far as Sumerian and Egyptian cultures, celebrates Imbolc (arguably from the old Irish, "in belly," referring to the pregnant ewes). The Gaelic tradition of St. Brigid's Day honors the Christian saint associated with fertility. Groundhog Day calls upon animal wisdom to intuit just how long the icy days will last. Maybe all this celebrating doth protest too much… February, the very heart of winter, sometimes feels like Atwood's "month of despair," and most of us relate to the big smoke signal of her last line, "make it be spring." If that's where the poem ends, it begins by rhyming "dead" "head" and "bed" and the wonderful, irreverent line, "Winter. Time to eat fat." We can all relate to this particular form of in-belly-Imbolc, which Atwood shamelessly extends from a craving for vinegar fries to the notion of eating our own young.

The repetitive, insistent striving for a hockey goal—"Over and over / again, *He shoots he scores!*"—models a hopeful, if desperate, scooping up of the life principle. Humor, irreverence, and reoriented priorities aren't just respite from the gloom, but part of a staunch belief in the possibility of renewal. Not much is as simple and quick as the sudden lift we get from a laugh. Chuckling at a cat's pink bumhole is a radical practice that enthrones life and love in the face of all the forces that drag us toward stagnancy right now. Atwood's cat and Pennsylvania's own Punxsatawney Pete are undercover agents of the life force, which is stubbornly building somewhere underground. We may all have, like the month of February, "a skewered heart in the center," but it continues to beat. Political climate irrevocably screwed? Covid got ya quarantined? A good belly laugh scoops the Imbolc right up into the heart. It's love, Atwood tells us, that does us in and by implication saves us (from eating our young among other things). We can still cling to hope, as she does when she commands her cat to make it be spring already.

The current of death rising back up toward renewal is configured differently in Tamiko Beyer's "February." Instead of externalizing the life principle as an animal, she herself embodies a human-out-of-hibernation beast: "I'm climbing out of this season, / fingernails ragged, belly soft." The stem of mint behind her ear "to remind myself" transports us along with her back to warmer times. Spring starts in the roots: feet, dirt, and arugula's "alchemical veins / pulsing sun and dirt and / water." Deep down in the veins of the earth, underground interactions of sun, dirt, and water are creating new life. This elemental alchemy is central to Chinese medicine, in the transition from winter, governed by water, to the wood element of spring seeds and saplings. Wood stands in not just for vague hopes and dreams taking shape in the manifest realm, but also stands for the very principle of expansion and potential.

The poem's form mimics the way the stubborn, halting life principle is striving to expand and rise, continually swatted down by frost. After the introductory stanza about emergence and memory, each stanza takes us through the swing between past and present. Beginning with one word that throws out a marker of time like "Once" or "Now," each section throws out some warm-weather phenomenon to be reversed by winter: "I pinned summer light up in my hair" becomes "in such a cold / place, my hair thinning / against winter." Or winter hopelessness is reeled back in, as when rabbit tracks in the snow yield to the memory of red clover, murmuring hopeful encouragement about flow and nourishment and grit. We rise and fall with each stanza through "sunbound" summer memories reaching upward toward the "potent sky of the longest day," down via the low, hanging winter sun that "rolls low on the / horizon" and "dips / back down again."

The final stanza of "February" offers a meta-reflection on these reversals, capitalizing on Beyer's image of the sun as a ball of twine. Here at the end of the poem the metaphor appears fully developed: "I reel the memory out, let it linger on the horizon, then reel it back in. I play it out and reel it back in. Some kind of fishing, some kind of flying—again and again." The "erratic rhythm" makes sense now: Beyer's poem instantiates a kind of parabola, where an object thrown out against gravity returns in a symmetrical curve.

Maybe the parabolic line (a fishing term) is useful for thinking about the dip-and-rise of fishing for hope this month. After two springlike days, it's snowing outside my window as I write this. Grr. The figure of the parabola is a nice way to imaging our actual breath, bringing the poem's abstraction into concrete embodiment. We cast the breath out and draw it back in. This rhythm of breathing is the truest moment-by-moment tether to the life principle. The comforting cadence rocks us like the soothing words of Beyer's red clover: "we've got this."

PRACTICE

How might we facilitate the returning current and, in Atwood's turn of phrase, "get going / on a little optimism around here"? I think of the much-quoted line from Wendell Berry: "practice resurrection." Here's a resurrection practice for stimulating the parabolic turn in the energy system, dipping down to rise back up like Beyer's fishing line. The Returning Current acupressure point relates to Hexagram 24 of the *I Ching*, which describes a turning point after a time of decay. Banished light returns. There is movement without force. The old is transformed and the new is introduced. Also known as Kidney 7, this acupressure point helps the downward energy turn around and ride back up toward the torso. Related to the power of rebirth, the physical point is used to stimulate childbirth. And isn't the crowning of a baby's head the perfect manifestation of spring, new life emerging from the mysterious darkness of the birth canal? Stimulating this acupressure point, about two thumbprints up from the inner ankle bone, might help renew the feeling of upward current. As you tenderly knead this spot, you might visualize loops of breath around the torso, inhaling from the pelvic floor up the spine and around the top of the skull, like reeling in the thread of energy, and exhale it down the front, as if playing out the fishing line again.

Also you might just need the remedy of laughter. I hate to say locking into a screen counts as embodied practice, but if you can't watch a cat (or some other living thing you associate with the life principle), you might hunt for a few funny online videos of your favorite creature to study its magic. Does this beast have a superpower that might help you through the last bitter weeks of winter?

FEBRUARY WEEK 2
HEARTBUILDING

Billy Collins
"Aimless Love"

This morning as I walked along the lakeshore,
I fell in love with a wren
and later in the day with a mouse
the cat had dropped under the dining room table.

In the shadows of an autumn evening,
I fell for a seamstress
still at her machine in the tailor's window,
and later for a bowl of broth,
steam rising like smoke from a naval battle.

This is the best kind of love, I thought,
without recompense, without gifts,
or unkind words, without suspicion,
or silence on the telephone.

The love of the chestnut,
the jazz cap and one hand on the wheel.

No lust, no slam of the door—
the love of the miniature orange tree,
the clean white shirt, the hot evening shower,
the highway that cuts across Florida.

No waiting, no huffiness, or rancor—
just a twinge every now and then

for the wren who had built her nest
on a low branch overhanging the water
and for the dead mouse,
still dressed in its light brown suit.

But my heart is always standing on its tripod,
ready for the next arrow.

After I carried the mouse by the tail
to a pile of leaves in the woods,
I found myself standing at the bathroom sink
gazing down affectionately at the soap,
so patient and soluble,
so at home in its pale green soap dish.
I could feel myself falling again
as I felt its turning in my wet hands
and caught the scent of lavender and stone.

———

Dorianne Laux
"Heart"

The heart shifts shape of its own accord—
from bird to ax, from pinwheel
to budded branch. It rolls over in the chest,
a brown bear groggy with winter, skips
like a child at the fair, stopping in the shade

of the fireworks booth, the fat lady's tent,
the corn dog stand. Or the heart
is an empty room where the ghosts of the dead
wait, paging through magazines, licking
their skinless thumbs. One gets up, walks
through a door into a maze of hallways.
Behind one door a roomful of orchids,
behind another, the smell of burned toast.
The rooms go on and on: sewing room
with its squeaky treadle, its bright needles,
room full of file cabinets and torn curtains,
room buzzing with a thousand black flies.
Or the heart closes its doors, becomes smoke,
a wispy lie, curls like a worm and forgets
its life, burrows into the fleshy dirt.
Heart makes a wrong turn.
Heart locked in its gate of thorns.
Heart with its hands folded in its lap.
Heart a blue skiff parting the silk of the lake.
It does what it wants, takes what it needs, eats
when it's hungry, sleeps when the soul shuts down.
Bored, it watches movies deep into the night,
stands by the window counting the streetlamps
squinting out one by one.
Heart with its hundred mouths open.
Heart with its hundred eyes closed.
Harmonica heart, heart of tinsel,
heart of cement, broken teeth, redwood fence.
Heart of bricks and boards, books stacked
in devoted rows, their dusty spines
unreadable. Heart
with its hands full.
Hieroglyph heart, etched deep with history's lists,
things to do. Near-sighted heart. Club-footed heart.
Hard-headed heart. Heart of gold, coal.
Bad juju heart, singing the low down blues.
Choir boy heart. Heart in a frumpy robe.
Heart with its feet up reading the scores.
Homeless heart, dozing, its back against the Dumpster.
Cop-on-the-beat heart with its black billy club,
banging on the lid.

POETIC THEMES

Let's flip the script on our love objects this Valentine's Day. Don't worry, I'm not going to launch into a description of some kind of facile "self love." Could anything be more sinister than the thriving "self-care" industry, with its pricey baubles and spa treatments and pleasure excursions that feed care right back into the mouth of the capitalist vortex? How instead might we use this holiday to renew our capacity for loving? These poems invite us to move away from the idea of love as aimed, directed, lusting or craving, and toward a notion of love as open receptivity.

Billy Collins is the perfect poet to create some space for lightness and pleasure (surely this was an intention in placing Valentine's Day at the heart of this gray month). "Aimless Love" takes us along on an adventure of falling in love with the world, opening our sense of what counts as lovable all around us. Collins' humor charms us into falling for each and every object, from wren to dead mouse to clean white shirt. The change in feeling-state as we read one disarmingly sweet image after another is like being wooed, line by line, till we identify with Collins' wonderful image of the heart as a bullseye target, waiting for Cupid's next arrow. This focus on receiving love is what the poem actually enacts. In reading these lines we come to share his uncomplicated adoration for the highway that cuts across Florida, or the miniature orange tree. His disarming ability to render things lovable reaches a kind of perfection when the last stanza brings us to gaze affectionately along with him at a bar of soap, "so patient and soluble / so at home in its pale green soap dish." He confesses, "I could feel myself falling again," and we fall too. We can feel in our own hands the slippery stone, smell the wet scent of lavender. Perhaps Collins' presumed aimlessness is a bit coyly disingenuous, as any good seduction always is: each line of the poem aims its arrow at the bullseye of the reader's heart, transferring its sticky, sweet capacity for loving the world.

Dorianne Laux takes this one step further, in a poem about falling in love with the ability to still fall in love. Learning how to dote on our heart's capacities is fundamentally different from "self love." It's kind of like the far end of non-dual: we identify with what's not us until we merge with it, achieving sufficient distance to perceive our own caring with tenderness. When the potential for love becomes the love object, the heart takes shape in natural and otherworldly form: from a sleepy bear to a curling worm to the afterworld maze of rooms and hallways for ghosts. The merging of self and other fold back in on themselves like a mobius strip, and we can fall back in love with our heart, one step removed.

Laux shapeshifts the heart from a mythical form with "its hundred mouths open" and "its hundred eyes closed" to the quotidian, lazy shape we take when watching movies bored. Laux seems to suggest the endless possibilities for our capacity to love, as the pace of her poem picks up to rapid fire and our heart shapeshifts from harmonica to tinsel to cement to broken teeth and on and on. One of these objects is bound to get under our skin, and by the end of the poem we are stuffed with images, maybe feeling a lot like the "Heart / with its hands full." Whether via Laux's wild artillery fire or Collins' more drawn-out Cupid arrows, the images in both poems invite us to engage our heart's capacity to fall back in love with the world. When we do, we don't actually need diamonds or flowers or greeting cards, because we are already replete.

PRACTICE

Riffing on the image of the heart as a bullseye, I'd like to adopt a psychodrama technique taught by Leticia Nieto. Nieto adapted this group exercise for individual practice to accommodate the online format of Transformative Change's Embodied Social Justice Summit. I'm adapting it further to synch with this week's theme of the skills required for loving. Please note: this is NOT an exercise on the skills required for drawing. If, like me, you're no artist, just use chicken-scratches like stick figures and simple symbols.

*Begin by drawing a circle on a piece of paper, and at the bullseye, draw your heart.

*Label it with a name that stands in for a special quality you identify in your soul of souls, or in a version of you from your past — one that is central to your capacity for loving but does not receive adequate reinforcement in your life (for example: vulnerability, courage, softness, confidence, trust, joy).

*Identify the specific people or phenomena that have challenged or undermined this quality (what Nieto calls "the pulls"). Draw them outside the circle, and then draw lines connecting them to the heart at its center. It's best to choose for these figures not vague, overarching phenomena such as patriarchal white supremacist culture, but its incarnation in the people places and things from your personal history. Like that creepy church your great-aunt dragged you to, or that vicious fourth grade math teacher. Wassup, Mrs. Avery.

*"Resource the circle with auxiliaries," in the language of psychodrama, by populating the inside of the circle with companions. (Like supportive figures

from childhood; objects from nature, elements from your upbringing or ancestry; or communities you feel safe in. So much love to that Arizona hotel housekeeper who saw my 13-year-old Queer potential and introduced me to Suzanne Vega.)

*Jot down a few key lines that encapsulate the demand or pressure being placed upon the heart quality by each figure outside the circle. (For example, the accusation that your laziness makes you unlovable; that if you cry, you're weak; or that you're worthless unless you win. I'd give my mom a line I still can't shake, "Only boring people get bored.")

*Scan the field on this "map of pulls" to imaginatively place yourself at the center, holding the connective threads (as you would do in a live group exercise). Physically mime holding imaginary cords in your hands so that you can experience what it would feel like to let them go. To ritualize this, speak aloud the lines you have written—the pull being made—and enact the experience of actually physically setting the cord free with your hands, releasing that pull. You might become aware of which of these cords are particularly hard to let go —the more "gnarly elements" as Nieto puts it. These ties probably live deep in the body, wrapped up in personal and/or ancestral history. What is the energy or charge that arises when we dialogue with these pulls? What is the emotional quality or body sensation that comes up?

Give yourself some time to breathe and integrate the experience.

When I first did this exercise, the snipped cords recalled an early nightmare image of mine from some movie where an astronaut is floating alone into space after his line to the mothership was snipped. I've been balancing this feeling using a Kundalini yoga technique where you visualize a snakelike coil of energy at the base the spine, rising up the central axis of the body and winding around the heart center. Perhaps imagine the gnarly cords on your map instead as golden threads, and you are sucking them back into your body with each inhale, hoovering spaghetti style, reclaiming them and wrapping them around the spool of your Suzanne Vega heart, your boring-because-bored heart, your fuck-long-division heart. Give your heart some volume. Bolster it. Make it sturdy and real and thick. Maybe this process of heartbuilding will lend you new eyes for what's lovely and enticing all around you. I think of love scenes you see in the cartoons, where somebody's eyes shoot big hearts all over the place, usually with a sound that's something like "A-OOOO-GA!" May you see your world this Valentine's Day with Billy Collins aooga goggles.

FEBRUARY WEEK 3
PISCES SEASON

Eleanor Stanford
"Instant Message from Salvador, Bahia"

Today was sunny and the beach
at Itapuã was crowded and I thought of you.
I cut my foot on the coral beneath the tide pools.

On the screen, the greenish script glitters
like the dolphin who flipped
his body up into the sun. Suddenly
appearing, then
it's gone again.

I saw the whales last week, passing through.
Their backs and haunches turning over,
like a slow thought
in the mouth of the Bay of All Saints.

Here it's dark already: austral winter.
Can you see our shadows
flit against the unlit
background? I see your sons
move in and out of the frame—

their faces older,
Changed.

Do the whales make their way that far north?
Is it possible we move
in that same dark medium,
that same ponderous physical world?

———

Eleanor Stanford
"The Poem I Meant to Write"

It breathes among the breakfast dishes, gilled
and fickle. Gurete in the kitchen wields
a knife: a scythe of scales gathers on the floor.
"Today is your day off," she says. "Therefore
you can help clean fish." The lines
that caught my waking in their tangled twine
unreel. The poem turns a silver fin and dives
for darker water. I roll my sleeves and give
my hands to the rhythm of slit and gut.
Talk skates the mirrored surface of the skin. Gurete
laughs as words keep slipping from my grasp.
The shiny bodies split themselves in heaps: what's
useful and what's not. The thin blood
spreads and darkens. In my hands, the bones unclasp.

Even as the Chinese elemental system of nature takes us from water to wood, this week the astrological calendar plunges us from Aquarian air into the water of Pisces season. Both systems share the theme of the call in early spring to birth something new out of watery creative gestation. This week the Northern Hemisphere enters the final trimester of winter, harkening back to our own fishy prehistory in the womb where we all knew how to swim. The first poem sets us on the beach at Itapuã, with its long fishing and whaling history, during the reproductive period of the humpbacks—a great time and place to see them breach. The texts to and from her beloved are compared not to a breaching whale but to the sudden display of a dolphin who "flips his body up into the sun," like the transient messages flashing on her green screen.

The poem then follows the gradual roll of the whales by slowly rolling out a thought about her sons, moving in time toward maturity "in and out of the frame." The ambiguity of the referenced frame is haunting, like staring into the sea: is it the frame of her own imaginings, where her shadow flits with her absent love? Or the containing frame of the cell phone, which might catch a shadow of her sons, there wandering with her on the beach at Bahia? The poem turns us slowly in the "dark medium" of its own uncertainty, until the last lines reveal the implied analogy between the swimming whales and our own movements in the "ponderous physical world." The murkiness of this movement blends time and space, one lover North of the other, inside a temporal flow where their sons grow and change and ultimately drift away. Part of creation, of fertility, of continuance, is a kind of burdened, sorrowful release, like the pull of the womb each month as it strips itself.

The tone of "The Poem I Meant to Write" couldn't be more different. Here, writing a poem is like catching and gutting a live fish. They're slippery things, thoughts! We dream the lines that elude us in our waking, and we have to cast the line out, tangle them up, pull them into the shore of our minds. The process isn't pretty: it requires that roll our sleeves up, wield knives to slit the skin, blood spreading as we struggle to grasp the slipping words, splitting the bones into what's useful and what's not, mercilessly discarded into the "scythe of scales" on the floor. The labor involved in creating anything at all is not for the faint of heart.

These two Stanford poems are characteristically and gorgeously enigmatic. We could trace many of the same elements in Mary Oliver's three best-known fish poems: "The Fish," "Dogfish," and "Humpbacks." Oliver's Piscean view of creativity contains all the stages: bodies feed one another, tangle and slide through cracks, and rip through their watery surround to finally break through the surface. In "The Fish," the fluidity of container and contained—the speaker is the fish, and the fish is in her—reminds me of Maurice Sendak's *In the Night Kitchen*, "I'm in the milk and the milk's in me! I'm Mickey!" In this poem, the pattern of old life feeding other, new life, is not only the mystery of nourishment but a mystery that nourishes—we need this cycle, like food. Science is only beginning to glimpse the scope of the co-mingling that takes place in pregnancy: microchimerism, or the two-way flow of cells between mother and fetus, reveals some wild phenomena. But we all, breeders and non-procreative adults alike, are chimeric beings, constantly absorbing and becoming the amalgam of cellular material we take in through food, breath, skin, and fluids. Science has yet to determine definitively how the body absorbs cellular information from sexual partners, but this too might be part of your intuitive experience. Note the poem's blunt carnality, cousin to Stanford's poem, when the fish is eviscerated and eaten. Oliver, like Stanford, acknowledges the darker side of bringing anything new into the world. The degree to which we are mingled with all the stuff we absorb is something we are only beginning to comprehend.

"Dogfish" is a candid depiction of the realities of the food chain. The scene of big fish hunting little ones becomes an analogy for self-renewal, where one version of the self must die for another to be born. The poem ripples from the big shadowy dogfish and the impossibility of kindness to the waterfall metaphor for plenitude (of sunlight or life's song). We can revive our capacity to love, but it happens slowly, like the pace of the dogfish. Oliver splits the poem neatly into three parts, with lines that issue a punctuated direct address to the reader, like a wake-up call that drags us into the struggle. We're scooped from our comfortable witness seat and thrown in to swim with the fishes. We can't just float around complacently waiting for something simpler. The poem's urgent message: to really stay alive, we must meet the exigencies of our changing world. It's a picture of movement and regeneration as high-stakes hard work.

The breaching whales in "Humpbacks" are likened to the human soul, which can barely be held back from flight. Against stable-izing gravity, the whale flies straight up toward the open sky, like Stanford's dolphin. It's not that this poem is about birth, but its tone is transportable: the incredulous glee with which the speaker celebrates the awesome spectacle is a pretty good description of the birth scene. I'll never forget my mom's voice ringing out like a bell when my daughter hit the scene: "IT'S A BABY!" And that wasn't even the first time she saw me give birth.

"Humpbacks" echoes this kind of breathless wonder at nature shaking out her mane. Part of the poem's superlative mode are the repetitions of key words leaping up off the page. Creativity can feel like this, too—the barely-held-down pull of soul against bone, always longing for flight. I think of the poem's

Biblical reference to the fifth day of creation, ending just like the others in a vision of goodness. Whatever my dog does, I find myself exclaiming, "Good dog! What a good yawn! Such a good belly." It's like the bottomless well of fascination and surprise that we have with sunsets, or ocean waves, or our creations: it's a baby! (or sculpture or non-profit or whatever-is-your-thing!)

PRACTICE

Assuming that you're not going to gut a fish or dash over to the pool for a swim, the next best thing for embodying these themes would be a bath. Epsom salts? Great! Fishify yourself! You are mostly water! And for the first six months of your life, you were a master of the innate primitive reflexes that enabled you to be right at home underwater, decreasing heart rate, closing the glottis, and chilling out your need to breathe. These amphibious reflexes, which humans share with seals and dolphins, can be strengthened by bathing in cool water. Warm water has its own perks though, affecting blood pressure and the autonomic nervous system, for starters. No matter how you go about it, the health benefits of bathing are huge (as many cultures, from Japan to Rome, have always known), and its effects are related to processes of renewal. The rising body temperature actually (I read somewhere) grows and repairs the cells in your body. You are, in short, rebirthing yourself.

Perhaps you could create a ritual around this fact. You might begin by just living into the quiet stillness of your submerged body, occasionally moving as a fetus might, suspended in the warm amniotic fluid. Getting out of a bathtub isn't much of a birth canal struggle, so you might embody the active motion away from the past and toward what is to be by sloughing off dead skin cells, perhaps with a loofah sponge. When you breach and rise, are you more tuned in to the dreams of your body-made-new?

FEBRUARY WEEK 4
MODELS OF SPIRITUAL STRUGGLE

Rainer Maria Rilke
"The Man Watching"

I can see that the storms are coming
by the trees, which out of stale lukewarm days
beat against my anxious windows,
and I can hear the distances say things
one can't bear without a friend,
can't love without a sister.

Then the storm swirls, a rearranger,
swirls through the woods and through time,
and everything is as if without age:
the landscape, like a verse in the psalter,
is weight and ardor and eternity.

How small that is, with which we wrestle,
what wrestles with us, how immense;
were we to let ourselves, the way things do,
be conquered *thus* by the great storm,—
we would become far-reaching and nameless.

What we triumph over is the Small,
and the success itself makes us petty.
The Eternal and Unexampled
will not be bent by us.
Think of the Angel who appeared

to the wrestlers of the Old Testament:
when his opponent's sinews
in that contest stretch like steel,
he feels them under his fingers
as strings making deep melodies.

Whoever was overcome by this Angel
(who so often declined the fight),
he strides erect and justified
and great out of that hard hand
which, as if sculpting, nestled round him.
Winning does not tempt him.
His growth is: to be deeply defeated
by ever greater things.

Doreen Gildroy
"Dung Beetle"

Be kind to me, a mess. I represent
persistence—in the
dirty thing;
things larger than me
I do not fear.

Whatever you think, or like—
I live. Oh,
marvel!

Pushing up the hill—
rolling around.
I feel myself at work.

You are larger than I think,
and that is very comforting to me.

POETIC THEMES

Since this book sets March as the beginning of a new year, the last week of
February is a good time to look back and think about the internal work we've
done. We could review the processes of gestation and reflection and paring
down that will, hopefully, yield new life in the spring. The long dark hours of
wintertime demand a kind of psychic reckoning that can be imagined several
different ways.

Take Rumi's famous analogy of the chickpea cooked in the spiritual fire.
Translating this poem is a whole debate unto itself. Since it's hard to get a taste
of Rumi's actual language, we'll just stick to the poem's conceptual level.
When chickpea tries to hop out of the boiling pot, the divine chef swats her
with a spoon. The poor lil' pea is reassured that a delicious dish will come out
of it all. The realm of childhood simplicity is represented like the plant
drinking rain in the garden, and we are only fully human when cooked. That's

when our true flavor emerges. So ultimately, the chickpea surrenders and becomes thankful for the process of becoming a delectable human being. This model of spiritual transformation is about the least Sufi thing imaginable—gone is the embrace of pleasure and sublime ecstasy. But there it is.

The second paradigm might be more familiar to the Western way of struggle and machismo. The Judeo-Christian example is that of Jacob wrestling all night with the stranger who turns out to be an emissary of the divine. Even when his hip is broken, Jacob hangs on, insisting that he be blessed and given a new name. Rilke tweaks the tale, typically read as a rite of passage where a man is redefined by struggle, ultimately receiving the blessing he sought. "The Man Watching" flips the script to denigrate small conquests in favor of the power of surrender. If we allow ourselves to be dominated as if by "some immense storm, / we would become strong too, and not need names." Becoming a full-grown adult requires that we understand the universe is not going to submit to human will. The eternal, the extraordinary, is not for us to bend. But in this reverential approach to failure and loss, whoever struggles with and is beaten by a superhuman force comes out of it "proud and strengthened." Rilke stretches Jacob's sinews like the steel of a musical string. Even when we are stretched to our human capacity, extraordinary forces aren't wresting with us, but playing us like an instrument—deliberately, feelingly, with sublime artistry. It's in being stretched that our very being is transformed into music.

Lastly, here's a much humbler poetic offering with an equally ancient and expansive cultural tradition behind it: the dung beetle. Ellen Skilton (one poet from December Week 4) returned from a trip to Egypt with a gift for me: a little turquoise scarab. Being a nerdy professor, she expounded on the significance of the scarab in Egyptian culture until I too had fallen in love with it. The scarab is a representation of the dung beetle and a talisman of the potential for rebirth. Looking for something to represent the wondrous power of spiritual transformation? Hear Ye Hear Ye: A bug.that rolls.its.poop. Pushing a sizable ball of excrement significantly larger than itself, the dung beetle diligently presses on across the desert, ducking down under the sand at night, feeding off its own mess. It then plants its seed in the poop, which nurtures the new life, and lo and behold: a baby dung beetle emerges. The Egyptians were smitten. Like the sun, pushed across the sky, dipping below the surface at night to rest! Holy dung beetle, born complete, with everything it needs to be born again! I asked Ellen for a scarab poem, and she found me Gildroy's "Dung Beetle."

Like the humble bug, and like Ellen's little scarab, this tiny poem holds something huge. Gildroy celebrates the mess, our "persistence—in the dirty thing." Unlike Rilke's wrestler, this small pusher of poop does not fear the divine, in fact it maintains an ignorant remove from the larger forces at work and just keeps its head down, pushing along. Consider Existentialism's dour adoption of Sisyphus as the spokesperson for the human condition, eternally pushing the rock uphill to watch it roll down again. This is really different: the dung beetle's worldly work yields new life! In the words of Gildroy, "Oh, marvel!" Marvelous enough to compare to the sun, reborn each day. Marvelous enough to gain a Pharaoh access to the underworld, buried as he is with a scarab as his key to enter. The beetle in this poem addresses divine forces in the final couplet: "You are larger than I think, / and that is very comforting to me." I think of Stephen Mitchell's interpretation of the story of Job as a tale of surrender, not submission. The sacred is larger than we can think—larger than we are capable of holding in our minds. So we might do well to acknowledge that we can never truly know divinity, and take comfort in the limits of human understanding. We have permission to narrow our scope, to relax the struggle. When we can rest our focus more humbly on our own limited mortal powers of transformation, we can then begin to see our potential for change as itself miraculous. With this shift in perspective, we displace divinity and bring it home to earth, in our messy, human work.

Three models of persistence with such very different flavors. We can ask ourselves this week: which rings truest to our own process of transformation?

PRACTICE

If you were to take the spirit of these first two poems about struggle and distill them into some kind of movement exercise, it would be unpleasant. How to find the palpable experience of keeping our head down in the water while being boiled? Maybe call your insurance company. In fact, do *any form* of adulting. To capture the physical strain of wrestling, you can't get more pinprick specific than Rilke's stretched tendon. 99% of us could find all of Jacob's discomfort in having his sinews stretched, simply by trying to get into a full split. But do we really need to? We could instead practice *not* choosing to be stretched so thin. And there ain't no more literal experience of the Rilkean sweetness of failure than accepting that our body will never "do the splits."

Let's instead embody Gildroy's dung beetle. We have only to practice "persistence in the dirty thing." Feel free to get down and dirty on your belly or crawl on hands and knees while pushing an object forward with your head. "I feel myself at work" best, personally, rolling around in a ball on my back. One could read that line as "when I work, I feel myself." What a wonderful way to celebrate our daily human endeavors! Sometimes we work, whether it's writing a book or washing dishes, in order to feel ourselves simply *being*. In the phasing of this poem: "I live. Oh, / marvel!" This isn't so distant from Camus' conception of Sisyphus after all, but so much more sustainable as a model of vitality and pleasure!

This circular movement is a modification of an Ashtanga yoga exercise. If you want to try it, lie on your back, pull your knees in, and try to rock and roll up and down your spine, pivoting your whole body to make a full circle. (So with the first 180 degrees, your head winds up where your butt was, and the next 180 degrees complete the circle to return you to your starting position.) Does this playful work feel different than wrestling with your own body in an excruciating pose like a split? Which is more like your process this past year? I think we could all benefit from reconfiguring our change-making into a kind of merciful, joyful, humble play.

"It turns out poetry does, in fact, do the thing I want it to do…it helps me return to the world, to experience it, to pay attention…. People love to make big pronouncements about poetry saving us. And I want to believe that, but for now, what I can say is…poetry can make us feel. And right now, maybe that's enough. It doesn't have to bring us hope or joy, it just has to remind us that we feel. That we are alive, and here, and feeling the world."

— Ada Limón

AFTERWORD

What's the sound of a Rolodex turning?
THWT. PHHBT.
Sometimes the calendar turn is the sound of raining sunlight a V of geese honking and thwacking across the sky. Most days it's a whip crack. You wake up with a defib jolt to some new gray morning of the world. A hundred cigarettes later and a hundred broken bones of trust you still haul out the smile. Igneous feeling, like you're laminated.
And then the words arrive
a watsu-surround of angels awash
there has never been, in the long song since the big bang
a ticklier more loving touch
feathery wing-fingers to carry you, softly
back to hug the wall. Like Daddy,
water droplets in his beard, bobbing after each lap
I'd be prone at the end of the pool
concrete granules sticky on my palms
mimicking his goldfish gulp with my face all up in his
fishy Hongi Daddy I miss you
I still hear your breath
in the sound of water

ACKNOWLEDGEMENTS

To those who helped this book through to the finish line: Anne Sydor and Angela Flores for permissions guidance, Rebecca Heider for last-minute editing, Bryan Simon for formatting, Katherine Soutar for the gorgeous cover art, and Doug Smock for cover design

To my teachers, who kneaded me into something like edible

To my collaborators who I'd never call "students," for savoring some ideas and spitting out the rest, suggesting a pinch of this or a whole new batch

To my friends, who put up with my braininess to hold up the heart I'm getting to know

To my love, I bet you're psyched this thing is a wrap—time for rock and roll, baby

To my family, I don't know where to start, so I'll just say, Mommy, you're my best friend. Dani and Seth, thank you for sticking by me, and Kelly for sticking with all of us. Ani and Skye, there are words for everything under the sun and there are no words for this love